# Teacher's Resource Book
# The Church
## A Spirit-Filled People

## Second Edition

**Catherine Romancik, S.N.D.**

**General Editor: Loretta Pastva, S.N.D.**

*"Then there appeared to them tongues of fire, which parted and came to rest on each one of them"* Acts 2:3.

**Benziger Publishing Company**
Mission Hills, California

*Theological Consultant*
The Reverend Ronald A. Pachence, Ph.D.
Associate Professor Practical Theology
Director, Institute for Christian
Ministries, University of San Diego.

*Nihil Obstat*
Reverend Paul J. Sciarrotta, S.T.L.
Censor Deputatus

*Imprimatur*
Most Reverend Anthony M. Pilla, D.D., M.A.
Bishop of Cleveland
Given at Cleveland, Ohio, 17 September 1990

The nihil obstat and imprimatur are official declarations that a book or pamphlet is free of doctrinal or moral error. No implication is contained therein that those who have granted the nihil obstat and imprimatur agree with the contents, opinions, or statements expressed.

*Revision Editor*
Celia Rabinowitz, Ph.D.

Send all inquiries to:
Benziger Publishing Company
15319 Chatsworth Street
P.O. Box 9609
Mission Hills, California 91346-9609

ISBN 0-02-655836-X
Printed in the United States of America.

1 2 3 4 5 6 7 8 9   99 98 97 96 95 94 93 92 91

# TABLE OF CONTENTS

# GENERAL INTRODUCTION

*The Church: A Spirit-Filled People* attempts a challenging task. It aims to present the mystery of the Church to young people growing up in a scientific and technological age, and to show the relevance of its history for a "now" generation. It suggests that, with imagination and effort, even the large parish complex can fulfill the contemporary hunger for the intimacy and warmth of community in a highly depersonalized society. The task is further complicated by the fact that we stand at a time when Church theology and practice, which were the main foci of Vatican II, are in flux, with scholars continually lighting up new facets of the mystery, bishops assuming new leadership, and a more educated laity now beginning to exercise fuller responsibility for both their Church and their world.

## Teacher's Resource Book

The Teacher's Resource Book (TRB) is designed to be used closely with the Student Text and the Teacher's Annotated Edition (TAE). Each chapter of the TRB includes the following standard sections:

1. TEACHER'S PREVIEW
2. TEACHER'S RESOURCE
3. ANSWER KEYS
4. ABRIDGED LESSON
5. ADDITIONAL RESOURCES

Each of these standard sections is clearly marked in the TRB by the use of one of the symbols below.

Each of these standard sections is described below.

## 1. TEACHER'S PREVIEW

 The TEACHER'S PREVIEW section is always the first material the teacher sees in the TRB for that particular chapter. It contains as standard features:

- **Focus:** brief statements of the Doctrinal and Personal foci of the chapter.
- **Objectives:** brief statements of the Cognitive and Affective learning objectives of the chapter.
- **Chapter Outline:** a listing of the heads and features in each SECTION of the chapter.

## 2. TEACHER'S RESOURCE

 The TEACHER'S RESOURCE correlates to the RESOURCES in the Teacher's Annotated Edition. Each resource mentioned in the TAE will appear in this section of the TRB. Each TEACHER'S RESOURCE is a blackline master that can be reproduced for student use, either as a handout or an overhead. The Chapter Test, which is always a Teacher's Resource, includes a blackline master of the test for student use, and the answers for the teacher to use.

## 3. ANSWER KEY

 An ANSWER KEY is provided for every question which appears in the text:

SECTION 1—text questions and Checkpoint!

SECTION 2—text questions and Checkpoint!

SECTION 3—text questions and Checkpoint!

CHAPTER Review

Each ANSWER KEY is clearly marked for quick reference.

## 4. ABRIDGED LESSON

 A complete lesson plan for each chapter appears in the TAE. However, time constraints and other situations may make it impossible to use an extended lesson. For these situations, an ABRIDGED LESSON is provided. When using an abridged lesson, keep in mind the following ideas:

- The abridged lessons are aimed at assisting the teacher in presenting the contents of the text in sessions of one to one-and-a-half hours in length.
- The abridgements are specifically designed for teachers in parish schools of religion.

- Each lesson includes a prayer experience, a sharing of student experiences, some writing, some reading, a student activity, and, when needed, a review of the previous material.

- When preparing for this lesson, read the Teacher Preview given for the regular lesson. You may also wish to read over the regular lesson suggestions.

- Finally, plan your class using the suggestions given in the abridged lesson.

## 5. ADDITIONAL RESOURCES

 Under the title ADDITIONAL RESOURCES, the teacher will find other ideas for teaching the chapter, along with references to articles beneficial to the teacher.

# Overview of the Student Text

**Chapter 1** sets the stage by examining negative and positive Church images and how they are formed. It shows the need of holding valid images of the Church in order to respond openly to Christ's personal call.

**Chapters 2–4** examine the mystery of the Church through Biblical, contemporary, and traditional images.

**Chapter 5** invites the students to explore their personal experience of Church in their own parish and local Church. After presenting, both by concepts and by example, this investigation will initiate or reinforce student involvement in the local Church community.

**Chapters 6–11** trace the Church in its origin and historical unfolding. In Chapters 6 and 7, the question of the divine institution of the Church is treated in detail and the activity of the Apostolic Church is shown as divinely inspired and, therefore, the norm of the Church in every subsequent age. The remaining chapters of this section highlight the main events of the Church as it unfolds in four time-periods: The Rise to Power; Catholic Christendom; the Reformation, and Modern Times. The influence of individual personalities in the Church is emphasized both to engage the natural interest of adolescents and to demonstrate the human constitution of the Church. The power of the Spirit to work in the midst of the human situation is likewise pointed out.

**Chapters 12–14** present the mystical image of Church as Christ still active in announcing and bringing about the kingdom through his living members. The students are encouraged to develop an evangelizing mentality, not only to spread the kingdom by word but also to intensify it within themselves. They are called to the witness of holiness and to service of their brothers and sisters in Christ. The text is completed by a Handbook on mainline Protestant Churches which teaches the ecumenical thrust of today's Church.

The content of the student text can be understood as being grouped into four areas of thought.

- **Chapters 1–4:** The nature of the Church in Biblical, contemporary, and doctrinal images.

- **Chapter 5:** The experience of Church in the contemporary local Church and parish.

- **Chapters 6–11:** The Apostolic Church as the norm and, viewed in the light of that norm, the unfolding of the Church in history.

- **Chapters 12–14:** The mission of the Church— Christ in his members today in the process of teaching, sanctifying, witnessing, and serving.

## ADDITIONAL NEEDS

Throughout the course of this text, the teacher will have opportunities to have the students work with a personal journal and with the Bible.

### Journal

Encourage the students to keep a journal-notebook throughout this course to:

1. Clarify ideas and feelings;

2. Trace growth in their prayer life;

3. Voice opinions privately.

You may offer the following directions on how to organize the entries to have a neat, orderly, easy-to-study journal:

1. Write all journal entries on standard two- or three-ring notebook paper and keep them in a folder.

2. Write your name, in ink, on the cover.

3. Keep your journal neat. Avoid extraneous markings or doodles. Write all entries in ink.

4. Keep your journal up-to-date, ready to hand in at any time.

5. For each entry, write the date in the margin.

6. Skip two lines between entries.

7. Use both sides of the paper.

8. Be creative. Occasionally illustrate your entires with a drawing, a photograph, a picture, or some special lettering. Use colored pencils for artwork.

9. When entries are related to your text book, include the text page or exercise number.

10. Use the pockets of your journal folder to store materials related to this class.

11. Your journal is for this class only. No other subject should be included.

12. To make your journal last longer, put a waterproof covering on it.

## Bible

Scripture reading plays an integral part in the development of this course. Teaching suggestions presume that students will have a copy of the Bible in hand, or, at least, that there will be class copies. The student text offers many incentives to Bible reading. *The New American Bible with Revised New Testament* published by Benziger is recommended, since that is the translation used within the student text itself.

# Teaching the Church to Adolescents

The following suggestions will make teaching this subject more enjoyable to students.

## Dignity and Freedom of the Individual

The entire thrust of Vatican II was ecclesial. This resulted in radical shifts in Catholic life which have not as yet been fully absorbed by the people in the pews, nor even by all of the clergy. One of the most fundamental concepts to be highlighted was the dignity and freedom of every human being. This has wide implications both for the Church and its relation to the world.

## Within the Church

Vatican II saw the Church as a people, each of whom is important to the unfolding of God's plan. Adolescents must grow up understanding that they are the Church. They share the mission of Christ directly and not as a participant in the mission of the clergy (who are only a part of the People of God set aside for a special function).

Although deep concern was given to human freedom—the right of each person to decide in matters of faith or morals—it must be noted that a false or uninformed conscience is not free. Therefore, adolescents must hear the importance of and means for arriving at an informed conscience. Here the guidance of the Spirit in the Church is a means that cannot be ignored.

## Relation to the World

The Council's vision of the kingdom as an entity wider than the visible Church stems from its recognition of Christ working secretly everywhere—that is, in all hearts and in the heart of creation. Teenagers reared in a pluralistic and democratic society will heartily endorse a view of the world that is humbly oriented toward intercommunion, outreach, learning, and love. Although service is not much honored in an affluent society, service as an ideal is always appealing to young hearts. It must be held up as a key image of Christ.

Accordingly, concern for the world, involvement in politics, direction toward professions with social impact, and activities for peace and justice will be important for upcoming generations of Catholics. This, not only by necessity, as third and fourth world nations demand equal rights, but also for love of and in imitation of the healing service of Christ.

The Catholic Church in the United States is likewise in a time of transition. It is passing from a nurturing and maintenance stage necessitated by its minority status in a sometimes hostile Protestant environment, to a great outreach of evangelization. Because of the focus on the role of the laity in Vatican documents and the revised code of Canon Law, and the dramatic decline in the numbers of clergy, this task will be accomplished mainly by the laity.

But the world is ambiguous. It is wounded. Therefore, Christians are called to be a sign and sacrament to it, to critique its values in the light of Christ's teachings and to be salt and leaven. All Christians are called to evangelization and to personal holiness. This requires the courage of a prophetic stance. The example of the many saints, contemporary and of old, can serve as example and stimulus. Adolescent energy and rebellion can be channeled against all that threatens the kingdom.

The students must be alerted to the fact that the wonderful progress of science is Christ as healer continuing to work in history because his Spirit is behind all good. But they must see, too, that the Spirit relies on them to keep progress moving under God's law if it is not to become destructive. Adolescents need to see meaning and purpose to their lives and efforts.

## Using Images

In an era that looks on all institutions with a jaundiced eye, the only acceptable presentation of the Church will be that of a dynamic organism, animated by the Spirit. Church is not so much taught, as caught. It is for this reason that the text focuses on images as the vehicle of transmission. Images involve those who contemplate them. Playing on imagination and emotion, and teasing the mind, they elicit a response of the total person. Therefore, whatever you do to bring alive the images presented in the text will be beneficial.

Since a television generation is visually oriented, you will want to use color, line, and form. Word pictures are helpful to some students while tactile images speak to others.

The central image is the risen Christ, alive and working in his Body: the Church. This pivotal image is highlighted in the final chapters of the text so that the students can take it away with them.

But even more fundamental to the existential grasp of Church is the experience of Christ's presence—more than symbol or image. A shift away from a tendency to rely on a magical-religious presence in the sacraments to a "real" presence in human relations and activities springs from a Christology "from below" and is the natural outgrowth of the new ecclesiology.

## Preparation for Change and Growth

Each person's relation to Church is unique. Although images change, Christ is the same yesterday, today, and forever. Grace invites us to closer intimacy, greater understanding, deeper involvement, and truer service with Christ. To prepare students to expect and see the value of change must be a priority of religious educators today.

## Focus on the Christ Connection

Life is a journey. As we can't decide what individual roads to take unless we know where we're going, so a foundational understanding of the connection between Christ and the Church and global dedication to Christ in his Church are essential for knowing what particular decisions to make "en route."

## Participative Learning

Whatever content is taught ought to lead the student not merely to be intellectually aware of what a discipline deals with, but to participate in the process of the discipline. In learning mathematics, students should be given the tools, skills, and methods mathematicians use, not just the information needed to complete exercises. Teaching must become discovery learning. This requires that the students participate in the unearthing of knowledge. It is not how much the students know, but how they view and react to evidence or information uncovered with the aid of the teacher. Content and method must work together. The purpose of education is a dynamic interaction of teacher and student in a continuing process of discovery. No longer can the teacher simply tell the students what they need to know. Both teacher and student must embark on a quest of truth and knowledge which leads both to a more rational and compassionate appreciation of this world.

Students must be prepared to direct their own future, not to defend the past. The educational process must evidence more intimate personal concern between the student and the teacher.

The involvement questions and opportunities for student response in suggested activities—especially the experiential projects such as actual investigation of the parish, contact with church leaders, and reports of experiences with other Christian Churches—bear out this philosophy.

10

**CHAPTER 1**

# FINDING AN IMAGE THAT WORKS FOR YOU
(Text pages 6–29)

## FOCUS

**Doctrinal:** Only a living and loving image of the Church can adequately support a lifetime faith commitment to it.

**Personal:** Is my image of the Church valid? Personal? Conscious? Deliberate?

## OBJECTIVES

**Cognitive:** (a) to learn how images are formed and how they influence our lives; (b) to uncover and understand my own image of the Church.

**Affective:** (a) to want to grow toward a valid, loving image of the Church; (b) to respond to Christ's call to discipleship in my present life situation.

## Chapter 1 Outline

### SECTION 1
**The Impact of Images**

What You See is What You Get

The Power of Images

*On This Rock* (margin feature)

*Iconography* (text feature)

A Changing Mosaic

### SECTION 2
**Examining Your Ideas of the Church**

A Definition of Church

*Communion of Saints* (margin feature)

Definitions Through the Centuries

Experiences Contribute to Attitudes

*Identifying Your Feelings for the Church* (text feature)

Unconscious Feelings

### SECTION 3
**Need For A Guiding Image**

Forming an Accurate Image

The Church as They

*A Test of Knowledge* (feature)

Your Call to Discipleship

*A People at Prayer* (margin feature)

Knowledge of the Course

# 1A TEACHER'S RESOURCE

## Historical Notes

In addition to the definition of Church formulated at the Council of Trent (1545–1563), other definitions and decisions were made. Among them are reaffirmations of the roles of Scripture and tradition in the Catholic Church, of the seven sacraments, of the Mass, and of the priesthood. This Council resulted in a harmony of past and present and the Catholic Church emerged with a renewed sense of stability.

## Pedagogical Notes

1. Unconscious images can become destructive to ourselves and others unless we recognize them personally. Students need to learn to become aware of their own unconscious images. The resources for this chapter offer activities aimed at developing an awareness of images.

2. Erik Erikson has identified the psychological thrust of adolescence as the achieving of intimacy. Therefore, a recognizable deepening of intimacy with God can characterize this period of human development.

# 1B TEACHER'S RESOURCE

## Theological Notes

Any study of the Church at the end of the twentieth century necessarily involves a discussion of both continuity and development. We have to talk about continuity because, as Catholics, we believe that the roots of the Church reach back two thousand years to the one who called himself "the vine", and us, "the branches" *(John 15:51)*. To speak of our continuity as a Christian community is to profess our constant claim that the foundation of the Catholic Church was laid by Christ and the Apostles. The Church is Apostolic; that's one of its four "marks."

In the wake of Vatican II, however, no investigation of the Church's nature, function, and mission is complete without reference to its development. There is no way of getting around it. The Church of the 1990s **is,** and at the same time, **is not** the Church of the 1950s and 1960s. For high school students, appreciating this era of transition and understanding it from a historical perspective may be quite a challenge. They can't

remember the days before Vatican II and anything that happened before the Council is bound to be perceived by teenagers as ancient history.

The discussion of images in this chapter can help you introduce your class to the topics of continuity and development in Church history. As the term itself suggests, images are born, not in the intellect, but in the imagination. They are "verbal photographs" that isolate the attitudes and activities of the Christians who passed them on to us. We might even think of images as the self-portraits of our spiritual ancestors.

In the next four chapters of the text, several specific images of the Church are reviewed. Before moving on to them, however, it is important to establish three things that will guide your students in the study of this material:

1. The fact that images are generated by the human imagination (rather than the intellect) does not mean that they are less important than definitions, theologies, philosophical concepts, or other cognitive activities. Quite the contrary. Once an image gains acceptance by the community, it becomes a kind of shorthand expression of what it means to be a Christian. It can move people to deeper understanding, more faithful commitment, and even to radical conversion to Christ. The power of images should not be underestimated.

2. Images reflect experience. When we study images from the past, we gain access to how other people lived and how they interpreted the meaning of their lives. This window on the past is a valuable tool for helping us understand the continuity and development in the Church.

3. Images fade. Their power to reflect the meaning of life may diminish with time. That's because people have new experiences and their self-understanding changes as they grow older and wiser. When this happens, it's important to recognize that the older images were not necessarily wrong or bad, and they certainly should not be discarded. Instead, we can use them as points of reference and comparison to help us understand how we "got here from there" and even as a guide to help us stay on course during periods of rapid change.

12

*Suggestion:* Using the old image of "America, the melting pot" as an example, discuss with your class the three reflections on images mentioned above. This exercise can help students get a feel for the concept of images and for how the concept is developed in subsequent chapters. First, clarify the "dictionary meaning" of melting pot as it was once used to describe the United States. Then talk about why this image expressed what it meant to be an American.

How did it encourage people to live up to some specific ideals that it implies? Next, have the class suggest how the melting pot image has changed in light of a renewed emphasis on ethnic diversity in America. Finally, invite discussion about the place this image has in our thinking about the United States today. What new images better express what it means to be an American?

# How Images Are Formed

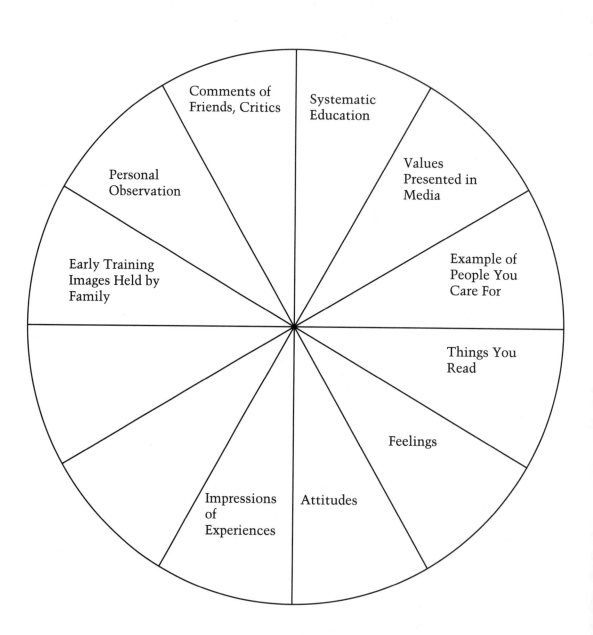

Comments of Friends, Critics

Systematic Education

Values Presented in Media

Personal Observation

Early Training Images Held by Family

Example of People You Care For

Things You Read

Feelings

Impressions of Experiences

Attitudes

# Identifying Your Feelings

**1.**

| Image of the Church | Feelings It Creates |
|---|---|
| a. Large factory turning out a stereotyped product | |
| b. Friends conversing comfortably before a cozy fireplace | |
| c. A stately, beautiful marble building with a golden dome | |
| d. A black-robed judge in a crowded or empty courtroom | |
| e. A responsible, warmly loving parent | |
| f. A DC-10 filled with noncommunicating passengers on their way to Bermuda | |
| g. An elderly person hobbling on a cane | |
| h. Other: | |

**2.** The image that best ties in with my feelings about the Church is Image _____ because

_____

_____

**3.** My real feelings about the Church _____

_____

_____

**4.** Things I dislike about the Church.          Reasons why:

a. _____          _____

b. _____          _____

c. _____          _____

Name: _____ Score: _____

**① CHAPTER 1 Test**

## Finding an Image that Works for You

I. **Completion:** Write the word or term needed to complete each statement correctly.

1. A (An) _____ is a concept of someone or something held by an individual or the public.

2. Images grow out of our _____ , _____ , and

   _____ .

3. One definition of Church is a congregation of those who profess the same

   _____ , partake of the same _____ , and are governed

   by one visible _____ .

4. Our attitudes toward the Church are formed by our unique

   _____ of it.

5. Because our image of the Church influences our value, priorities, and

   actions, it needs to be_____ .

6. Just as Jesus called his first followers to form a (an) _____ , we are also called to be members of the Church.

II. **Incorrectly classified:** Write the letter of the answer that does not belong.

____**1.** Images are (a) always changing, (b) not important, (c) based on experiences, (d) related to our actions.

____**2.** Our image of the Church needs to be (a) ideal, (b) authentic, (c) related to life, (d) conscious and deliberate.

____**3.** Images can be (a) constructive, (b) invalid, (c) ignored, (d) changed.

____**4.** The Church's definition of itself (a) changes, (b) reflects the historic situation of the times, (c) was pinpointed by Trent, (d) was ignored by Vatican II.

____**5.** A valid image is based on (a) knowledge, (b) experience, (c) growth, (d) other's feelings.

**III. Short answers:** Briefly explain each of the following statements.

1. As long as you are alive, your vision and love of the Church are capable of growing.

   _____

   _____

2. You are called to beam your light into the world and so to swell the brightness of the Catholic community of believers, who are set on a hill for all to see.

   _____

   _____

**IV. Essay**

1. What is your present image of the Church? Out of what experience and feelings has it grown?

2. What is meant by a call to discipleship? What does that call demand of you?

# CHAPTER 1 Test
## Finding an Image that Works for You
### I. Completion
1. image
2. experiences, feelings, and attitudes
3. faith, sacraments, head
4. experience
5. authentic
6. community

### II. Incorrectly classified
1. b
2. a
3. c
4. d
5. d

### III. Short answers
1. Answers will vary.
2. Answers will vary.

### IV. Essay
1. Answers will vary.
2. Answers will vary.

# CHAPTER ONE

## SECTION 1
### Text Questions (Student text pages 8–11)
#### Page 8
(1) Answers will vary—attitudes are formed at home, by experiences, or the media.

(2) Yes—a bad attitude closes a person off, and they will learn less.

#### Page 10
(3) Answers will vary—parents, friends, siblings all contribute to our self-image. The Church gives us values and a place to belong.

#### Page 11
(4) Answers will vary—images of parents, politicians, friends, or ourselves change over time. The cause may be maturity, error, or education.

## SECTION 1 Checkpoint! (page 12)
### Review
(1) Images influence our perception and attitudes and affect our motivation, efforts, and relationships.

(2) Images affect how we perform in school or on the job, how we treat others, and how we relate to them.

(3) How we are seen by others can provide us with an ideal to live up to, or cause us to underachieve.

(4) Images come from everyday experiences and from our family, friends, school, society, and the media.

(5) Images are never finished because we are continually changing, maturing, and developing.

(6) Words to Know: *subconscious* (without awareness or knowledge); *image* (a concept held by an individual or the public; the way you look at something); *attitude* (a feeling or emotion toward a fact or experience); *mosaic* (small pieces of colored material inlaid to form a picture or decoration); *icon* (a physical image often used in art, a visible image of God's presence).

### In Your World
(1) Example of the power of images over young people could include clothes, cosmetics, or music. Get students to think about what those images do, such as entice teenagers to spend money they earn on new sneakers, a CD, or a movie.

(2) Point out images used in advertising such as music, clothes, or books. Note also images of stability, family life, investments, cars, types of insurance, or other images which might be in one magazine and not in the other.

### Scripture Search
The images in these Scriptural passages include God as creator, lawmaker, judge, protector, parent, giver of power, and supernatural being. Some of the adjectives that could be used are powerful, awesome, angry, destructive, loyal, fair, faithful, and loving. Encourage discussion of all these images and how they contribute to our overall image of God.

# SECTION 2

## Text Questions (Student text pages 13–19)

**Page 13**
(5) Answers will vary—answers may include the building, ritual, belief, or creed.

**Page 15**
(6) Answers will vary—get students to say how churches are alike and how they differ. Note that by the end of the year, the similarities and differences should be clear.

(7) Answers may include the sacraments, priesthood (and its distinctive dress), Scripture, and the pope.

**Page 17**
(8) Answers will vary.

(9) Answers may include a birth or death, communion, confirmation, ordination of a family member, or religious education.

## SECTION 2 Checkpoint! (page 20)

## Review

(1) Robert Bellarmine was a Jesuit priest who defended the Church against Protestantism. His definition of Church is a people who profess the same faith, have the same sacraments, and are governed by the same head.

(2) Acts 2:42 describes the Church as followers of the Apostles living in a community, believing together, and sharing bread.

(3) The Church is a "universal sign of salvation," and "a sign and instrument . . . of communion with God and of unity among all [mankind]."

(4) A definition creates a mental image. An experience is an encounter you have with the Church that contributes to your feelings about it.

(5) An experience may add to your definition of Church which then becomes part of your image. A feeling is a response that is spontaneous. Attitudes are formed over time.

(6) Our attitudes are formed by a combination of our education, experiences, and feelings.

(7) Our images of the Church reflect our feelings, which may be subconscious.

(8) Words to Know: *Doctor of the Church* (honor given by the Church to a person because of his or her integrity, faithfulness, and learning); *Council*

*of Trent* (meeting of the bishops of the Church in sessions held between 1545 and 1563 to pray, discuss, and make decisions about the life of the Church); *sacrament* (an outward and visible sign of the inward grace given to us; there are seven sacraments in the Catholic Church).

## In Your World

The dialogue might focus on the value of education in its teaching of history and morality, and its role in developing the minds and hearts of students and preparing them for adulthood. Disagreement might focus on the need to grow continually as a person of faith.

## Scripture Search

(1) Answers will vary about Paul's use of body imagery. Point out that today's society is very body conscious. Our physical differences can contribute to a unity of all people. People's gifts are joined together like pieces of a puzzle to make a picture. Unity of spirit means unity of body and soul.

(2) The Beatitudes focus on a life of service based on the desire for righteousness and peace. They offer a total vision of human life in response to Christ. Mercy deserves mercy; reward is offered to all who live for others.

# SECTION 3

## Text Questions (Student text pages 21–26)

**Page 22**
(10) Answers will vary.

(11) Some facts may include knowledge about the beginnings of the Church or information about the specific diocese in which students live.

(12) The secretary means that the Church is the people, not just the hierarchy.

(13) "They" automatically excludes the speaker from the group. It removes any responsibility from us.

**Page 25**
(14) Answers will vary.

(15) Discipleship requires Christians to read and reflect on Scripture and its role in our lives, participate in the life of the Church, and commit ourselves to spreading the Word of God.

## Page 26

**(16)** Influence may come from parents, pastors, teachers, or friends.

## A Test of Knowledge (feature) page 23

**(1)** The Church is the Body of Christ. It includes all who accept Jesus' teachings and the authority of his representatives, and who share his sacrifice and sacraments.

**(2)** Laity are Church members who are not ordained. Their role is to live the Gospel in their daily lives, thus making Christ present in the world.

**(3)** The pope is John Paul II. He is the head of the Church, the representative of Jesus Christ, the chief bishop of the Church, and successor to Saint Peter.

**(4)** Answers will vary. A bishop is a successor of the Apostles who usually governs in some area in union with the pope. A diocese is a geographic region under the authority of a bishop

**(5)** Answers will vary. A pastor is a priest placed in charge of a parish community. A parish is a specific geographical area (territorial) or group (non-territorial) within a diocese identified as a community of believers.

**(6)** Catholics believe all Jesus taught as preserved in the Scriptures and the Apostolic tradition of the Church. Basic doctrines are summarized in creeds.

**(7)** The Ten Commandments provide our basic moral code. They tell us to worship only one God, not to take God's name in vain, keep the Sabbath holy, honor our mothers and fathers, not to kill, not to commit adultery, not to steal, not to lie, and not to covet our neighbor's spouse or possessions. They are found in Exodus 20:1–17.

**(8)** Jesus is the Son of God who died to atone for the sins of all humanity. His commandment is "love one another as I have loved you" *(John 15:12)*.

**(9)** The laws of the Church tell us to participate in the Eucharist, to abstain and fast on the appropriate days, to receive the Eucharist during Easter, to confess all serious sins once a year, to support the Church, to obey the marriage laws, and to participate in the missionary activity of the Church.

**(10)** The sacraments are Baptism (new life in Christ); Eucharist (body and blood of Christ); Confirmation (spreading the kingdom); Penance (forgiveness of sins); Holy Orders (episcopacy, priesthood, diaconate); Matrimony (marriage); Anointing of the Sick (healing).

**(11)** The Church's purpose is to bring all humanity into the Paschal Mystery of Christ.

**(12)** Answers will vary.

## SECTION 3 Checkpoint! (page 27)

### Review

**(1)** A guiding image is a personal vision of the Church that largely determines how the Church affects you and how you affect the Church.

**(2)** A guiding image must be accurate if one's Church participation is to grow and deepen.

**(3)** An accurate guiding image includes some knowledge of what the Church is, how it came to be, why it exists, and an awareness of how others view it.

**(4)** A depersonalized image perceives the Church as a "they" rather than as a "we."

**(5)** A conscious, deliberate image of the Church can help you to commit yourself totally to it, and to deepen your understanding of its mystery of divine strengths and human weaknesses.

**(6)** The call to follow Christ is both communal and individual because each individual is called to form a community.

**(7)** Jesus calls his disciples to follow him and spread the Good News throughout the world.

**(8)** Words to Know: *disciple* (one who follows someone and spreads his or her teachings); *perception* (a mental awareness); *paranoid* (a tendency of a person to be unnecessarily distrustful or suspicious of others); *personality* (the characteristics that distinguish an individual; the sum of a person's behavioral and emotional characteristics); *guiding image* (an image used as a foundation for other images or behavior); *depersonalized* (to lose a sense of personality, made impersonal).

### In Your World

**(1)** Get students to think about how another Church might be different (e.g. no rituals, no school, or more frequent attendance at religious services).

**(2)** For example, "Serving, not selfish."

20

## Scripture Search

When Matthew is called, he responds immediately by following Jesus. John the Baptist points out Jesus to Andrew and John, and Andrew summons his brother, Simon Peter. Philip answers the invitation of Jesus, and then invites Nathaniel. All the disciples sense an attraction to Jesus and follow him without hesitation. Some encounter Jesus directly, others (like Peter) were first aroused by the promise of finding the Messiah. Jesus attracted people of diverse backgrounds, personalities, and values. He used acceptance, curiosity, and leadership to attract the disciples. The variety tells us that Jesus adapts himself to each person, respecting individual strengths and weaknesses.

## CHAPTER 1 Review (pages 28–29)

### Study

(1) Your image of the Church will influence your attitude towards the Church.

(2) How you are seen by others can provide you with a positive image to "live up" to or a negative image to live "down to."

(3) Images come from everyday experiences, from families, friends, school, society, and the media.

(4) Because people continually grow and mature, their images grow and mature as well.

(5) Icons are a spiritual form of art. They are visible images of God's presence among us. The role of icons is to help connect us with the divine.

(6) Answers will vary.

(7) A definition creates a mental image. An experience is an encounter you have with the Church that contributes to your feelings about it.

(8) Feelings arise from experiences. All experiences and feelings influence a person's attitudes and thus a person's image.

(9) Guiding images shape our lives by influencing our choices and actions.

(10) An accurate image of the Church is developed through an accurate understanding the Church's history, its reason for existing, and an awareness of others perceptions of it.

(11) The call to follow Christ is given to each individual. Part of the call is the need to form community.

(12) Jesus expects disciples to follow his teaching and proclaim the Gospel.

(13) Our images of the Church change as we mature because we learn and come to understand the meaning behind certain actions, and our own role in the life of the Church.

(14) When the Church is referred to as "they," it places responsibility for what happens on someone else. When the Church is "us," responsibility is claimed by each individual.

### Action

(1) Answers will vary. As parishes vary, so will the students' responses. Students from inner-city or rural parishes will probably have different images than do their suburban counterparts.

(2) This creative assignment could be writing, music, drawing, sculpture, or some other medium.

(3) What images do students have of Church music—in their own church and in others? If there is time, bring in examples (of Gregorian Chant or gospel singing) or just discuss the variety.

### Prayer

This activity is important. You may want to reintroduce the passage from 1 Corinthians about the unity of the body, and to discuss the role of the physical and visible in representing that which is invisible and spiritual. Talk about the value of sight, hearing, and smell in the experience of prayer.

# Finding an Image that Works for You

**OVERVIEW:** The aim of this chapter is to make students more aware of how they form images and attitudes, especially those about the Church.

**OBJECTIVES:** The students will:

- Generate examples of images that influence their lives.
- In small groups, make a list of definitions of Church contained in Section 2.
- Formulate a class definition of Church which reflects the class's images of Church.

**TIME FRAME: One to one-and-a-half hours.**

**MATERIALS: Poster board, markers, religious statue or icon, candle, Bibles.**

**PROCEDURE:**

*Into:* Prayer—Begin class with a prayer from the feature "On this Rock" (page 8).

*Through:*

Activity One:

1. Ask students about their image of school. Use questions 1 and 2 on page 8 to guide this discussion.

2. Then ask students to describe their images of an inanimate object, a historical figure, and a living person. How do these images influence their lives?

3. Conclude this activity with a discussion of the students' images of God, the Church, and themselves. Use question 3 on page 10 to guide this discussion.

Activity Two:

1. Ask the students individually to write their own definitions of "Church."

2. Form the students into groups of three. Have the students find the nine definitions of "Church" found in Section 2 of this chapter, pages 13–19.

3. Have each group share at least one definition with the class, and why they, as a group, "prefer" it.

Activity Three:

1. Discuss the definitions of Church and decide, as a class, which reflect the students' image of Church from Activity One.

2. Based on these images, formulate a class definition of "Church." Write this definition on a poster board and display it in class.

*Beyond:* Suggest that students read "Your Call to Discipleship," focusing on question 15 on page 25. Encourage them to complete "In Your World," activity 2 from SECTION 3 Checkpoint! on page 27.

*Prayer:* Close class with the prayer found in CHAPTER 1 Review, page 29.

# Analyzing Attitudes

| Person | Attitude | Experience That Triggered It | Part of Your Experience | |
|---|---|---|---|---|
| | | | Yes | No |
| 1. Alanna Wack | | | | |
| 2. Greg Markovitch | | | | |
| 3. Frank Han-Chinh | | | | |
| 4. Fred Smith | | | | |
| 5. Bessy Parker | | | | |
| 6. Philip Sanders | | | | |
| 7. Rosaria Sanchez | | | | |
| 8. Theresa Martin | | | | |
| 9. Beth Spencer | | | | |
| 10. Barbara Leigh | | | | |
| 11. Cheryl Larson | | | | |

Name: _____     Score: _____

**CHAPTER ONE QUIZ**
# Finding an Image that Works for You

Mark true (+) or false (o).

____  **1.** Images exert a powerful influence in our lives.

____  **2.** Our images are a result of our experiences.

____  **3.** Images never change.

____  **4.** The Church can be defined in many ways.

____  **5.** Attitudes toward the Church are formed by our experience of it.

____  **6.** We are always conscious of our feelings.

____  **7.** Our image of the Church largely determines how we will relate to it.

____  **8.** The closer an image comes to reality, the better it is.

____  **9.** Depersonalized images produce the most growth.

____ **10.** Studying the Church helps one develop a true image.

# CHAPTER ONE QUIZ
Answer Key

**1.** +
**2.** +
**3.** o
**4.** +
**5.** +
**6.** o
**7.** +
**8.** +
**9.** o
**10.** +

## The Power of Images
At the kindergarten open house, Macy Higgs's parents were puzzled by their daughter's artwork displayed on the bulletin board. It was a crayon drawing of their family—the two parents, Macy's brothers, Macy, and Timbo, their Scottie. The figures were childishly spindly and sticklike, except that they all had massive shoulders and chests. Largest of all was the thorax of the dog. Miss Spencer, the little girl's teacher, reported that when asked about her drawing, Macy had said, "I left a lot of room because my Mommy told me in our family we all have big hearts."

What image of her family had the mother instilled in the little girl? Do you think it will affect the kind of person she becomes? Why or why not?

## Defining Your Identity
The modern novelist James Joyce, in the book *A Portrait of the Artist as a Young Man*, has Stephen Dedalus, a student in a school in Ireland, write in his geography book:

Stephen Dedalus

Class of Elements

Conglowes Wood College [boys' schools were called colleges in Ireland]

County Kildare

Ireland

Europe

The World

The Universe

He read the column "from the bottom to the top till he came to his own name. What was he?

And he read down the page again. What was the universe? Nothing. But was there anything round the universe to show where it stopped before the nothing place began? It could not be a wall but there could be a thin line there all round everywhere. Only God could do that."

Like many young people today, Stephen Dedalus was asking the basic questions: Who am I? What am I? Why am I? Direct the students to write the most inclusive identification of themselves that they can.

After the exercise, lead them to see that their relationship to God in Christ can only be made through the Church. But you might caution them that a relationship with God—being baptized in the Church—is not merely a matter of going to Church on Sunday or observing Church feasts. All these plus their personal prayer, sacramental participation, life activities, and service to neighbor must tend toward one thing—growth in intimacy with God.

## A Mathematical Definition of Church
Write these words vertically at the chalkboard:

**God =**

**Jesus =**

**Church =**

Below, write the answers:

me, Jesus, Church.

Ask the class to complete each equation by lining up the answers correctly. The result should be:

**God = Jesus**

**Jesus = Church**

**Church = me**

## Using Imagination to Express What the Church Is to You
Invite students to think of their parish church, the Church of their diocese, or the Church universal in the image of a bird, a plant, or an animal and draw the image in pencil, pen, crayon, or paint. After completing the drawing, have them explain their choice of metaphor to a partner and hear their partner's explanation.

Ask: What does your image say about you? What kind of Church member might you one day be if you retain this image?

**①**

## The Iceman and the Crucifixion

In Eugene O'Neill's *The Iceman Cometh*, the traveling salesman Hickey finally shot his wife because she always forgave him when he returned after being unfaithful to her. Ask: "Why would her unfailing love nourish his hate?" (Because it made him feel so guilty that he couldn't forgive himself, and so he had to kill the source of his suffering.) Help the students to see the parallelism with the crucifixion and the deepest reason why some people are so angry with the Church—Christ's Body—here on earth. Stress the urgency of self-knowledge and response to grace.

## Some Ways to Handle Discussion

### A. Class or Open Discussion

1. Have the class prepare ahead of time by reading and thinking through some lead questions.

2. If possible, after a few teacher-led demonstrations, have students lead the discussions.

3. The leader should try to get as many as possible to participate, gently put down any who monopolize, draw out the timid, prevent detours, and keep the discussion moving and open-ended.

4. Someone can be appointed to summarize the main points raised in discussion, either at intervals or at the end.

### B. Panel Discussion

1. In advance, four to six selected students are assigned different aspects of a topic. The class also gathers general background on the topic ahead of time.

2. A chairperson introduces the panel members and their respective viewpoints, if appropriate. Members then present their discussion.

3. The chairperson opens the discussion to the class (floor). Individuals then address a specific panel member with coments or questions. A panel member may address other panelists or members of the class or make additional comments.

4. The chairperson summarizes the main points of the discussion.

### C. Round Table Discussion

1. Small groups of from three to eight persons sit around tables or in circles and freely discuss a prepared agenda of questions on a designated topic.

2. Each group's secretary takes notes and presents them to the class, after which individuals from the class may ask further questions or add to the discussion.

### D. Phillips 66

This activity is also known informally as a "Buzz Session." Many teachers have their classes permanently divided into groups of four, five, or six students for group activities during the quarter. Each group has a permanent chairperson. A different secretary may be named for each group session. The students may review or give highlights of a topic, present their answers on a topic or question for four to six minutes. Different groups may have different topics, phases, or pages to discuss; or half the group may be given one section and the other half another section. The secretaries then report to the entire class.

## Surfacing Unconscious Images

Much has been written in psychology and religion journals about the value of images for arriving at truth in a world ruled by logical thought. Although youth are bombarded by images from the media, and are quite at home with visual images, they often lack the imagination of those who grew up with the spoken or written word alone.

You may want to devote time at the outset of the course to give the class a perspective on these ideas. Stress the need for a knowledge of history, and the importance of being open to models of Church other than those they already know from their limited experience.

As already formed persons, adolescents have images of the Church buried in their unconscious. If unrealized, these images can become destructive to the young people and to others. Since material in the unconscious is not always known to the conscious mind, it might be well to lead your class to ways of locating their unrealized images.

Although the royal road to the unknown life is within us and the main way we compensate for neglected areas of personality is through dreams, dream analysis demands some specialized knowledge and may not necessarily relate to Church. But attending to other sources—such as projection, feelings, and active imagination— might prove helpful.

By *projection* we hurl unowned parts of our self into the environment. We "project" on others and they begin to represent ourselves without our realizing it. For instance, strong admiration for the work, talent, or qualities of others may contain a hint that we too have similar abilities which we need to recognize, accept, and develop. The calling to particular Church ministries may begin in this manner. Attraction to certain qualities in persons or institutions of other denominations may be impulses of the Spirit to bring those qualities, through oneself, into one's own parish. These images in our environment call us to our responsibilities.

Intense dislike of certain people, features, mannerisms, appearance, qualities, or situations may be just as revealing. When we do not admit that we need healing, greater wisdom ,or forgiving, we tend to find these needs in others. We attribute these needs to them, not to ourselves! Thus when the apparent domination of a committee head, organization president, pope, pastor, or bishop seems unbearable, it may be our own unrealized tendency to dominate what we see in them. Of course, the Church and its people can possess very real faults. But more often than not, our images of Church may reflect a projection which, if scrutinized objectively, becomes a window to the self we do not know. The purpose of this activity when done in connection with the Church is not so much to obtain self-knowledge, as to be enabled to recognize when criticism is objective and valid, when it is partially or purely subjective.

Along with dreams and projection, feelings are an important source of images. One process frequently suggested by psychologists is to sit quietly with eyes closed and see ourselves marching as if in a parade, allowing images to surface from within us on an imaginary screen inside our head. By noticing those images that recur and seem to vibrate with the emotions of our head, we enter more deeply into our true motivations of and our true responses to experience.

Once we recognize our emotional needs, we become less compulsive in our reactions, less likely to lash out at the Church for our own failures to integrate our lives. Lack of self-knowledge often is at the root of alienation from the Church because of actions and rules we have judged as unjust.

A mother who consistently conjures up images of cruelty may find the need to acknowledge that both her excessive permissiveness with her son and her anger at the firmness of the sister who disciplines him stem from the unowned vice lodged deep within her own character. On the one hand, unprincipled kindness compensates for the unconscious guilt of evil inclinations; on the other, anger is the result of projecting the heart's evil on another.

A person with a poorly developed thinking function may view a thinking-type person as in an ivory tower. Someone with a poorly developed feeling function may judge another as a "bleeding heart" or "all sentimentality," when, in actuality, that "bleeding heart" actually has a well-integrated feeling function.

A third way to find unconscious images is through active imagination expressed in patterns of dance, drawing, or other art forms. Even the gospel stories that touch us find the unconscious corners within us. Soon students may be able to act out their images of Church imaginatively. Outrage at some real or alleged injustice or hurt done by some significant person in the Church may more easily be expressed in crushing a piece of paper, stamping a foot, or drawing a violent scene than in words. The comments of those who love us can be a help to identifying our problems in relating to Church.

The real issue, of course, is our anger with God—our need to crucify Jesus—because of our humiliating unlikeness to him and the guilt and shame of our failure to respond to his love. This often is projected onto his Body, the Church—Christ among us. To give students a glimpse of this truth can possibly be the most liberating thing you can do for them. You can help them understand the reasons for their anger or fear, and offer them suggestions on ways in which they can develop new and healthier attitudes.

27

## CHAPTER 2

# BIBLICAL IMAGES AND MYSTERY

(Text pages 30–57)

**2**

## FOCUS

**Doctrinal:** The divine-human mystery that is the Church is best explained and understood through images.

**Personal:** Am I willing to grow in my understanding of the mystery of the Church?

## OBJECTIVES

**Cognitive:** (a) to understand that, by its nature, the Church shares in the mystery of God; (b) to grow from experiencing some images of the Church used in Scripture and from what they reveal about the Church.

**Affective:** (a) to discover a meaningful image of the Church to which I can relate; (b) to accept the divine-human nature of the Church and to grow in love for it.

## Chapter 2 Outline

### SECTION 1
#### The Wonder of a Mystery
The Church: A Religious Mystery

The Mystery of God

Saint Paul and the Mystery

Jesus and the Mystery

*On This Rock* (margin feature)

Biblical Images of the Mystery

The Sheepfold and the Good Shepherd

The Vine and the Branches

*Images in Art* (text feature)

### SECTION 2
#### A Community of Disciples
Disciple and Teacher

Faith Supported in Community

*Communion of Saints* (margin feature)

Our Church Community

The Call of Discipleship

The Body of the Church: Paul's Image

Our Union with God in Christ

Our Union with One Another

*A Pilgrim Church* (text feature)

Diversity of Gifts

## SECTION 3
### People of God

The Chosen People
*Chosen and Choosing* (text feature)
Imperfection among God's People
Early Church Leaders
*A People at Prayer* (margin feature)
The Work of the Holy Spirit

❷

# TEACHER'S RESOURCE 2A

## Historical Notes

The concept of mystery has a long history in the culture of Greece. Concretely, mystery implied something secretive. Just as the initiation rituals of the ancient Greek mystery religions were held in secret, early Christian celebrations of the Eucharist were open only to the baptized. All others were required to leave worship before the Eucharist.

Biblical images have always been important in Christianity. The images found in the Hebrew Scriptures were identified as types of New Testament figures. These links enhanced the relationship between the Hebrew Scriptures and the New Testament, and thus between Judaism and Christianity.

## Pedagogical Notes

1. Only selected Biblical images are developed in this chapter. You may wish to work more extensively with some of the images suggested for research in the Scripture Search on page 40. All the images given in the text and many others are well developed and interrelated in the final chapter of *Images of the Church in the New Testament* by Paul S. Minear (Philadelphia: Westminster Press, 1977).

2. Your class might need a review of the history of Israel as a background for understanding the biblical image of the People of God—rooted in the event of the Exodus and the giving of the Law on Mt. Sinai.

# TEACHER'S RESOURCE 2B

## Theological Notes

Right from the beginning, the Christian community recognized that its self-definition necessarily involved a relationship to God and God's son, Jesus. So, instead of trying to develop complicated intellectual definitions of the Church, Scripture simply records images that describe this relationship. Three Biblical images are particularly helpful for our understanding of how the first Christians understood themselves; disciples, the Body of Christ, and the People of God.

A disciple is a student—a learner. Because those who followed Jesus accepted him as their rabbi or teacher, they felt comfortable with the image of disciple. Christians are women and men who are anxious to learn all they can about the "Good News" Jesus came to proclaim. We recall the stories Jesus told, the wisdom about God's Kingdom that he shared, and the challenges he offered us to think about life in a brand new way.

The Body of Christ is an image for the Church that comes from Saint Paul. It too describes a special relationship that Christians enjoy with Jesus. The important thing to remember about this second Biblical metaphor for the Church is that it suggests an organic relationship with Christ. The Body of Christ is one, although it has many parts, and no single part can claim to be the whole. Only by working together can we disclose Christ to the world. What is more, this image implies an obligation that we have to be the earthly Body of Christ now that he is no longer present among us as he was two thousand years ago. If we are not the Body of Christ, we deprive the world of the witness that Jesus intended us to make.

The third Biblical image that indicates the Church's relationship with God is the "People of God." One of the most startling pieces of good news that Jesus brought us is that we should no longer consider ourselves servants of God. Rather, he said, we are members of God's household—God's family. The first book of the Bible, Genesis, reveals that we were created in God's image and likeness. We are God's daughters and sons.

Though this intimate relationship with our creator was obscured by sin, God never gave up on us. Like the loving father in Luke 15, God welcomes us home, no matter how far we go astray. This was Jesus' word to us, and we express our reliance on his word by claiming the name of God's people. This claim is not a boast or an act of presumption on our part. It is simply a recognition, made in faith, of God's boundless mercy.

Each one of these ancient images for the Church stresses that the Church is far more than an organized institution. It is, above all else, human beings who have been called by the Father and the Son to hear the Gospel, to proclaim it, and to rejoice in it. While it is certainly true that the Church has grown and become a more complex organization over the centuries, its nature and mission have never changed.

Church is people. It is people who have been called by God to receive the gift of God's love and to accept the task of sharing that love in the name of Jesus Christ. There is much more that we can say about the Church, but as Scripture indicates, we dare not say less.

**②**

# Biblical Images of the Church

"The inner nature of the Church is now made known to us in various images"
*(Constitution on the Church, 6).*

Sheepfold

A Pilgrim People

Vine and Branches

People of God

Church

Community of Disciples

Body of Christ

Name: _____   Score: _____

# Study Guide, Chapter 2

Directions: Using your text as a guide, fill in the missing terms.

**2**

**I.**   To express the inner nature of the Church, Vatican II felt the need to use
_____ to help bridge the gap between our _____ and the
true meaning of the Church. Because of belonging to the category of
things sacred, the Church is a profound _____ reflecting the
inexpressible mystery of _____. We all _____ mystery, and
although we cannot put it under a microscope, it is not _____.
Mystery involves _____, the acceptance of things unseen based on the
acceptance of God's _____ .

The mystery of the Church lies in the unfathomable design of God's
_____ and _____ , and in the desire to share the divine _____.
God first revealed the _____ plan to _____ , and through Jesus,
showed that all peoples were included. Those who accepted Jesus and
lived out his _____ became known as the Church. In trying to
communicate the mystery of God, Jesus used familiar images. Their
power calls forth our _____ as they instruct us in the mystery and
reflect many _____.

**II.**   John's Gospel compares the Church to a _____ with Jesus as the
_____. The _____ image is found in the _____ and expresses
God's loving care of us. Another image of the relationship of Jesus'
followers to himself is the _____ and the _____. The mutual
_____ which it portrays is perhaps the deepest mystery of the
Church. Christ dwells in it as a whole and in each of his _____.
Through the actions of the _____ we are inserted into Christ's
community and transformed into partakers of _____.

The Gospels show Jesus as gathering a community of _____, each
called _____. Jesus called himself a _____ in relation to his
heavenly Father because he _____ to the Father and did the Father's
_____. In a community of disciples, _____ in Jesus is
the core. Members _____ each other in living _____ lives.

**III.** In calling Christians the Body of Christ, Paul emphasizes both our
_____ and our_____. Jesus, as _____ of the body, is
closely united to all the _____ , and becomes the _____ for
our own lives. Paul suggests that this close union with Jesus is as intimate
as that of _____ and calls the Church the _____ of Christ.
The Church as the Mystical Body of Christ is bound together by the
_____. Members have different _____ but remain one
_____. One image for the Church, used in Apostolic times and
restored by _____ , is the _____. It was first applied to the
_____ and then to _____. Israelite tradition shows that being
specially chosen by God is a _____ experience and a heavy
_____ . Members of God's people often have not, and still do not,
live up to _____. But despite our failings, the _____
continues to work through weak and sinful people. We have Christ's
_____ , "I am with you _____ until the end of the world"
*(Matthew 28:20).*

## Study Guide, Chapter 2
### Answer Key

**I.** religious mystery

images

experience

God

need

irrational

faith

word/wisdom

goodness

mercy

life

divine

the Jews

"new way"

images

emotions/sides.

**II.** sheepfold

gate

shepherd

Hebrew Scriptures

vine

branches

abiding

members

sacraments

his divinity

disciples

individually

disciple

listened

will

faith

support

Christian

**III.** unity

diversity

head

members

pattern

marriage

bride

Holy Spirit

gifts

body

Vatican II

People of God

Hebrews (Jews)

Christians

humbling

responsibility

expectations

Holy Spirit

promise

always

## Summary Sheet

1. A mystery goes _____ our ability to fully _____ .

2. God is reflected in _____ mystery.

3. Paul used the word for mystery to mean _____ , God's plan for

   our _____ and the _____ which ensure our entry into

   the _____ of Christ.

4. The _____ is a community of disciples who

   follow _____ and support others in the _____ .

5. The Church is composed of many _____ , all different,

   but _____ in faith. Paul used the _____ of

   the _____ to symbolize this _____ .

6. The _____ community is identified as the _____ of

   God.

7. The image of the _____ People suggests _____

   and _____ .

8. The _____ of the Spirit can bring about _____

   and _____ . But as a _____ organization, the Church

   may display _____ .

## Answer Key for 2E

1. beyond, understand
2. religious
3. knowledge, salvation, rites, community
4. Church, Jesus, community
5. individuals, united, image, body, relationship
6. Church, People
7. Chosen, faith, responsibility
8. power, unity, strength, human, weaknesses

Name: _____  Score: _____

## CHAPTER 2 Test

## Biblical Images That Light Up the Mystery

**I. Matching:** Write the letter of the term that corresponds to the description given.

**a.** Body of Christ      **e.** *musterium*      **i.** sheepfold

**b.** disciple            **f.** mystery          **j.** sin

**c.** failure             **g.** pilgrim          **k.** unity in diversity

**d.** faith               **h.** religious initiation   **l.** vineyard

____ **1.** Something beyond our ability to comprehend.

____ **2.** Being brought into the community through sacred rites.

____ **3.** The Greek initiation ritual whose name was applied to the sacramental rites of Christianity.

____ **4.** Image of the Church in which Jesus is the gate.

____ **5.** Image of the community of Israel.

____ **6.** Blocks God's kingdom.

____ **7.** Jesus' relationship to the Father.

____ **8.** The core of discipleship.

____ **9.** Saint Paul's image of the Church.

____ **10.** Characteristic of the Church as the Mystical Body.

**II. Multiple choice.** Place the letter of the best answer on the line.

____ **1.** The Church is a profound religious mystery because (a) it cannot be defined, (b) it belongs to the category of things sacred.

____ **2.** The first revelation of salvation was made (a) to the Jews, (b) to the followers of Jesus.

____ **3.** The presence of Christ in his Church is primarily (a) revealed in the miraculous, (b) hidden in the ordinary.

____ **4.** Images are powerful because they reflect (a) a single aspect of a reality, (b) many sides of a thing at the same time.

____ **5.** Shortcomings among the followers of Christ (a) have always existed, (b) were unknown in the early Church.

**III. Matching.** Write the letter of the Church image most closely associated with the characteristic(s) given. Answers may be used more than once.

**a.** Body of Christ     **c.** People of God     **e.** Sheepfold and Shepherd

**b.** Community of Disciples     **d.** Pilgrim People     **f.** Vine and Branches

____ **1.** Sacrificial love and tender care

____ **2.** Foreshadowed in the Israelites' desert experience

____ **3.** Identification of Christ's union with Christians as head

____ **4.** Old Testament imagery related to mutual abiding

____ **5.** An individual call which requires a daily response

____ **6.** The mystery of group choice made by God

____ **7.** Union with Christ brings forth fruit.

____ **8.** Members are interrelated but have a unique diversity

____ **9.** The way to becoming saints is one of constant conversion and renewal.

____**10.** Involves mutual support and presupposes instruction and initiation

**IV. Essay.** Choose two.

1. Why is mystery a need of human beings? How does the Church fill it?

2. Explain your favorite biblical image of the Church and tell why it is your favorite.

3. How do you help or hinder God's plan for yourself? the world?

## Chapter 2 Test
## Answer Key

**I.**

1. f
2. h
3. e
4. i
5. l
6. j
7. b
8. d
9. a
10. k

**II.**

1. b
2. a
3. b
4. b
5. a

**III.**

1. e
2. d
3. a
4. f
5. b
6. c
7. f
8. a
9. d
10. b

**IV.**

Answers will vary.

# CHAPTER 2

## SECTION 1
## Text Questions (Student text pages 31–39)
### Page 33

(1) Answers will vary—emotions may range from confusion to fear to awe to excitement.

(2) Those who share the inner vision of faith perceive the mystery of the Eucharist and participate in the life of the Church.

### Page 35

(3) The images include love, terror, salvation, and danger.

(4) The difference lies in the role faith plays in reinforcing the images. The image of salvation may be missing in the image of non-members.

(5) Images are like clues; they link concepts and make connections.

### Page 37

(6) Other relationships might be teacher and student, parent and child, or even elected official and constituent.

(7) As shepherd, Jesus is concerned about the sheep in his flock and those outside it. Jesus acts as protector and savior. As savior, he gave his life as a sacrifice like the sheep Abraham offered for Isaac.

### Page 39

(8) The human body is probably the next best image.

(9) The image of the vine demonstrates the full integration of all who come to Christianity and accept its truths. Each person is like a branch, fully grafted onto the main vine of the Church.

## SECTION 1 Checkpoint! (page 40)
### Review

(1) Images are used to describe mysteries because they reflect different aspects of that mystery. This way several angles of the mystery are illustrated at the same time.

(2) Mystery reflects reality. It touches the sacred and pushes us to the limits of life.

(3) Religious mystery reflects the sacred and the mystery of God.

**(4)** *Musterion* means a religious ritual of initiation involving reenactment of events in the life of a god.

**(5)** Paul uses the word to mean the Church as a mystery hidden for ages and unfolding according to God's plan to restore all things. It can also refer to the sacramental life of the Church.

**(6)** Jesus used images familiar to his followers from the Hebrew Scriptures and from the daily life of the culture.

**(7)** Words to Know: *etymology* (the study of word origins); *musterion* (the rites of the Catholic Church); *mystery* (something beyond our ability to comprehend); *pastoral* (relating to the countryside and the raising of livestock); *sacred* (holy or divine, different from everyday).

## In Your World

**(1)** Some new images might include a friend or older sibling. These images carry the ideas of trust, someone on whom to rely, intimacy, and protection.

**(2)** Have students pick out some terms. Use an unabridged dictionary and show them how to find the root of the word and its original language. Some terms might include sacred, secular, divine, Eucharist, communion, Church.

## Scripture Search

**(1)** Matthew 13 (the image used is of a fishing net and the process of sorting out its contents); Luke 6 (the image is of a house and how the type of foundation on which it is built determines how permanent it will be); John 15 (this is the image of vine and branches discussed in the chapter).

**(2)** Students will need a Bible. Discuss the apparent contradiction between leading and being led and how they are successfully combined in these images.

## SECTION 2
## Text Questions (Student text pages 41–47)
### Page 42

**(10)** Answers will vary and may include family, profession, friends, and material possessions.

**(11)** Answers will vary—volunteering to work with the homeless or in a soup kitchen, education fundraising, etc.

### Page 43

**(12)** Answers may include counseling, shelter, or friendship.

### Page 44

**(13)** Answers may include being a good friend, showing compassion to someone in need, or cooperating at home.

**(14)** While one might advise them to go to a counselor, priest, or teacher who can help them, it's important simply to be a friend to the person, pray together, and be a good listener.

### Page 46

**(15)** The head controls and sends messages to the other parts of the body and the members make the entire body function well and together.

**(16)** The Church shelters the poor and concerns itself with issues of war, justice, and peace throughout the world.

**(17)** We are united in our faith, our obedience to the Holy Father, and in our religious observance. We differ in culture, language, and customs.

### Page 47

**(18)** Diversity gives variety to the Church and makes it more complete because it then reflects the different types of people who make up the Body of Christ. Human society is more interesting and benefits from diversity. Each person can make a unique contribution to society.

## SECTION 2 Checkpoint! (page 48)
### Review

**(1)** Jesus called his disciples as individuals by challenging them to community life.

**(2)** Jesus was a disciple of God and of Joseph while he was growing up. He acted as an apprentice: listening, learning, and being obedient.

**(3)** Answers will vary and may include the support of friends and interaction with others.

**(4)** The Church offers support because it knows people are tested in their faith. It offers support and reconciliation to those who hurt from physical, emotional, or spiritual causes, and to those who are in doubt.

**(5)** Discipleship is offered to us daily.

**(6)** Jesus is the head united to all the Church's members who form the body. It is a united organism that works together by the individual contributions of its members.

**(7)** Words to Know: *disciple* ( one who accepts and spreads the teachings of Christ); *patriarchal* (society where authority is given to male members); *diversity* (being different).

## In Your World

**(1)** Make a list of the gifts and note how many different ones there are (the diversity). Encourage the students to reflect on their own gifts as well as those of others. Discuss how this diversity can lead to completeness, but also sometimes to jealousy.

**(2)** Encourage students to think about what would cause a crisis of faith for someone—especially a young person—and how they would respond.

## Scripture Search

Initiate a discussion of how the body is seen as both good and bad by most people. Relate this to secular images of the body, especially in advertising. Reread the creation narrative in Genesis 1–2. What other organizations could use the body imagery (the family—with both parents as head is an example). Finally, discuss Paul's imagery and our ability to cooperate with God's grace to overcome the limitations of our bodies.

## SECTION 3

## Text Questions (Student text pages 49–55)

### Page 50

**(19)** Jews and Christians have all had: (a) a common faith experience and history; (b) a covenant with God; (c) struggles with infidelity and persecution. For Christians, the Jewish people prepared the way for them, and the expected Messiah is Jesus. For Christians, Jesus' sacrificial offering saved the people from sin.

**(20)** Answers will vary but should focus on the active role of responding to God's offer of a permanent covenant. Responses God demands may include obedience, faith, trust, or strength.

### Page 52

**(21)** Answers will vary and may include negative ones such as greed, weakness, or laziness; and positive ones such as honesty, caring

involvement, and strong faith. Look for specific instances, not hearsay.

**(22)** Answers will vary but should focus on the point that the failings of one person do not affect the holiness of the entire body.

## SECTION 3 Checkpoint! (page 55)

### Review

**(1)** Answers will vary—the experience focuses on our reliance on God, our responsibility, and our need to live up to expectations.

**(2)** The Church community must fulfill its moral and social obligations in imitation of Christ.

**(3)** The Church is rooted in humanity, which is imperfect and therefore displays weaknesses.

**(4)** The diverse group of Jesus' followers reflects the wide appeal of his message and the variety of gifts brought into the Church.

**(5)** Words to Know: *People of God* (image of the Church based on the Jews as the people specially chosen by God); *mercy* (compassion); *zeal* (eagerness in pursuing something); *Nicodemus* (Jewish leader who became a follower of Jesus); *Inquisition* (court established to uncover heresy within the Church).

### In Your World

**(1)** Discuss this in class and then have each student ask at least one other person. Go over the results in class. Focus specifically on the term as it applies to the Jewish people and then to the Church. Be sure to encourage students to see the passive and active aspects of this concept.

**(2)** Some things which threaten the Church today might be greed, disobedience, the lure of secular society as a result of television programming, peer pressure, and weakness. The Church can respond with strength, faith, and active discipleship on a daily basis.

### Scripture Search

A covenant is a pact or agreement in which each party has a particular responsibility. If either side does not live up to the agreement, the covenant may be broken. The covenant in this passage focuses on God's promise of a homeland and prosperity in response to the faith, trust, and obedience of the Jewish people. Christ limited the commandments to two and made the covenant universal by offering it to all people. He mediated God's message of an emerging kingdom of God.

## CHAPTER 2 Review (pages 56–57)

### Study

**(1)** People often use images and symbols to explain things which they don't understand.

**(2)** Religious mystery means that the true inner nature of the Church is known to us only through our experiences and images, not by its true meaning.

**(3)** Saint Paul applied the word "mystery" to the Church and to the sacramental life of the Church.

**(4)** One comes closer by affirming faith, by saying yes daily to discipleship, and by being open.

**(5)** Biblical images act as mirrors to reflect the mystery; they need to be examined carefully.

**(6)** The shepherd represents Christ as caring for his people (the flock). Jesus protects the members of the Church, but also acts as the sacrificial lamb, dying in order that its members can live.

**(7)** Images come from within a culture so that the people will be able to relate to and understand those images. The images must be familiar so that people can make the connection between the image and the reality.

**(8)** Jesus was a disciple of his human father and of God, and also a master to his own disciples.

**(9)** The Church is Christ's body on earth. It witnesses the living Savior to all people.

**(10)** People are called to discipleship on a daily basis and should respond continually. Discipleship is a challenge that allows us to demonstrate our faith.

**(11)** It is successful in that it suggests how the Holy Spirit binds Christians together under Jesus. If taken literally, the image suffers.

**(12)** Through the diversity of gifts, the Church is able to meet the needs of the whole body collectively. Everyone is needed; no one is indispensable.

**(13)** Being part of the People of God means being part of a community that has been gifted with God's grace.

**(14)** The Church can disillusion some people when it displays the imperfections of all human beings and human organizations. We must remember that, while we should try to live up to Christ's standards, people still fail.

### Action

**(1)** Some images might include a dove (for the Holy Spirit and peace), or a family. Encourage creative images. Require an explanation of what each image means and why it was chosen.

**(2)** This can be done individually or as a group. Stress every step of the journey as part of the spiritual experience, not just the time spent in the place itself.

### Prayer

Try to encourage discussion of these experiences. Is one form of prayer necessarily better or more effective than the other? How do they complement each other and work together to give the Christian community a sense of completeness? Perhaps the class might meet before school to attend Mass every day for a week.

# Biblical Images and Mystery

**OVERVIEW:** The aim of this chapter is to present the concept of images to students and to show how biblical images are used to illustrate the mystery of the Church, the relationship between Jesus and the Church, and the call to discipleship.

**OBJECTIVES:** The students will:

- Discuss the idea of mystery in life and in the Church.

- In small groups, examine the biblical images of the mystery.

- As a class, discuss the concepts of People of God and being a disciple by showing how individual and community are linked.

**TIME FRAME: One to one-and-a-half hours.**

**MATERIALS: Poster board, markers, Bibles.**

**PROCEDURE:**

*Into:* Prayer—Begin class with a prayer, possibly from Deuteronomy 6:4–9.

*Through:*

Activity One:

1. Ask students to define a mystery like certain emotions such as love or happiness. Use questions 1–2 on page 33 as a guide.

2. Have students define or describe God. How does the notion of mystery apply here?

3. Conclude by looking at some of the biblical images and discussing how they work effectively to communicate the mystery. Use question 5 on page 35.

Activity Two:

1. Ask for a definition of a disciple. Have students ever thought of Jesus as a disciple as well as a master?

2. Discuss the role of the Church community. Break into groups and have each provide at least two functions for the community. How do they relate to all aspects of life including prayer, faith, and support?

3. Have each student answer the following: "I am a disciple because ____." What makes each of us a disciple?

Activity Three:

1. What does People of God mean? Write down responses. Discuss the concepts of chosenness, superiority, choosing, and responsibility, and then apply them to the Jewish people and to the Church.

2. Discuss the humanity of the Church as composed of human beings and make a list on poster board of characteristics of the Church and its members.

*Beyond:* Suggest that students read "Chosen and Choosing" on page 51, and follow up by doing activity 1 from Section 3 "In Your World," page 55.

*Prayer:* Close class with the same prayer with which it opened.

**CHAPTER 2 QUIZ**
# Biblical Images that Light up the Mystery

Mark true (+) or false (o).

___ **1.** No one definition of the Church is totally satisfactory.

___ **2.** Mystery is a necessary part of life through which we are called to grow.

___ **3.** Since the Church is a mystery, we should not waste time trying to understand it.

___ **4.** God is revealed in Jesus and continues that revelation in the Church.

___ **5.** Images reflect many sides of a thing at once.

___ **6.** Jesus was the first to present God in the image of the shepherd.

___ **7.** The image of the vine and branches speaks only of our union with Christ, not with one another.

___ **8.** Discipleship involves listening and doing.

___ **9.** Jesus was a master, never a disciple.

___ **10.** The image of the body brings out the Church's unity in diversity.

___ **11.** The title "People of God" applies to both Hebrews and Christians.

___ **12.** Being God's people frees us from failings.

## CHAPTER 2 QUIZ
Answer Key

**1.** +

**2.** +

**3.** o

**4.** +

**5.** +

**6.** o

**7.** o

**8.** +

**9.** o

**10.** +

**11.** +

**12.** o

### Moments of Mystery
We all have moments when the mystery of our existence breaks in on our daily lives:

• A display at the natural history museum of the bones of a dinosaur that walked the earth 200 million years ago.

• In a state park, the rock formation and sandy path which show that, at one time, millions of years back, the area you are hiking in was once completely under water.

• The millions of years it took to form a diamond.

• The perfectly formed tiny fingernails of a neighbor's new baby.

• The intricate color patterns of feathers on the wild geese that landed on the lake where you were camping.

• The exquisite soft beauty of a lowly pansy.

• The innocent giggle of a child, communication by satellite, your own growth.

Pause now to recall when you experienced mystery in your life.

### Experiencing Images
Because the point of using images is not so much intellectual as experiential (that is, emotional and spiritual) before exploring the biblical images of Church, you may want to help the students place themselves in a receptive mood for the experience of images. This can be done in several ways:

• A stilling exercise in which extraneous "noises" are quieted and the whole being is poised for encounter with the image.

• An imaginative description of a setting can make the image more meaningful.

• Use of a secular poem:

Any of Emily Dickenson's, but a discussion of "What mystery pervades a well!" (#1400 in her collection) might lead into the mystery of a simple thing like water. The last line of "A Narrow Fellow in the Grass" describes the experience of mystery.

If your class is able to handle it, use Stephen Spender's poem, "The Landscape Near an Aerodrome," where not only is the rape of the land told in image, but also the place of the church in the modern landscape is suggested.

Two "mood-creating" old standbys are Gerard Manley Hopkins' "God's Grandeur" and Elinor Wylie's "Velvet Shoes."

### Main Events in God's Plan of Salvation
*Prehistoric times*

Promise of victory over evil [Genesis 3:15 ]

Covenant with Noah [Genesis 9 ]

*Israel's Early History*

1900 B.C.: Covenant with Abraham: Many Nations [Genesis 12:2–3, 15:18, 17:2,5–7]

1250 B.C.: Covenant with Moses: My People—12 Tribes [Exodus 3:4–10, 19:5–6, 19–20; Deuteronomy 6,7, 26:16–19]

1000 B.C.: Covenant with David: David's House [2 Samuel 7:8–17]

750 B.C.: Early Calls to Renewal: Fidelity [Amos 5:7–15; Hosea 11:1–8]

*Israel's Exile and Return*

(Hints of the Coming One)

740 B.C.: Prophecy of Immanuel for all nations [Isaiah 11:1–5,10–11]

625 B.C.: Prophecy of a New Covenant [Jeremiah 3 1:3,33]

575 B.C.: Prophecy of a New Spirit [Ezekiel 36: 26–28 ]

540 B.C.: Prophecy of the Suffering Servant [2 Isaiah 42:1–4, 49:1–7, 50:4–11, 52:13–53:12]

450 B.C.: Renewal of the Covenant [Ezra 10:2–3,12; Nehemiah 8:2–6,9]

165 B.C.: Prophecy of the Son of Man [Daniel 7:13–14]

Prophecy of all the Kingdoms [Daniel 7:27]

*Age of the Messiah*

6–4 B.C.: The Savior Appears [Luke 1:30–33, 35; Matthew 1–2]

4 B.C.–A.D. 30: Jesus Gathers His Disciples [The Four Gospels]

A.D. 30–110: The Spirit Calls the Church into Being [The Acts of the Apostles]

A.D. 110 to Present: The Church Unfolds in History [Writings of the Fathers; Church Practice]

Have individuals or groups look up and summarize the Scripture quotations connected with each event, or simply draw from the class the meaning of each event. Point out the narrowing process leading up to the one man, Jesus, and the widening process after Jesus.

Conclude with a prayerful reading of Isaiah 9:1, 5–6 and Psalm 22:2–3, 8–9,17–19 or Philip's instruction to the Ethiopian in Acts 8:26–39. Why should Christians know the history of Israel?

In your journal note the effect on you of the thought that God has been preparing the Church for you since the beginning of time.

Psychologists say that the development of each individual parallels the development of the species. The same can be said about history and the individual. People experience "desert times" and times when they seem, like David, to have everything under control. They fall into the slavery of sin and experience restoration and prophetic insights in hard times. What stages traveled through by the Chosen People have you known? Which do you think you are experiencing now?

In one parable Jesus speaks of the kingdom of God as a seed. What parallels do you see between the stages of seed growth and the unfolding of God's revelation?

## A Liturgical Summary of the Story of Salvation

*Prayer:* Father, we acknowledge your greatness: all your actions show your wisdom and love. You formed us in your own likeness and set us over the whole world to serve you, our creator, and to rule over all creatures. Even when we disobeyed you and lost your friendship you did not abandon us to the power of death, but helped all people to seek and find you. Again and again you offered a covenant to us, and through the prophets taught us to hope for salvation. Father, you so loved the world that in the fullness of time you sent your own Son to be our Savior.

Eucharistic Prayer IV (adapted)

## Church as Community

1. The evangelists saw the Church as a community of disciples. Look up any set of five references, summarize each, then state the theme of discipleship which the five reflect. For example, a disciple must always be willing to learn, as a child learns.

   Luke: 1:26–38; 5:1–9, 11, 27–28; 6:12–16; 8:1–3; 9:1–6, 23–26, 46–48, 57–62; 10:16; 12:29–31; 14:25–26; 19:5–8; 24:11.

   Matthew: 8:21–22; 9:13b; 10:20, 24–25, 34–39; 10:40–42; 12:46–50; 16:18–19, 22–23; 18:1–5, 19–20, 22–23; 19: 23–26; 28:16–20.

   Acts 6:2.

   John: 1:43–50; 4:2, 29–30; 20:29; 21:19.

2. A popular image in the New Testament centers around the Wedding Feast and the proper choice of clothing. Read the following passages. What does the feast suggest to you about Christian life/heaven? What do the robes signify in each instance?

   Feast: Revelation 19–9; Luke 12:36; Matthew 22:1–10

   Robes: Revelation 20:11, 7:9–11, 1:14; Mark 9:3; Galatians 3:27; 2 Corinthians 5:2–3; Ephesians 6:11; Colossians 3:12f.

## Illustrating Biblical Images of the Church

Have individuals or small groups read and illustrate these brief parables. Supply the information given under symbols and actions. Ask them to formulate their own reflections. If those chosen below were not included, add them.

1. LEAVEN: Matthew 13:33—Symbols: (a) dough: our neighborhood, city country, (b) leaven (yeast): each Christian, a cell—Action: mixing together—Reflection: all look alike but Christians have the power to change the dough; suffering is the fire or oven in which change occurs.

ADDITIONAL
RESOURCES

**2.** WEED AND WHEAT: Matthew 13:24–30—
Symbols: (a) field: the Church; (b) wheat: people
living in truth sown by Christ; (c) weeds:
people living in sin, sown by Satan—Action:
wait until the harvest to gather them in—
Reflections: each person has a chance to show
if he or she is weed or wheat; both exist in the
Church and we must live with both; God gives
everyone time to grow; the end of the world
represents the sorting.

**3.** TREASURE IN THE FIELD: Matthew 13:44—
Symbols: (a) treasure: divine love in Jesus;
(b) field: human members—Action: God hides a
treasure in the dirt of the field—Reflection: the
treasure is invisible so the field looks
worthless; a person sells everything for the
hidden treasure.

## Culminating Discussion

**1.** Agree or disagree: The faults of Church
members spoil God's plan for the salvation of
the world.

**2.** One modern hymn asks where we would be
without Christ. Where would Christians be
without Israel?

**3.** What is the final mystery God has in store for
us? Will the Church still be needed? Why or
why not?

**4.** In the novel, *My Name is Asher Lev*, a
professional artist shocks his Jewish parents by
using the crucifixion as a symbol in his
painting. Why do you think he resorted to this
central Christian symbol?

**5.** The modern psychiatrist Carl Jung concluded
from his study of disturbed patients that we
need to face and accept the dark side of
ourselves to be healed. What prominent
symbol, often used to characterize the Church,
expresses this psychological-religious truth?

## Additional Reading

The following books can provide additional
information on a variety of topics covered in this
chapter:

Ferguson, George. *Signs and Symbols in Christian
Art.* New York: Oxford University Press, 1981.

Origen, *On Prayer* 12.2 in *Origen. Classics of
Western Spirituality.* Translated by Rowan A
Greer. New York: Paulist Press, 1979.

Montefiore, G. G. and Loewe, H. *A Rabbinic
Anthology.* New York: Schocken Books, 1974,
p. 78 (for midrash).

Rauff, Edward A. *Why People Join the Church.*
Glenmary Research 1979.

Trigg, Joseph W. *Origen: The Bible and
Philosophy in the Third Century Church.* Atlanta:
John Knox Press, 1983.

## CHAPTER 3

# Contemporary Images of the Church

(Text pages 58–83)

**3**

## FOCUS
**Doctrinal:** Models help us to uncover new dimensions and depths in the mystery of the Church.

**Personal:** How can I become more open to all that the Church is?

## OBJECTIVES
**Cognitive:** (a) to learn how models can help us to understand various aspects of the mystery of the Church; (b) to realize that each model, with its strengths and weaknesses, mirrors only a part of the total reality.

**Affective:** (a) to appreciate the variety of ways in which believers participate in the life of the Church; (b) to grow in openness and acceptance of others' points of view.

## Chapter 3 Outline

### SECTION 1
**Understanding God's Message**

Using Models to Build Images
What Is a Model
The Primary Model: The Trinity
*On This Rock* (margin feature)
Five Contemporary Models
The Church as an Institution
*Light of All Nations* (text feature)

### SECTION 2
**Examining Other Models**

The Church as Community
Community as Relationship
The People of God
The Church as a Unique Community
The Church as Sacrament
The Sacramental Church
Using and Abusing the Model
*Understanding Scripture* (text feature)
The Church as Herald
*Communion of Saints* (margin feature)
The Word in the Church
Integrating Models

## SECTION 3
### Being of Service

The Church as Servant
The Serving Church
*A People at Prayer* (margin feature)
Pulling the Models Together
Your Special Gifts
*Follow the Star* (text feature)
A Community of Disciples

# TEACHER'S RESOURCE 3A

## Historical Notes

The Trinity has been studied and used as a model since the time of the early Church. Saint Augustine, among others, wrote a treatise on the Trinity examining its use in psychology and relating the trinities in our relationships to the divine Trinity. Early Christian theologians used exegesis of Scripture in order to clarify theological concepts.

## Pedagogical Notes

1. Models are used in all aspects of human expression. Students should become familiar with the use of models in a variety of fields. Discuss or bring in familiar models: for example, Picasso's use of multi-faceted drawings, Einstein's theory of relativity, or any modern music (such as that of Charles Ives) which incorporates several melodies at the same time.

2. Encourage students to place themselves into the story of the text, particularly in Section 3. At this stage in development, students have more of a wish to conform to their peers than to recognize gifts which may separate them. Focus on the positive value of difference.

# TEACHER'S RESOURCE 3B

## Theological Notes

As the topic of contemporary images is discussed in this chapter, it may be useful to explore why there are so many different approaches to understanding the Church today. The teacher would not want to leave students with the mistaken impression that bishops and theologians don't understand the Church. Quite the contrary; bishops and theologians understand the Church very well. However, the more complex an organization is, the more difficult it is to explain. For example, the better we understand ourselves, the more complex—even mysterious— we appear to be and the more difficulty we encounter in attempting to explain who we are. It is next to impossible to determine a simple, comprehensive definition—hence, the need for new and more varied images.

A good example of this development might be the way Americans understand themselves today.

If you asked the class to define what it means to be an American, any number of contrary (not necessarily contradictory) images are likely to surface. No single image would say it all about the United States; and yet all of them together are still insufficient to define the nation and its people.

Yes, we are the "land of the free," but some Americans still feel disenfranchised. America is the "land of opportunity," yet the doors to opportunity are not always open for everyone. People in the United States are, by all accounts, materialistic, but then, they are also among the most generous and altruistic people in the world. Our currency proclaims trust in God, while our public schools disallow prayer to God.

If a country just over two hundred years old is complex, so our two-thousand-year-old Church is much more so. Just as Americans strive to define who we are as a people, the leaders and teachers of the Church are continually trying to "catch the spirit" of Catholicism with new images and models.

In developing contemporary models for the Church, it is interesting to note that the bishops at Vatican II, as well as post-Vatican II theologians, have shown a preference for what might be called *functional* models and images. That is to say that the Church's self-understanding these days is frequently expressed in images that express what Christians do (or should do!).

The Body of Christ image, so popular at Vatican II, is a good example. So are Fr. Avery Dulles's models—particularly communion, herald, and servant. "The Church is as the Church does" seems to be the message. If this kind of contemporary imaging of the Church is practical, it is also Biblical. Scripture reveals that Jesus "defined" who he was for us by doing the works of the Father. He healed the sick; he gave hope to those who had despaired; he fed the hungry, and he challenged whoever would listen to him to take a fresh look at the meaning of life.

Taking our cue from the founder of the Church, Catholicism today seems to be returning to its roots for modern self-descriptions. Like Jesus, we are asking ourselves what we must *do* in our world to image the Father and the Father's kingdom. As we determine those tasks in light of the Gospel, we express who we are by using the more functional models current these days.

Our appreciation of who we are as Catholics will surely continue to develop over the centuries, just as it has developed since the last book of the Bible was written. But no matter what models and images are developed now and in the future, their purpose will always be the same: to help us to remember Jesus and what he sent us out to do. We are a people called to proclaim the Gospel of salvation for all women and men.

3

# Models of the Church: An Analysis (by Avery Dulles)

Name:

| Model | Mission of the Church | Major Strength | Major Weakness | What Keeps Members Together | Leaders (Experts) | Who Belongs |
|---|---|---|---|---|---|---|
| Institution | to baptize all in order to get eternal life | gives structure to the Church and a strong sense of identity | monopolistic tendencies, clericalism, juridicism, triumphalism | external discipline; pray, pay, obey | clergy (pastors) | Catholic Christians |
| Community | union with God in the Power of the Spirit | the Spirit is available to all | lack of formal structure leads to spiritualism | internal life of grace | lay people (ecumenists) | those faithful to the Spirit |
| Sacrament | to be a meaning-ful sign to all believers and non-believers | structure and availability of the Spirit | difficult to preach this model; too inward from a theological viewpoint | life of grace but externally manifested | those who witness (professional theologians) | those who really witness by prayer, integrity, good works |
| Herald | to proclaim the good news of salvation far and wide | rich theology of the Word, use of Scripture | the Gospel is for those who know their Scripture (almost too exclusive) | the preaching and acceptance of the Word of God | preachers (Scripture scholars) | believers in the preached Word of God |
| Servant | to renew the face of the earth in the vision of Christ | relevant social Gospel | secularistic, where is the spiritual dimension? | those linked in social renewal | prophets (those engaged in social work) | those active in works of justice |

■ Circle the items which reflect the theology of Church you have articulated .

Name: _____ Score: _____

## CHAPTER 3 Test

## Contemporary Images of the Church

**I.** Matching. On the first line, write the letter of the
model to which the statement applies. On the second
line, write an **S** if it is a strength and a **W** if it is a
weakness.

**a.** Community    **b.** Herald    **c.** Institution    **d.** Sacrament    **e.** Servant

___ ___ **1.** Evangelization, catechesis, theological studies

___ ___ **2.** Identifies the spread of God's kingdom with the alleviation of social ills

___ ___ **3.** Salvation is attached to religious actions and places, rather than to God's universal saving presence.

___ ___ **4.** Warm, caring spirit; shared responsibility; reaching outside the Church

___ ___ **5.** Relieves the lot of the poor and oppressed; Christianizes unjust social structures

___ ___ **6.** Establishes clear identity roles; cherishes tradition, clearly defined beliefs, and moral code

___ ___ **7.** Imitates the lifestyle of Jesus; utilizes cultural developments to fulfill human needs

___ ___ **8.** Highly organized; preserves rituals of worship; tends to create order, peace, and security

___ ___ **9.** May lead to separation from the institutional Church; fosters a too-private religion

___ ___ **10.** Gives and nourishes the life of Christ; reflects the role of Christians in the world as mediators between God and people

___ ___ **11.** Slow to change; subject to power struggles and other corruptions of authority

___ ___ **12.** May turn a group in upon itself to the neglect of the larger community

**II.** True or false. If the statement is true, write a plus
sign (+) on the line. If it is false, write a zero (o).

___ **1.** The institutional Church dominated the period before Vatican II.

___ **2.** Protestants emphasize the sacrament model of the Church.

___ **3.** The Church reflects the life of the Trinity by being united in truth and in charity.

___ **4.** A sacrament is an encounter with the life, death, resurrection, and Spirit of Jesus under visible signs.

___ **5.** Pluralism is a condition of society in which only two distinct groups coexist within a system.

___ **6.** An institution is a highly structured organization, established for a particular purpose, that usually ends with the death of its founder.

___ **7.** The primary model of the Church is Trinitarian Love.

___ **8.** As a rule, changes should be introduced gradually, with sufficient instruction, and, where possible, with options.

___ **9.** The Church is continually growing in its own self-understanding.

___ **10.** A model can simplify a reality so that one can deal with it in a limited way.

___ **11.** All models and figures of the Church may be drawn together in the model of the Church as a community of disciples.

**III.** Completion. Fill in the words needed to complete the sentence correctly.

Of the five models of the Church mentioned in Part I above, _____ and _____ serve as models of what the Church IS. The remaining three, _____ , _____ , and _____ , describe what the Church DOES.

**IV.** Essay. Choose two.

**1.** What model of the Church is best reflected in your own life? Explain why.

**2.** Which Church model has the greatest personal appeal for you? Why?

**3.** Explain why we need more than one model for the Church.

## CHAPTER 3 Test
### Contemporary Images of the Church

**I.**

1. b  s
2. e  w
3. d  w
4. a  s
5. e  s
6. c  s
7. e  s
8. c  s
9. b  w
10. d  s
11. c  w
12. a  w

**II.**

1. +
2. o
3. +
4. +
5. o
6. o
7. +
8. +
9. +
10. +
11. +

**III.**

community

institution

sacrament

herald

servant

**IV.**

Answers will vary.

# CHAPTER 3

## SECTION 1
### Text Questions (Student text pages 59–65)
**Page 60**

(1) Answers will vary.

**Page 61**

(2) Answers will vary and may include visions of God as protector, judge, source of hope, parent, or comforter.

(3) The Trinity is the source of our being in creation and in the beginning of salvation. It is also the goal of our salvation. The process has begun, but is not yet finished.

**Page 65**

(4) Have students offer reasons for their answers.

(5) Other institutions might include school, municipality, or federal government. They are all structured in a hierarchy or pyramid with leaders delegating and taking responsibility. The advantages are a shared sense of responsibility and opportunity for many people with varied talents to participate. The disadvantages include possibilities for some people not to fulfill their responsibilities, and for tension, jealousy, laziness, or greed to interfere with the running of the institution.

(6) Some of the advantages are that there is a clear identification of roles within the institution, there is clarity of beliefs and goals, efficiency, organization, and stability. The Church as institution cherishes traditions and preserves rituals of worship.

### SECTION 1 Checkpoint! (page 66)
### Review

(1) The Church must grow in its self-understanding in order to meet new challenges and to fulfill the spiritual needs of the people. The Church is a living institution and must grow in order to stay vibrant.

(2) Pluralistic society means many viewpoints and voices. This variety can lead to creativity and completeness. It can also lead to misunderstanding or rivalry.

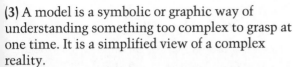

**(3)** A model is a symbolic or graphic way of understanding something too complex to grasp at one time. It is a simplified view of a complex reality.

**(4)** Multiple models present different aspects of that one complex thing. They give different views. One model, or aspect, may be clearer to one person than to someone else. All the models are complementary.

**(5)** We should use God's communication with us as a model for our own communication and relationships with others. We should relate to others selflessly and lovingly as a sign of God's presence among us.

**(6)** The hierarchy of the Church is the pattern of authority that extends from the Holy Father down to bishops, priests, and to all the baptized.

**(7)** Words to Know: *pluralism* (numerous groups living together in a single system); *model* (a simplified view of a complex reality); *hierarchy* (a system of authority organized into ranks); *institution* (highly structured organization begun for a particular purpose and intended to outlast its founders).

## In Your World

**(1)** Students might include pictures of photographs of the building itself, various people in the parish (pastor, acolytes, teachers, religious), the Holy Father, congregants, a baptism, or others. Be sure to encourage them to capture as many different aspects of the Church as institution as they can.

**(2)** Discuss the results of the poll in class. If the overall view of institutions is negative, discuss reasons. Why is it easy for institutions to become stagnant? How can that be prevented? Do people prefer to think of the Church as something other than an institution? How can this model become more positive?

## Scripture Search

**(1)** The Timothy passage discusses the need for ethical leadership. Paul is concerned about having good leaders with high morals. Since Church leaders act as Christ's representatives on earth and as examples to all, they must always maintain the highest standards. Paul makes an important connection between personal and community life. They are complementary.

**(2)** Through faith, Christ dwells within us and makes the Father known to us. The Spirit draws us into the endless circle of love between the

Father and Son. This is the Trinitarian model of the Church. We can be examples to the world by loving others and demonstrating that love by supporting our friends, being an active part of our families, and becoming involved in activities that reach out to the less advantaged in our Church and local communities.

## SECTION 2
## Text Questions (Student text pages 67–73)
### Page 69

**(7)** Answers will vary. Communities offer support, friendship, and completeness. Individuals contribute to the working of the community and everyone benefits from an individual's efforts.

**(8)** Answers will vary and may include references to outreach and educational programs. Students may not be aware of all the activities in their parish. Have them bring in a copy of the parish bulletin or newsletter.

**(9)** Answers will vary.

**(10)** The Church community differs in the bond of faith and discipleship that holds it together. Other forms of community are bonded by common secular goals, but not necessarily by a common faith and worship. It is the same in that all its members work together and rely on one another to achieve a common goal.

### Page 70

**(11)** Your presence shows your commitment and support for the Church and the community. It represents your willingness to be seen and to voice your faith.

**(12)** Scripture is kept alive through prayer, other forms of worship, and education.

### Page 73

**(13)** Learning and knowing about something like ecology or hunger may lead a person to act. Knowledge may give us the impetus we need. Neither action nor learning should take place in a vacuum.

## SECTION 2 Checkpoint! (page 74)
## Review
**(1)** A person grows through others because they can give us new perspectives about ourselves. We see ourselves differently through others.

**(2)** Within the large Church community there are schools, committees, classes, Bible study groups, and other smaller communities for those who share interests or concerns.

**(3)** A person can be a sacrament by being involved and active in the world, by living one's faith. This might mean volunteering, taking part in worship, or choosing the religious life.

**(4)** A sacrament reflects God's presence in the world. That presence can be detected every day in a multitude of ways, not just in the ritual sacraments.

**(5)** Education doesn't mean much if it isn't applied to life. It doesn't exist just for itself. Its purpose is to enrich us so that we become better people. If we just put our learning into its own world, we will never apply it to the problems of the world.

**(6)** Religious education can be applied to our daily lives. It provides us with a sense of history as well as with moral guidelines for making decisions and acting in society.

**(7)** Words to Know: *community* (a coming together of people to create a unity of goals); *sacrament* (an encounter with the life, death, resurrection, and Spirit of Jesus under visible signs within the institutional Church); *herald* (one who calls people forth to hear a proclamation); *fundamentalism* (a form of biblical interpretation that emphasizes the literal meaning of the text); *ecumenism* (efforts by churches to appreciate the validity of other religious traditions).

## In Your World

**(1)** The activity could be centered on a Bible study, soup kitchen, or change for a neighborhood such as a cleanup or a garden. Discuss the need for the two communities to share a goal and to share resources. How do you delegate responsibilities?

**(2)** Discuss the challenges of teaching. Can students appreciate the daily struggle of teachers after having tried it? Be sure students have preset goals for the class they are teaching. How should students go about transmitting those goals or trying to share them?

## Scripture Search

**(1)** Jesus is described as wise beyond his years in Luke when he questions adults and displays his knowledge of Scripture. Solomon solved problems using wisdom and foresight in 1 Kings. Matthew and Mark use the herald model of proclaiming and converting. The disciples are told to spread the word of the Gospel by teaching.

**(2)** Faith is a crucial part of the miracles. Faith in Jesus' power and ability is the key. Each person who is cured has expressed faith in Jesus and is rewarded for that faith. The Scriptures make God present to us in the miracle stories. This is part of their sacramental nature.

## SECTION 3

### Text Questions (Student text pages 75–81)

**Page 76**

**(14)** Answers will vary and may include images of slaves, lack of rights or freedom, a maid or a housekeeper.

**(15)** Today's sick and outcasts include people with AIDS, children, the poor and homeless, and political prisoners.

**(16)** Violence and injustice can be seen in the home, in inner cities, South Africa, Northern Ireland, the Middle East, and many other countries.

**Page 77**

**(17)** Answers will vary.

**(18)** People may act as servants just to get recognition or fame, and not in the true sense of the word. When people act like this, they are just using other people, not helping them.

**Page 80**

**(19)** Answers will vary. Have students provide examples to prove their answers.

**(20)** Answers will vary.

## SECTION 3 Checkpoint! (page 81)

### Review

**(1)** A true servant is a healer and a helper, someone who does good for others. He or she is humble and tries to imitate Jesus.

**(2)** The Church can work to restore faith, support those who are in doubt, and forgive. Outside the Church community, it can support the oppressed, speak out against injustice, and work to correct wrongs.

**(3)** Selflessness means doing things without thinking of personal gain such as money or

Copyright © Glencoe, Macmillan/McGraw-Hill

recognition. Real service is done in the spirit of living without thought of reward.

4) Some additional models might include family or home. Have students be creative, but expect explanation for answers.

5) Words to Know: *servant* (someone who answers the needs of others); *transformation* (the process of being changed from one thing to another); *disciple* (someone who accepts and assists in spreading the word of Christ).

## In Your World

1) This service can be in the area of education or meeting a social need. Perhaps the class can focus on a particular group such as children, adolescents, or the elderly. Be sure to clarify the existing situation and the transformation the class hopes to accomplish.

2) Make a montage of all the different aspects of the service of your Church. Be sure to capture as many as possible and to discuss the variety.

## Scripture Search

In Luke, Mary is described as servant because of her obedience to God in response to God's offer. The passage in Acts shows the willingness of the disciples to submit to punishment because of their service to God even though they do not fully understand. In Romans, the apostles are set apart as special servants who have a special mission. Matthew describes our traditional concept of servants who carry out the orders of a king. Mark describes servants who are laborers paid for their work. A new definition of servant will include all these concepts: servants can be put into voluntary or involuntary service to someone, they may be paid, their work varies, and the consequences of their actions may vary.

## CHAPTER 3 Review (pages 82–83)

## Study

1) Model may mean an ideal, a set of plans, or a simple way to describe a complex thing.

2) Multiple models present different aspects of one reality which may be hard to grasp. Together they clarify that reality.

3) The Church reflects the community of the Trinity. The life of the Trinity in us is an example of our life in the Church.

(4) We communicate with others as an outreach or arm of God. We reflect God's communication with us.

(5) Three components of the institution model are hierarchy (structure), common goals, and precise ways of worship.

(6) The institutional model contributes order, stability, links to tradition, and community.

(7) The characteristics of an institution are its large size, clear definition of roles, bureaucracy, rules, and authority.

(8) As a community, the Church has common goals which result in unity of purpose. People grow as a result of interpersonal relationships and mutual concern and love. Meeting human needs leads to a better Church community.

(9) Scripture reveals the grace of God and shows us Christ as a presence in the world. Liturgy sanctifies a time and also reveals Christ in and through the community, where faith is celebrated.

(10) The function of heralds in the Church is to proclaim the Good News, and share it with others as educators, missionaries, and preachers. Each person should be a herald by his or her daily example.

(11) Jesus fulfilled God's will in his life and death, and served his community in healing, forgiving, and addressing outcasts.

## Action

(1) *Trinity:* images might include grandmother/mother/daughter as representing the same blood and the renewal of generations. *Institution:* your class could be an image of a hierarchy, support system, and a group which develops its own moral and behavioral code. *Community:* a youth group is an image of community formed with a special interest and common goals. It can also reflect the importance of interpersonal relationships and the possibilities for tension. *Sacrament:* the individual is an image of the living model of a sacrament. That person can read, teach, and minister, but can only do so with others, not alone. *Herald:* You (the student) can be an effective herald in your response to the Gospel. *Servant:* a group such as Pax Christi which tries to meet the needs of others including their need to develop a sense of self-worth.

(2) Start with the class and other students or teachers. Discuss the possible reasons for the favorite choices.

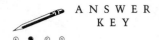

**(3)** Your actions will vary depending upon which model is chosen.

## Prayer

Before engaging in this activity, discuss the meaning of prayer. Be sure students see prayer as an expression of faith which has a set group expression as well as personal (and often spontaneous) expression. Encourage students to compose prayers that reflect their feelings, attitudes, hopes, or fears, and that they can share with the class. Do not insist that students read them aloud if they do not wish to. Explain that there is no special vocabulary or format for their own prayer. Try to collect enough to use for class prayer.

**3**

# Contemporary Images of the Church

**Overview:** This chapter aims to introduce students to the use of models and then details five specific models of the Church.

**Objectives:** The students will:

- Discuss the uses of models in general.
- Briefly examine each of the five Dulles models.
- Discuss how these models are unified into a whole.

**TIME FRAME:** One to one-and-a-half hours.

**MATERIALS:** Paper, Bibles, chalkboard.

**PROCEDURE:**

> ***Into:*** Prayer—Begin class by reading the Beatitudes featured in "A People at Prayer" (page 76).
>
> ***Through:***
>
> Activity One:
>
> 1. Ask for definitions of a model. List as many as possible on the board. Use question 1 on page 60 as a guide for discussion.
>
> 2. Explain the definition of model given in the text as complementary ways to view one reality. Use the Trinity as an example.
>
> 3. Focus on the institution model by asking students to give characteristics of an institution and to fit the Church into that definition. Be sure to note the positive and negative attributes by using questions 5 and 6 on page 65.
>
> Activity Two:
>
> 1. Have students write down a definition of community including its purpose and characteristics. Use these definitions to discuss the Church as a large community made up of smaller communities. Be sure to explain how it is both like and unlike secular communities.
>
> 2. Read through or summarize the section on "The Church as Sacrament" (pages 69–70), making sure students understand the importance of living and working this model.
>
> 3. Discuss the herald model and how many different activities fit into it.
>
> Activity Three:
>
> 1. Have students define servant in 2 or 3 words. Compare definitions and then add others which may have been left out. How can this term be made more positive by servants in the Church?
>
> 2. Study the Star model on page 79. Be sure its meaning is clear.
>
> 3. Have each students say which model she or he prefers and why.
>
> ***Beyond:*** Encourage students to read "Light of All Nations" on page 64 and "Understanding Scripture" on page 71. Suggest that they try activity 2 from Section 2 "In Your World," page 74.
>
> ***Prayer:*** Close class with a prayer composed by a student in advance or even said spontaneously in response to the material covered.

Name: _____   Score: _____

## CHAPTER 3 QUIZ
# Contemporary Images of the Church

Mark true (+) or false (o).

___ **1.** Models allow us to approach the mystery of the Church in a variety of ways.

___ **2.** Multiple Church models complement and enhance one another.

___ **3.** An individual parish may reflect aspects of several or all models.

___ **4.** Trinitarian love is the original model of what the Church is all about.

___ **5.** Every model has strengths and weaknesses.

___ **6.** Exaggerating any one model distorts the true nature of the Church.

*As institution ...*

___ **7.** The Church tends to focus on people.

___ **8.** It is associated with tangible, visible realities such as buildings, rules, and regulations.

___ **9.** It fails to provide a sense of identity or a clearly defined moral code.

___ **10.** It is most effective with large numbers.

___ **11.** Visually, it would resemble a circle.

___ **12.** It lacks order and a sense of security.

*As community ...*

___ **13.** The Church views members as a family joined in love.

___ **14.** It is seen as a dispenser of sacraments, without structure.

*As sacrament ...*

___ **15.** The Church tends to emphasize celebration and downplay service.

___ **16.** It confines the sacramental character to the seven sacraments.

*As herald ...*

___ **17.** The Church sees itself as a people who receive the Good News and share it.

___ **18.** It cannot go wrong since this model emphasizes education and Scripture.

___ **19.** The Church concentrates on the here-and-now.

*As servant ...*

___ **20.** The Church uses its resources to heal.

# CHAPTER 3 QUIZ
Answer Key

**Contemporary Images of the Church**

Mark true (+) or false (o).

1. +
2. +
3. +
4. +
5. +
6. +

*As institution ...*

7. o
8. +
9. o
10. +
11. o
12. o

*As community ...*

13. +
14. o

*As sacrament ...*

15. +
16. o

*As herald ...*

17. +
18. o
19. o

*As servant ...*

20. +

# Church Council: Simulation on Models of the Church

(Can be used with Teacher's Resource 3C.)

Divide the class into six communities: Romans, Thessalonians, Corinthians, Hebrews, Galatians, and Ephesians.

*Roles:* Each participant is a delegate to the ecumenical council representing his or her community. The teacher is the facilitator.

*Materials:* Large paper or poster board, magic markers for each group.

*Directions:*

1. Each group elects a bishop to act as spokesman to the larger enclave.

2. Each group selects a scribe to write responses on the poster board.

3. Each group is to arrive at a consensus on these questions (allow about twenty minutes):

   a. How does your community define the Church?

   b. What does your community see as the major mission of the Church?

   c. If your bishop were elected pope within the next six months, to what three pressing issues should he address himself?

4. Each community reports on its consensus. Minority reports may be filed. Hang up the posters.

5. After all reports have been given, communities may challenge the findings of any other group. As a part of this process, the entire council should try to arrive at a consensus of the three questions. A preliminary draft of an encyclical should be written, intended for the entire Christian community (20 to 30 minutes). The facilitator asks questions in order to clarify and firm up the group's position.

6. Distribute and read Teacher's Resource 3C. Based on their answers to the three questions discussed, ask each community to decide which model(s) of the Church it most closely resembled. Which model does the consensus of the council resemble?

## The Church: Images

Jesus ...

Your Church is not a rut, it's a road;

It's not a dormitory, it's a battlefield;

It's not a mirror, it's a lighthouse;

It's not a history book, but a newspaper

A designer's board, an inventor's dream.

Your church is not where I am comfortable, or even secure or safe from hurt or free to fatten;

It is your road to the world, your voice to the world, your light to the world.

And I, too, am your Church, so I must be a bit of all of these, Christ.

Discuss ways in which the Church is each of the images mentioned.

## Define Your Terms

1. **apostolic:** all priests and bishops trace their ordination back to the time of Christ

2. **authority:** a role of service in the Church; means "to give life"

3. **bishop:** successor to the apostles, governs a diocese

4. **body:** most important symbol of the Church; stresses unity in diversity

5. **community:** the Church is social by nature; no one can be a Christian while cut off from the Church

6. **collegiality:** sharing a responsibility and authority (pope with bishops)

7. **curia:** central administrative agencies of the Church in Rome

8. **diocese:** administrative division, territory under the jurisdiction of a bishop

9. **doctrine:** essential teaching or belief of the Church

10. **hierarchy:** the authority structure of the Church; various levels of ministry, service, and leadership within the Church

11. **holiness:** the Church, in union with Christ, shares Christ's love and goodness

12. **infallibility:** the Church as a whole cannot be wrong on essential matters of faith

13. **minister:** a servant of the needs of others

14. **parish:** smallest local unity of the Church

15. **pastor:** "shepherd"; priest in charge of a parish

16. **pope:** the vicar (representative) of Christ, "Holy Father"

17. **priesthood:** refers to the power to offer sacrifices mediating between God and man; some men are ordained to the priestly ministry; all baptized Christians share in Christ's priesthood

18. **unity:** an identifying mark of the Church; pertains to belief, moral code, and worship essentials which are the same the world over

19. **universality:** the Church is open to all peoples of all ages (catholic)

20. **witness:** to give example in your life of what the teachings of Christ mean

## Additional Reading

Abbott, Walter M., ed. *The Documents of Vatican II.* New York: Guild Press, 1966.

Coulson, John, ed. *The Saints: A Concise Biographical Dictionary.* New York: Guild Press, 1957.

Grant, Robert M. and David Tracy. *A Short History of the Interpretation of the Bible.* Philadelphia: Fortress Press, 1985.

Ramsey, Boniface. *Beginning to Read the Fathers.* Mahwah, NJ: Paulist Press, 1985. (Good information on other models and images of the Church.)

**CHAPTER 4**

# The Image That Others See

(Text pages 84–113)

## FOCUS

**Doctrinal:** God has gifted the Church with four characteristics essential to its makeup and present from its beginning: one, holy, Catholic, apostolic.

**Personal:** As a member of Christ's Church, how can I mirror these characteristics in my own life?

## OBJECTIVES

**Cognitive:** (a) to learn the meaning of the four characteristics that tradition uses to mark the Church of Christ: unity, holiness, catholicity, and apostolicity; (b) to understand how these marks are present in the Catholic Church today.

**Affective:** (a) to love and be grateful for the fullness of truth held by the Catholic Church; (b) to want to share the rich heritage of Catholic Christianity with others.

## Chapter 4 Outline

### SECTION 1
**The Visible Image**

Looking at the Church

How Others See it

*On This Rock* (margin feature)

What is Distinctive?

Incarnation of the Incarnation

The "Marks" of the Church

*The Church—A Visible House of God* (text feature)

### SECTION 2
**The Church Is One and Holy**

Unity of Teaching and Faith

*Church Teaching—How Much Do You Know?* (text feature)

Unity of Worship and Liturgy

Unity of Government and Obedience

Unity, Not Uniformity

Efforts Towards Greater Unity

*Communion of Saints* (margin feature)

The Church is Holy

The Church's Holiness

The Holiness of Christians

**SECTION 3**
**The Church Is Catholic and Apostolic**
>    The Mark of Catholicity
>    Finding Christ in the World
>    Universality Means Openness
>    The Church Is Apostolic
>    Apostolicity Is Continuity and Communion
>    Efforts at Apostolicity
>    *A People at Prayer* (margin feature)
>    The Call to Be Catholic
>    *"Born" Catholics Speak Out* (text feature)

4

# TEACHER'S RESOURCE 4A

## Historical Notes

The Council of Nicaea (A.D. 325) is known mostly for the creed which defined Christian understanding of the Trinity as one substance in three persons. That statement has remained constant and has helped the Church defend itself against those who tried to claim otherwise. It is also clear that the very foundation of Christian belief in Jesus as Lord and Church as one was forged early in the history of Christianity. Throughout history theologians have continually worked to develop better understandings, and to love the faith expressed in the creeds.

## Pedagogical Notes

1. The "objective" concepts introduced in this chapter (the four marks) need to be made present to each student on a more personal and subjective level as well. This chapter can introduce students to the need to understand the historical development of ideas, beliefs, and practices before they can make the concept their own.

2. The personal statement in the text feature of Section 3 can be used in conjunction with Teacher's Resource 4D, which is a personal survey sheet. Focus on how each respondent in the feature (and each student) incorporates the marks of the Church into his or her own life.

# TEACHER'S RESOURCE 4B

## Theological Notes

Over the centuries, Catholic leaders and scholars have developed a rich theology of the Church. This theology is called "ecclesiology," from the Greek word for Church, *ekklesia*. Theological insights are instructive because they are the fruit of careful reflection and disciplined thinking. The theologian seeks a deeper understanding of the faith professed by believers. This text, in fact, reflects a great deal of traditional and contemporary ecclesiology.

When it's all said and done, however, people do not usually get excited by all the hard work of theologians. They are not attracted to the Church because of its theological achievements any more than the first disciples were attracted to the Good News of Jesus because of his theological expertise. What "grabs" people is the image of the Church

that ordinary believers project. Sound theology is important, but so is sound witness.

This chapter discusses the four classical marks—the four ancient signs—of sound witness that Catholics are called to make. Our Church and its people are one, holy, catholic, and apostolic. As these marks are discussed, it may also be helpful to spend some time with three other signs that the Christian community can and should make. Saint Paul was the first to recognize their importance and the Fathers of Vatican II echoed Paul's words when they called the Church "the community of faith, hope, and love" in the *Dogmatic Constitution on the Church.* In I Corinthians, 13:3, Paul reminded us: "There are in the end three things that last: faith, hope, and love, and the greatest of these is love."

When people see the Church in action, it is important that whatever else they understand, they also get the impression that Church members are deeply committed to God (faith), accept life as worthwhile (hope), and are dedicated to the welfare of others (love).

These are simple signs that broadcast the meaning of Christian discipleship. They are unmistakable signs which all people can see no matter how well or how poorly educated they may be. That's why it is so crucial that Catholics take the signs seriously, for if others can recognize the faith, hope, and love that is in us, they can also experience the presence of Jesus in our Church.

Saint Paul told us that love is the greatest of these three signs, not because faith and hope are less important, but because love summarizes the meaning of faith and hope. We cannot love if we are unable to make and keep commitments. Faith, above all, is a commitment. We cannot love if we don't accept that all life is worthwhile and that we do have a future. Hope expresses this attitude of optimism in the face of a flawed and uncertain world.

Unselfish dedication to the needs of others (Christian love), therefore, expresses the type of people we strive to be in Christ Jesus. It is the clearest sign of what it means to be Church that we can make for others.

The story is told about a man who, when asked why he first decided to become a priest, would recall his mother's loving patience with him as he was growing up. "I always misbehaved in church," he says, "and when I did, my mother

would correct me and then give me one of those big smiles of hers. I guess that her love and patience eventually convinced me that church must not be that bad!"

A simple sign is an image that someone sees and responds to. Having a mark of holiness and Catholicism speaks more eloquently than does the most learned ecclesiology. Jesus made simple signs, and because he did, he attracted faithful followers. This is our mission, too; and we don't have to be theologias to accomplish it.

## TEACHER'S RESOURCE 4C

## Models

**4**

1. PARISH

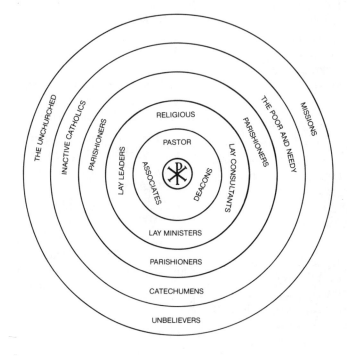

2. CHURCH

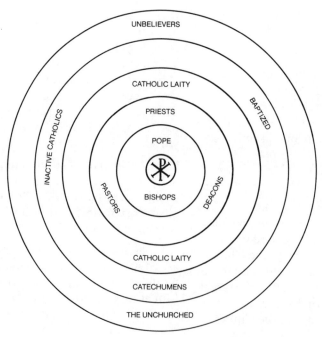

# Survey of Beliefs

**I.** Write an **A** on the line if you agree with the statement as it stands and a **D** if you disagree. Answer as thoughtfully and as honestly as you can. If you have a question or an objection to a statement, write it on the reverse side of the paper.

___ **1.** Christ founded the Church.

___ **2.** The Church is the extension of Christ's work and mission. It is meant to prepare individuals and the world for Christ's Second Coming.

___ **3.** The Catholic Church is the true Church of Christ.

___ **4.** The Church is holy in its purpose.

___ **5.** The pope and the bishops are lawful successors of Peter and the Apostles.

___ **6.** The pope can make infallible (free from error) statements binding in conscience regarding faith and morals.

___ **7.** The Church is necessary for salvation but every person who is saved does not necessarily belong to the Catholic Church.

___ **8.** The Church is a community of believers in Christ and his total message.

___ **9.** The message of Christ in the Gospels is for all people—not just the people who are labeled "holy."

___ **10.** Keeping the Ten Commandments is sufficient to obtain salvation.

**II.** Study the following reasons for being a member of the Church. Add others, if there are any.

Rank your reasons from 1–10. Consider #1 most important.

___ Baptized and educated Catholic

___ Mass and the sacraments fill a need

___ Family and friends are Catholic

___ Priests I know inspire me, help me

___ This is what I feel Jesus wants me to be.

___ Need the support of other believers

___ Catholicism really makes sense to me

___ Other: _____

___ Need the help and direction the Church gives me

___ Other: _____

Name: _____

**III.** Answer briefly. Be as honest with yourself as you can be.

**1.** Why are you a Catholic today?

**2.** Would you encourage your friends to join the Church? Why or why not?

**3.** Do you think that you will remain in the Church as an adult?

**4.** If you believe that Jesus is God, what alternatives to the Church are available to you for expressing your belief?

**5.** Is there anything young people have found that is a good substitute for what the Church stands for and is trying to achieve?

**6.** If there were something you could change about the Catholic Church, what would it be?

**7.** What do you like most about the Catholic Church?

## CHAPTER 4 Test

## The Image That Others See

I.  **True-False.** Write a plus sign (+) if the statement is true; a zero (o) if it is false.

___ 1.  The marks of the Church are gifts which challenge the Church to improve constantly.

___ 2.  All peoples are offered the gift of salvation.

___ 3.  Imperfections in the Church do not destroy its holiness.

___ 4.  Every human being's main task is to respond sincerely and wholeheartedly to God.

___ 5.  Most people remain Catholic out of fear of damnation.

___ 6.  Only baptized persons are incorporated into the Church.

___ 7.  Christ prayed for unity among his followers and we should do the same.

___ 8.  The Church makes up new doctrines to fit the needs of the times.

___ 9.  It is always possible to tell who belongs to the Church.

___ 10. The Church is most at home in all cultures.

II.  **Completion.** Write the word or phrase needed to make the statement correct.

1. The Church is one in its _____ and faith, in its worship and _____, in its _____ , and in its obedience.

2. The Church is holy in its _____ , _____ , _____ , and _____ .

3. The Church is universal in its _____ , _____ , and _____ .

4. When we say the Church is apostolic we mean _____

_____

5. Other names for the marks of the Church are _____ or _____ .

6. Unity allows variety; _____ means that individual things in a group are exactly identical.

7. The word _____ means "universal."

III. **Matching.** Write the letter of the mark of the Church most closely associated with the statement given:

A. apostolicity  B. catholicity   C. holiness     D. unity

___ 1.  The Catholic Church is a world Church.

___ 2.  There is an unbroken line of popes from Peter to John Paul II.

___ 3.  Pluralism of opinion enriches the Church.

___ 4.  The Church's purpose is to share Christ's saving mission.

Name: _____     Score: _____

___ 5.  The twentieth century has given the Church more martyrs than all previous centuries put together.

___ 6.  The Church absorbs and transforms elements of many cultures.

___ 7.  All in the Catholic Church celebrate seven sacraments using the same outward signs.

___ 8.  All Catholics believe that Jesus is Lord.

___ 9.  The Church is open to all, it cannot exclude anyone and be true to Christ.

___ 10. The Church today imitates the Apostles who circulated letters to the Christian communities and held a Church Council.


**IV. Essay.** Choose two.

1. How can diversity be present in a Church marked by unity?

2. Which mark of the Church has the greatest appeal for you? Why?

3. Give two specific examples of how each mark of the Church shows itself today.

4. Explain this statement: "There are different degrees of incorporation into the mystery of Christ."

# CHAPTER 4 Test
## The Image That Others See

**I.**
1. +
2. +
3. +
4. +
5. o
6. o
7. +
8. o
9. o
10. +

**II.**
1. teaching, liturgy, government
2. founder, purpose, ministries, members
3. duration, extension, teaching
4. it has an unbroken line of succession from Peter and the Apostles (it teaches and practices what the early Church did)
5. features, characteristics
6. uniformity
7. catholic

**III.**
1. B
2. A
3. D
4. C
5. C
6. B
7. D
8. D
9. B
10. A

**IV.**
Answers will vary.

# CHAPTER 4

## SECTION 1
### Text Questions (Student text pages 85–91)
**Page 87**

(1) Lumpy means that people keep their individuality, that one can see differences. Individual responses will vary.

(2) Answers will vary and may include beliefs, practices, moral codes, sacrament, and priesthood.

(3) The outward expressions of our faith are the reflection of God in us and make us active in the world just as Jesus was in proclaiming the Good News.

**Page 88**

(4) Answers will vary and may include social activism in groups such as Pax Christi or missionary work.

(5) Answers will vary depending on students' involvement in local parish church.

**Page 91**

(6) Members of other faiths participate in the fullness of Christ through their faith itself, their moral codes, love for others, or desire to understand and do God's will.

(7) Answers will vary. Have students attempt to offer a definition of each term.

## SECTION 1 Checkpoint! (page 92)
**Review**

(1) Stepping back offers perspective, objectivity, and a more complete picture than a close-up observation.

(2) All Catholics share the institution itself, beliefs, ways of worship, and an ethical code.

(3) Marty means that there is variety in the Church and individual expression. The Church is not a mass of people all saying and acting exactly the same.

(4) The internal faith life and visibility of the Church is an expression of the interior mystery of God working in the world. Faith is felt inside but expressed externally through worship and works.

(5) God is known to us through the Church, in creation, in Jesus, and in each individual.

**(6)** Mark means a gift of God, an essential aspect of something, a characteristic that cannot be changed.

**(7)** Words to Know: *perspective* (a view of something in its entirety); *paradox* (something which seems contradictory, but true at the same time); *to incarnate* (to give flesh to); *mark of the Church* (gifts essential to the Church's makeup; visible distinguishing characteristics).

## In Your World

**(1)** Discuss the results in class. Common responses will probably include priests and nuns, the sacraments, and Mary. Note how many of the answers are based on visible observation and not on doctrine or articles of faith. Focus on the importance of our observations in the way we form opinions.

**(2)** Some items might include a Bible, pictures of missionaries, chalice, or a Bible or lectionary in a different language. Be sure each mark is represented.

## Scripture Search

The images in these passages include God as creator, judge (or punisher), lawgiver, and bestower of mercy. The purpose of the images is to make God more understandable to us because of our human limitations. We give God characteristics that we can understand, and describe God's actions in ways that are familiar to us. We know that the true nature of God is beyond all these adjectives because God is perfect and completely other than what we are.

## SECTION 2

## Text Questions (Student text pages 93–101)

### Page 94

**(8)** Answers will vary and may include the recitation of the creed.

### Page 95

**(9)** The order of the Mass would be the same.

### Page 98

**(10)** Uniformity is discouraged so that individual gifts can be expressed and that all people can be a part of the Church—even if they come from many different cultures.

**(11)** Answers will vary.

**(12)** Answers will vary, and may include keeping dialogue and communication open, and being involved in the life of your family, church, and community.

### Page 101

**(13)** Answers will vary.

**(14)** Barriers to holiness include peer pressure to do, say, or wear certain things, the media and advertising, and human weakness.

## Church Teaching—How Much Do You Know? (feature) page 94

*Council of Jerusalem* (the first Church council held in A.D. 90); *Council of Nicaea* (A.D. 325, ecumenical council that produced the Nicene Creed); *barbarian* (member of one of the tribes that invaded the Roman Empire causing it to fall in the fifth century); *Edict of Milan* (A.D. 313 granted recognition to and toleration of Christianity in the Roman Empire); *A.D. 451* (date of the Council of Chalcedon which defined the relationship of human and divine natures in Jesus); *Saint Augustine* (important Christian theologian of the fifth century who wrote the *Confessions* and *The City of God*); *Saint Benedict* (author of the rules used to regulate monastic life); *A.D. 1545–1564* (dates of the Council of Trent called to enact reforms in the Catholic Church); *Joan of Arc* (patron saint of France and a martyr); *Teresa of Avila* (Carmelite nun who wrote about prayer and who is a Doctor of the Church); *Vatican II* (1962–65 council which led to important changes and developments in the Catholic Church).

## SECTION 2  Checkpoint! (page 102)

**(1)** The Church displays unity in teaching and faith, worship and liturgy, and government and obedience.

**(2)** Unity in faith is expressed in doctrinal confessions in worship, in teaching, and in acceptance of Church teaching.

**(3)** Unity of worship is made visible by gathering for worship and the celebration of the sacraments.

**(4)** The Bishop of Rome who is the pope has primacy over the Church.

**5)** Unity allows individuals to retain their identity in a group. Uniformity requires individuals to become identical to one another.

(6) The Church has the responsibility to engage in dialogue with other groups, understand them, and work with them to spread God's love by promoting peace and understanding.

(7) God is holy by nature inherently and we are holy only when God is present in us.

(8) The purpose of the Church is to share Christ's mission to save all people, and to transform the world.

(9) Words to Know: *unity* (oneness in essentials, oneness that allows individuals to remain unique); *primacy* (being first in rank); *uniformity* (exact identity of every individual in a group); *synod* (a council or assembly, especially one with governing power); *holiness* (being filled with the presence of God); *charism* (special power given to a Christian by the Holy Spirit for the good of the Church).

## In Your World

(1) Use the *Catholic Encyclopedia, Encyclopedia of Religion*, or other encyclopedia as a resource. Encourage students to study how the customs and traditions of a culture can be incorporated into their patterns of worship (include foods, dress, music, dance). Focus on the concepts of unity and uniformity.

(2) Be sure all four aspects are represented in order to present a holistic view.

## Scripture Search

(1) The oneness of God is reflected in the oneness of the Church. The passages in Ephesians represent calls to unity in the Father in faith, sacraments, and love. The verse from Deuteronomy reminds us of the unity of God which is an example for us of our own unity.

(2) Just as God's oneness and unity is an example, God's perfection is also an example. We should strive to be perfect as God is, even though we are limited. We participate in God's perfection through grace.

## SECTION 3
## Text Questions (Student text pages 103–110)
### Page 106

(15) Answers will vary.

(16) Until Vatican II, Latin was used for worship. Church architecture often reflects various European styles, music comes from a variety of times and places, artwork displays various influences.

(17) Answers will vary.

### Page 108

(18) Reading Scripture helps us understand the life of the Apostles and their actions in spreading the Gospel. Scripture provides a link to the past and an example for us so we feel a sense of continuity and can follow the unveiling of revelation.

### Page 110

(19) Answers will vary.

(20) Answers will vary.

## SECTION 3 Checkpoint! (page 111)
### Review

(1) The word "catholic" means universal—including all peoples everywhere.

(2) The Church's catholicity is seen in its steady spread throughout the world, its acceptance of all peoples, and its endurance.

(3) The Church is becoming more involved in the world by addressing specific issues such as nuclear war and the economy, and by acknowledging its mistakes of the past.

(4) Approaches to change include (a) standing in place and trying to prevent harm from the outside; (b) totally rejecting change; (c) trying to change things too much, too fast; and (d) gently moving forward steadily and slowly.

(5) The Apostles worked together, discussing the issues at hand. They issued letters and finally reached a consensus.

(6) The mystery is still being clarified because the Church is constantly growing in understanding as time passes.

(7) The four steps are (a) remain disposed to continuing inquiry; (b) adhere to Christ and the Church; (c) respect the teaching authority of the pope; and (d) try not to harm the common good.

(8) A free personal response is necessary for the act of faith. Faith is a free gift given by God, which requires a sincere response.

(9) Words to Know: *catholic* (universal, worldwide); *universal* (applying to everyone everywhere); *Babel* (a great tower built to try to reach God, see Genesis 11:1–9); *Holocaust* (the murder of 13 million Jews and others during

World War II); *apostolic* (descended from the Apostles in an unbroken line of succession).

## In Your World

(1) Write a script or allow students to improvise after having read the Scripture passages. Focus on the progress toward consensus made at the Council.

(2) Elements might include special holiday customs, particular foods made at festivals, the languages of parishioners, and more.

## Scripture Search

(1) These passages show that the distinctions which had divided people or made them stand out one from anothers are not important in the eyes of God. Faith makes people equal. Other opposites might include fat/thin, smart/average, or white/black.

(2) Paul responded to God's call by being converted or turned toward God in a new way. He responded positively. He began to preach fearlessly and took on his own special mission to spread the Gospel to the Gentiles (those who were neither Jewish nor Christian).

## CHAPTER 4 Review (pages 112–113)

### Study

(1) Outsiders often describe the Church as united, powerful, wealthy, or charitable.

(2) A lumpy Church means that it is diverse, real, and perceptible. Refined means that everyone looks and acts the same way, there is no individuality.

(3) Jesus was sent by the Father to take on our flesh and to save us. In the same way, in the Church Jesus takes on the flesh of his members and together with them saves the world.

(4) A mark is a permanent characteristic of something—an essential gift. The four marks of the Church are one, holy, catholic, and apostolic.

(5) The marks are still developing because they represent a goal. We grow toward them as individuals and as a group.

(6) The Church displays unity in faith and teaching, worship and liturgy, and government and obedience.

(7) Diversity leads to variety and to a wider appeal. By reaching out to all peoples, the Gospel message aims at a unity of all people.

(8) The role of the Church is to work with other religions to promote world peace and understanding, and to work out differences in order to spread God's love.

(9) The four facets of holiness in the Church are its founder, purpose, ministries, and members.

(10) The Church is holy in the four ways mentioned above even when some individuals may not be. The Church's holiness is in Jesus and has no limits.

(11) The Church continues to express social concerns, to teach, and to send out missionaries.

(12) The Church's apostolicity connects us to its founder (Christ) and to his earliest followers who are a source of authority, revelation, and its interpretation.

(13) Revelation unfolds in meaning through human reflection, clarification, and explanation in terms each generation understands.

(14) Vatican II teaches that all peoples possess saving gifts from God through Christ and can respond to those gifts.

## Action

(1) Discuss how the logo will incorporate the marks. It can use numbers (focus on 3 or 4), letters, or other symbols. You might keep this in the theory stage only, just asking for ideas, or encourage any artistically inclined students to try to create a logo.

(2) Discuss the process of the catechumenate in class before attending a session. Encourage an open discussion and follow up in class afterwards by discussing the reasons students think someone might want to convert.

## Prayer

Refer to a book on the lives of the saints if some students are not sure which saint to choose. They may want to look up the saint who shares their birthday. Encourage the students to read about the saint, to make that person real and to find the way that saint speaks to them. Also discuss what it means to incorporate veneration of saints in worship and prayer. Be sure students understand that saints are not God, and that their role is clear.

# The Image That Others See

**OVERVIEW:** This chapter identifies the four permanent distinguishing marks of the Church and puts them in historical and contemporary perspective.

**OBJECTIVES: The students will:**

- Talk about what makes the Church distinct from other organizations and religions.
- Discuss each of the four "marks" of the Church.
- See how each mark is still being expressed and developed in the Church.

**TIME FRAME: One to one–and-a-half hours.**

**MATERIALS: Bibles, chalkboard.**

**PROCEDURE:**

*Into:* Prayer—Begin class with a recitation of the Nicene Creed.

*Through:*

Activity One:

1. Ask students to say what they think about how non-Catholics describe the Church. Make a list on the board of the adjectives suggested.

2. Write the word "mark" on the board and ask for a definition. Then present the definition as given in the text. Relate the term to what makes each of us distinct (e.g. fingerprints).

3. Introduce the four marks of the Church and discuss how they form a goal for it. Use the concept of the Church as dynamic and changing. Use questions 6 and 7 on page 91 as a guide for discussion.

Activity Two:

1. Ask students what makes the Church one. Add to answers given by class by using material from the text.

2. Ask students if they think diversity is a good thing. Why or why not? Focus especially on the pressure put on young people to dress alike, listen to the same music, have the same hairstyles, and read the same books. Distinguish between unity and uniformity.

3. Break into two or three small groups. Have each group offer a definition of holy and give two examples of a holy person—one from the religious world, and one from the "secular" world. Discuss the holiness of the Church and the "unholiness" of some of its members. Use questions 13 and 14 on page 101.

Activity Three:

1. Have students define the term "catholic." Discuss the ways people confront change. Ask for examples of the ways people react to changes.

2. Have students define "apostle." Who is one and why? Link the Apostles to tradition and to continuity in the Church. Use the importance of tradition in the family unit as an example.

**3.** Why aren't all people Catholic? How do Catholics they know view non-Catholics? After discussion, present the views given in the text. Clarify the Vatican II position.

**Beyond:** Have students read " 'Born' Catholics Speak Out," on page 109 or do activity 1 from Section 1 "In Your World," page 92.

**Prayer:** Close class with the prayer in the margin feature "A People at Prayer," page 108.

**4**

A D D I T I O N A L
R E S O U R C E S

**CHAPTER 4 QUIZ**
# The Image that Others See

Mark true (+) or false (o).

___ 1. The Catholic Church is the largest religious body in the world.

___ 2. More than half the population in the United States are active Catholics.

___ 3. The Catholic Church answers human nature's need to express inner mystery in visible forms.

___ 4. The particular features that identify the Church today were present in apostolic times.

___ 5. No other Church shares in Catholicism's four marks.

___ 6. Unity is the clearest mark of the Church.

___ 7. The Church's unity is expressed in its faith and teaching but not in its worship.

___ 8. Before there can be unity of government, Catholics must obey all Church laws and precepts.

___ 9. Disciplinary laws of the Church differ from place to place.

___ 10. The Church's holiness exists primarily in its members.

___ 11. Holiness of life is probably the most important factor in attracting converts.

___ 12. The word "catholic" means the Church is at home in every culture.

___ 13. The Church has never rejected people on the basis of differences in race or belief.

___ 14. Being Catholic implies an openness to different points of view and levels of spirituality.

___ 15. Apostolicity means that the Church has been faithful to the teachings of the Apostles.

___ 16. Circumstances can change the truths of faith.

___ 17. Catholics are not free to differ with authority.

___ 18. The marks of the Church have always been present in the Roman Church in their fullness.

___ 19. Everyone is called to be an active member of the Catholic Church.

___ 20. There are degrees of incorporation into Christ.

# CHAPTER 4 QUIZ
Answer Key

1. +
2. o
3. +
4. +
5. o
6. +
7. o
8. o
9. +
10. o
11. +
12. +
13. o
14. +
15. +
16. o
17. o
18. o
19. o
20. +

## The Church Jesus Founded

*Directions:* Read and analyze each set of Scripture references, 1–8. From the list of statements, A–H, choose the one that best summarizes these references, and then write the letter to the left of the Scripture references.

A. **The Church is a community of believers.**

B. **The Church was founded by Christ on Peter and the Apostles.**

C. **The Church seeks to embrace all peoples.**

D. **The Church seeks to bring back sinners.**

E. **The Church centers its worship in Eucharist and in the priesthood.**

F. **The Church believes in one faith taught by the successors of Peter and the Apostles.**

G. **The Church suffers and endures in union with Jesus.**

H. **The Church is a community that loves others.**

___ 1. (a) I Corinthians 10:15–17, (b) Luke 22:19–20, (c) 1 Corinthians 11:17–29, (d) Colossians 2:6–7

___ 2. (a) John 15:12, (b) Matthew 25:31–46, (c) 1 John 4:20ff, (d) Matthew 5:42–45

___ 3. (a) Romans 12:4–5, (b) Romans 12:6–8, (c) John 17:21–24, (d) Acts 1:14

___ 4. (a) John 15:18–20, (b) John 15:15–17, (c) Matthew 5:10–12, (d) 1 Peter 2:19–20, (e) 1 Peter 5:8–9, (f) Mark 8:34

___ 5. (a) Matthew 16:15–18, (b) Matthew 16:18–19, (c) John 20:21–23

___ 6. (a) Luke 19:10, (b) John 10:11–18, (c) John 20: 21–23

___ 7. (a) Matthew 28:19–20, (b) Mark 16:15–19, (c) 1 John 3:1–2, (d) Colossians 3:12

___ 8. (a) 1 Corinthians 4:1, (b) Acts 4 :1–4, 33

## The Church Jesus Founded
Answer Key

1. E
2. H
3. A
4. G
5. B
6. D
7. C
8. F

## Why am I a Catholic?

"I am a Catholic because I am convinced that the Catholic faith contains the fullness of Truth. I believe in God, who is so good that he has reached out to humankind by sending his son. I believe that his Son Jesus Christ is truly God and truly man; that he lived and died in obedience to his Father's will to save us; and that he rose from death and sent forth his Spirit so that we, too, could share in his new life.

"I believe that Jesus still lives and loves through his Mystical Body, the Church, and that we are joined to him in loving union and empowered by his Spirit to carry out his saving work.

"In this Church-community, called 'Catholic,' I find signs of Jesus' love which I do not find in other religious groups. First, there are the seven sacraments, especially the Eucharist, which I believe is truly Jesus' body, blood, soul, and divinity and not just a symbol of it. Second, there is the positive teaching and leadership of the pope and bishops, successors of Peter and the other Apostles, communicating Christ's truth to us. Third, there is an unbroken historical connection between the Church Christ founded and the Roman Catholic Church today. We still uphold all, not just part, of what Jesus said his special community was to be.

"I also find encouragement in my faith by two historical facts. First, even though the Church has not always lived up to Christ's expectations, even though it has had some unworthy leadership, even though many members of the Church are sinners instead of saints—this Church has not only survived, but actually spread throughout the entire world.

"And, second, many of her members have shed their blood as a testimony of their faith in Christ's complete message. Both of these facts prove to me that God is with the Church, upholding her and giving strength to us to live Jesus' way faithfully.

"The seed of this belief was planted in me at baptism—it was God's special gift to me. Through long years of probing, reflecting, and praying—sometimes amid doubts and fears—I have grown from merely tolerating this gift to accepting it with joy and conviction. There are still many unanswered questions in my mind, but I trust that God in his wisdom and goodness will send his Truth in his own way and time."

Sister Mary Karita Ivancic, S.N.D.

## What Makes Our Family Catholic

"We share in the life of our parish, especially in the Sunday celebration of the Eucharist. Today, for many Catholic families, parish is as much a frustration as a blessing. But it is part of being Catholic, in one way or another. So we serve on committees…We try to be the parish.

"As a Catholic family we pray in ways natural to our life together: around the family table; parental blessings for the kids at bedtime; special liturgical goings-on for special liturgical seasons. Every year these are transformed, depending on the ages of the children. In this, parental faith benefits every bit as much as that of the children. Maybe more.

"But the basic thing is trying to live in our home, and in our relationships with extended family and friends, a spirit that is frequently at odds with the dominant culture…That is the essential thing for us as a Catholic family: trying to live in a wide-open vision of the gospel that we have learned during the years to love; a vision of God, one another, and the world that is Catholic and so Christian; a vision that helps us to make sense out of life (most of the time) and be glad for it."

Mitch Finley, *National Catholic Reporter* (Spokane, WA, May 15,1981).

## What Has the Church Done for Me

"Without the Church should I have learned to serve, to pray, to love, to adore? She offered me the main direction of my life. She taught me why I was in this world and what I had to do while I was in it. She taught me the right use of the body, without despising it, and its subjugation to the soul. She taught me spiritual ambition, in virtue of my high destiny. She taught me to remember my own weaknesses and my inability to fulfill that destiny unaided.

"She taught me that God was my portion, and she offered me priceless help in the attainment of that portion. She told me what sin was, and she expected me to fall into it, but she offered me daily and hourly means of recovery from it. She spread out her sacramental system, with its visible and corporeal means of spiritual regeneration and strength and growth.…She taught me what Christ was and ever has been to mankind, and she kept his living remembrance in the sacrament of the Eucharist. She told me of those who had almost transcended the bodily senses and heard words not given to man to utter. In one word, she has taught me how to seek God."

Maude Dominica Petre in "Maude Petre Modernism" by Clyde S. Crews, America (May 16, 1981), p. 406.

## For Discussion
1. One reader of *U.S. Catholic* (May 17, 1979, p. 11) commented: "Being Catholic makes a difference for me. After talking to my children who are in Catholic grade and high schools, I feel it will make less of a difference to them as they become adults." Why might this be so? Is it good or bad?

**4**

2. The oneness of the Church is not based on the uniformity of its rites or language, but upon unity in which diverse entities form a unit. Where in your parish do you see unity but not uniformity?

3. If others are to be attracted to the Faith, the Church must make its faith credible. Our worship, witness, and loving service are signs by which others can know the reconciliation that God wills for all creation. Is the modern Church characterized by unity and love?

4. Elizabeth Anne Seton was attracted to the Church by the strong Eucharist-centered faith of Catholic friends. Do you know of anyone who came into the Church through the example of others?

5. Do you think most teenagers feel a vital part of Christ's Church? Why or why not?

6. What characteristics of the Church do you appreciate most? Why? What other features of the Church appeal to you?

7. A friend of yours threatens to leave the Church because a highly popular priest has left to marry outside the Church. What can you say?

## Marks of the Church

### The Church is:

1. ONE in teaching and faith, worship and liturgy, government and obedience.

2. HOLY in its founder, purpose, ministries, and members. It encourages prayer, offers community celebration, and Mass. It has retreat houses, contemplative monks and nuns, and insists on charity and justice.

3. CATHOLIC in its duration, extension, and teaching.

4. APOSTOLIC in its communion with the Holy Father and all other Catholic communities. There is an unbroken line of bishops in communion with the teaching and practice of the early Church.

## Special Problems:

1. If teachers teach error...they may be forbidden to teach, yet allowed to stay with the community.

2. Teachers who sin...Jesus said the weeds and wheat remain: if they won't listen, treat them like publicans—do as they say, not as they do.

3. Catholicism may not *be* everywhere in the world, but it is *open* to all people.

4. Bishops who stray from the Church are still validly ordained and may ordain other bishops unless they change the essentials of their beliefs.

## Additional Reading

*The Rites of the Catholic Church as Revised by the Second Vatican Council. Study Edition.* New York: Pueblo Publishing Co., 1983. See especially p. 59, #123 for use with the margin feature in Section 3.

Hellwig, Monika K. "Living Tradition in the Living Church." *Chicago Studies* 19:2 (Summer 1980), 161–70.

McBrien, Richard P. *Catholicism.* Vols I, II. Minneapolis: Winston Press, 1980.

## CHAPTER 5

# Experiencing the Image

(Text pages 114–143)

## FOCUS

**Doctrinal:** Each parish is part of a diocese and is the ordinary way in which the Church ministers to its members.

**Personal:** How can I contribute to making my parish a better representative of Christ's Church?

## OBJECTIVES

**Cognitive:** (a) to understand parish roles and how parishes organize to minister to their people; (b) to see the relationship between parish and diocese as one of mutual support and help.

**Affective:** (a) to appreciate the new roles to which the laity are being summoned; (b) to want to contribute to the growth and improvement of our parishes.

# Chapter 5 Outline

### SECTION 1
**The Image in Action**

A Living Community

What is a Parish?

Ways Parishes Differ

Master Plan for a Parish

*On This Rock* (margin feature)

A People

Clergy and Laity

Priest and Parishioner

*A People within a People* (text feature)

A Mission

### SECTION 2
**Evolving Parish Structures and Programs**

New Parish Structures

Leadership

The Pastor

*Communion of Saints* (margin feature)

Parish Committees and Programs

*Baptizing Adults—New Life for the Church* (text feature)

Parish Vitality Today

Portrait of a Parish

Some Parish Activities

**SECTION 3**
**The Parish: How it Developed**

**❺**

# TEACHER'S RESOURCE 5A

## Historical Notes

Church organization as we know it did not begin to develop until the second and third centuries A.D. The earliest followers of Jesus anticipated his return within their lifetimes and did not focus on organization. Within two generations the need to develop or impose some structure became apparent as communities of Christians grew, especially in urban areas. The three-tiered ministry described in the text feature of Section 3 is the earliest evidence we have of the emergence of an organization. The concept of Apostolic Succession became the backbone of the emerging Church.

## Pedagogical Notes

1. The purpose of this chapter is to get students aware of and involved in their parish. Add one or more of the following activities to those suggested throughout the text: (a) Hold a "parish day" in class where each parish is represented by a student(s). Be sure various aspects of parish life are represented; (b) Ask students to collect their parish bulletins for two weeks and to describe the concerns of their parish based on the contents of the bulletins; (c) Survey 5–10 people on the importance of the parish in their lives. Compare the results in class or as a written assignment.

2. For more information on the Roman Curia, obtain *Catholic Update*, UPD 102 (October, 1982). Other details about the Roman or Eastern Catholic Churches can be found in the Catholic Encyclopedia.

# TEACHER'S RESOURCE 5B

## Theological Notes

When discussing how Catholics might best experience Christ's presence in the Church, the image of family is often introduced. Pastors, educators and theologians frequently speak of the "the parish family"—no doubt because Jesus himself sometimes used the familial model in his preaching about the kingdom of God. He spoke of God as "Father" and he told us that we are "heirs" of the Father's kingdom.

There is a great deal to be said for this kind of language about the Church, but some religious educators are suggesting that this image is not without its liabilities. These days, many of our students come from family situations that are not particularly good models of the Church. Families are broken by divorce. They are dysfunctional because of parental substance abuse. The traditional nuclear families, with their clear sense of values and stability, can no longer be assumed as normative.

Calling the parish a family, therefore, may be giving the wrong message to many of our students who come from wounded families. In this case, we would be saying too little about the Church. But there's more. For students who come from relatively healthy family situations, the family image may say too much about what it means to be Church. This model, for example, can establish unreal, perhaps even unhealthy, expectations of intimacy and group interaction. When Fr. Dulles critiqued the "mystical communion" model in his book *Models of the Church*, he outlined reservations that may also apply to the family image.

Speaking of the Church in these terms can imply that the primary beneficiaries of the relationship—the family—are the family members themselves. In this, calling the Church a family might suggest that charity not only begins at home, but is also primarily directed toward the household of faith.

If we use the family image, therefore, to talk about what we experience as members of Christ's Body, we should be careful not to say too little or too much. One way to achieve this balance, would be to "stretch" the family metaphor. Just as youngsters grow up and grow out of the close confines of their nuclear families, so too do Christians hear Christ calling them to go forth to all people with the Good News of God's kingdom. Christ invites us to leave behind the safe and familiar; to follow him as ministers of the Gospel. This means that the family image can be balanced with a ministerial image of the Church—what Fr. Dulles called the servant Church and the herald Church. Members of the servant Church attend to the needs of the family's guests and friends as gracious hosts and hostesses—no strings attached. They look for ways to witness Christ's love, even to those who are not part of the family circle. Members of the herald Church proclaim God's

Word in the marketplace, on the job, among their acquaintances, and by their social and political involvements.

In a sense, the Church may be described as a kind of family, but to speak of ourselves in this image does not say it all. Jesus always loved Joseph and Mary. He loved his heavenly Father.

But he left them to be about his Father's business. This is also our vocation. Any image or images we use to help people experience the meaning of life in the Church should include this challenge to maturity, with all the risks involved in "leaving the nest."

**5**

# Using Your Imagination

Imagine that you are president of your parish council and that your parish has been asked: (1) to send suggestions to the Holy Father and your bishop, and (2) to make some decisions regarding priorities in the parish itself. How would you answer these questions?

**The Holy Father asks:**

1. What kind of a person should I try to choose when I appoint a new bishop?

2. To what three important concerns of the Church would you like to see the pope direct his time and energies? Explain your answers.

3. What immediate changes do you feel are needed in the Church? Prioritize your suggestions.

**Your Bishop asks:**

1. What can our parishes do to deal with the lack of faith among so many of our young people today?

2. How can we continue to meet the needs of the diocese for priestly ministry? There are just not enough priests and it seems the number will continue to decrease in the future.

3. Our diocese, and many of our individual parishes, have larger expenses than incomes. How can we balance our budget and keep it out of the "red"?

**Your Pastor asks:**

1. The parish has been made the beneficiary of a wealthy widow's estate. Funds will cover *five* of these projects or programs. How should the parish spend this money? Give reasons for your decision.
   a. The parish school needs a full-time secretary.
   b. The parish needs a music director to help improve the quality of liturgy.
   c. The parking lot needs resurfacing and enlarging.
   d. The church roof is leaking and causing interior damage.
   e. There are many hungry people in the area. The parish has been asked to sponsor a soup kitchen twice weekly.
   f. The carpeting in the Church is wearing out.
   g. The diocesan seminary suffered huge damages from a fire. All parishes have been asked to help restore it to full use.
   h. The CYO needs a new gym and shower facilities.
   i. Parents are asking to have a kindergarten beginning next September. This will mean an additional teacher's salary.

2. How can we better involve young people, ages 14–18, in parish life?

3. What do you consider the surest signs of a healthy, growing, and caring parish? Why?

Name _____

# Build a Parish: A Simulation Game

*Directions:* Your group members have just been assigned to a NEW PARISH. You are the ones responsible for all decisions regarding running and organizing of the parish. Below are some of the "problems" that you experience. Together, figure out how you would handle them.

**I.**  From the members of your group, choose the following:

a pastor:_____

a principal:_____

a parish council president_____

The pastor should be prepared to give a report on the parish tomorrow for the diocese.

What role or function would the other members of your group serve (that is, which other duties would be necessary in running the parish)?

_____

_____

**II.**  List the following information:

**1.** Name of parish and reason for your choice: _____

**2.** Number of families: _____

**3.** Location: _____

**4.** Percentage of people over 60: ____ and people under 18: _____

**III.** Each parish is equipped with the basic materials needed (e.g., altar, tabernacle, organ, stations, etc.) You have been given an additional gift of $25,000 by a benefactor. You are to use it to purchase something that will be an inspiration to your parishioners. What would you purchase?

**IV.** Although you as a group realize that there are many things you will want to accomplish, set one major goal for this year and tell how you propose to accomplish it.

**1.** Goal:

**2.** How to accomplish:

**3.** Write a motto to fit your goal:

Name _____

**V.** You realize that one very important element in your parish community will be the opportunities offered to your parishioners through parish-sponsored activities.

**1.** List five regular religious activities your parish will sponsor:

**2.** List five regular educational activities your parish will sponsor:

**3.** List five regular social activities your parish will sponsor:

**VI.** Finally, one main problem you have noticed in other parishes is the fact that so many young people have not been involved. What would you do to involve people your age in the parish?

Be specific.

# The Rites of the Church

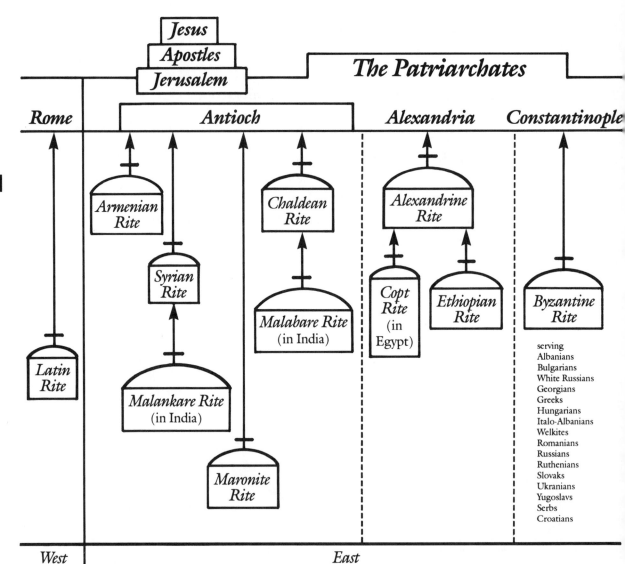

Note: Many of these rites have an Orthodox "twin."

Adapted by permission of the Diocese of St. Maron—U.S.A.

## CHAPTER 5 Test

## Experiencing the Image

I.  **Matching.** In the blanks below, write the letter of the correct answer.
    Answers may be used more than once or not at all.

| | | |
|---|---|---|
| a. archbishop | g. deanery | l. priest |
| b. auxiliary bishop | h. diocese | m. primary |
| c. bishop | i. evangelization | n. rite |
| d. coadjutor | j. parish | o. structure |
| e. collegiality | k. pastoral team | p. territorial parish |
| f. curia | | |

___ **1.** People who express their communion with God and one another

___ **2.** Section of the People of God entrusted to a bishop

___ **3.** Local church

___ **4.** Local ordinary

___ **5.** Bishops and pope working together

___ **6.** Ordained minister whose authority to preach, administer the
         sacraments, and make laws depends on a bishop

___ **7.** Bishop in line to succeed when a bishop dies or resigns

___ **8.** Assistant for the local ordinary; shares his authority

___ **9.** Head of a group of dioceses

___ **10.** A group of parishes usually close together geographically

___ **11.** Diocesan council, primary office for assisting the bishop

___ **12.** Supreme authority of the pope

___ **13.** Members are assigned by geographical boundaries

___ **14.** Level at which ordinary Catholics experience "the Church"

___ **15.** Determines the way in which a parish community will grow and
          carry out its mission

II. **True or False.** If the completion to the statement is true, write a plus sign
    (+); if false, write a zero (o).

**Parishes ...**

___ **1.** differ widely in personnel and organization.

___ **2.** are meant to be the Church in miniature.

___ **3.** reflect the patterns of residential segregation in American society.

___ **4.** function independently of the diocese.

___ **5.** are always headed by a pastor.

___ **6.** have less and less need of lay ministry.

___ **7.** exist to carry out Christ's mission.

Name: _____ Score: _____

**Pastors and priests ...**

___ **8.** must instruct and form parishioners in the Christian life.

___ **9.** need to help parishioners reach out beyond the parish to build a just society.

___ **10.** are meant to supply leadership and call others to roles of leadership.

___ **11.** supply whatever kind of ministry their parishioners need.

___ **12.** need to control the programs and activities being carried out in the parish.

___ **13.** should avoid getting involved with other Churches and community organizations.

___ **14.** should give priority to parish renewal and the people's spiritual development.

___ **15.** can keep financially afloat only if they frequently talk about money.

___ **16.** are independent of the bishop.

**The bishop ...**

___ **17.** is head of the local Church.

___ **18.** governs the diocese in his own name.

___ **19.** needs the assistance of priests, religious, various offices, and consultants.

___ **20.** is sometimes assisted by an auxiliary or coadjutor bishop.

**III. Essay.** Choose two.

**1.** Describe the "ideal parish"—its spirit, structure, activities, and aims.

**2.** Explain the office of bishop and the organization of a diocese.

**3.** In what practical ways could you help to move your present parish toward being the "ideal parish"? Identify your parish by name and be as specific and detailed as you can.

# CHAPTER 5 Test
## Experiencing the Image

**I.**

1. j
2. h
3. h
4. c
5. e
6. l
7. d
8. b
9. a
10. g
11. f
12. m
13. p
14. j
15. o

**II.**

1. +
2. +
3. +
4. o
5. o
6. o
7. +
8. +
9. +
10. +
11. o
12. o
13. o
14. +
15. o
16. o
17. +
18. +
19. +
20. +

**III.**

Answers will vary.

# CHAPTER 5

## SECTION 1
### Text Questions (Student text pages 115–123)

**Page 117**

**(1)** Answers will vary and may include roles such as student, acolyte, or teacher.

**(2)** Answers will vary and may include references to linguistic and ethnic differences, or age and economic differences.

**Page 121**

**(3)** Answers will vary. Groups might include old and young, unemployed, widowed, single, and physically challenged.

**(4)** Answers will vary.

**(5)** Town, county, state, country, American Roman Catholics, the worldwide Church.

**Page 123**

**(6)** Answers will vary—counseling, shelter, soup kitchen.

**(7)** Answers will vary.

**(8)** Answers will vary.

## SECTION 1 Checkpoint! (page 124)
### Review

**(1)** Parish life reveals God's love in all its activities. It mirrors the universal Church in its ministries.

**(2)** The purpose of a parish is to become more fully a People of God by sharing Christ's mission and developing the structure necessary to support its community life and to carry out its mission.

**(3)** Two parishes might differ in location and type of community for whom they minister (race of parishioners, age range, level of education, values, ways they seek God).

**(4)** Pastors encourage community, counsel, lead, express concern, and provide union with Christ in the sacraments. Parishioners work with priests in

prayer and activities to live the Gospel and witness to Christ's presence in the world.

**(5)** Parish members can become part of the leadership in lay ministry, being involved in family support, outreach to the alienated, or catechesis.

**(6)** Words to Know: *parish* (the Church in miniature; a group who gather to express their communion with God and one another); *ecclesial* (having to do with the community of the Church); *diocese* (a section of the People of God entrusted to a bishop to be guided by him with the assistance of the clergy); *laity* (all the faithful except those in holy orders); *pastoral ministers* (lay men and women who tend to parish needs).

## In Your World

**(1)** Have students create a parish that is significantly different from their own in ethnic, economic, and geographical terms. Then have them think about the types of programs this parish would need and how those programs would differ from the ones found in their own parish. Stress here diversity or individuality within an overall unity (concepts from previous chapters).

**(2)** Focus first on the issues that might cause the alienation. Have students be honest about their own feelings of alienation or those of people they may know. Now discuss the support a member of the parish can offer. Be careful not to have the student playing the parish member try to dismiss or demean the feelings of the alienated one. Stress the need for support and willingness to work toward an understanding.

## Scripture Search

**(1)** These passages focus on the need to pray—a need all people have, especially our leaders and teachers. They also stress action, hearing and doing the Gospel, treating all members of a congregation equally regardless of their background or wealth, and working at not judging anyone.

**(2)** The covenant was formed as a pact between God and the people present at Mt. Sinai. All the people present and their descendants form the community of the faithful. Moses' brother Aaron was designated as a priest. The function of the priests was to distinguish between holy and unholy things and actions, and to teach the new community the law.

## SECTION 2
## Text Questions (Student text pages 125–133)
### Page 127
**(9)** Answers will vary.

**(10)** Answers will vary.

### Page 129
**(11)** Answers will vary.

**(12)** Issues might include homelessness, civil rights, war and peace around the world, the environment, poverty, and world hunger.

**(13)** Answers will vary but may focus on the importance of the involvement of young people to ensure that the parish will stay alive. Even younger people will look up to teenagers who are active in the parish and try to follow their example.

### Page 133
**(14)** Some suggestions for meeting parish financial needs might include raffles, donation of time, a fair, holiday crafts sale, or making donations to your church in honor of a friend's or family member's birthday, confirmation, or baptism.

**(15)** Answers will vary.

## SECTION 2 Checkpoint! (page 134)
### Review
**(1)** A non-territorial parish brings people together who do not live together, but who may work in the same vicinity. It is usually found in a city.

**(2)** Parish leadership works to make the mission of the parish clearer, and calls forth the leadership and gifts of others.

**(3)** Pastor and parish council contribute to shared decision making, foster community, and facilitate the parish's mission. They also engage in policy-making.

**(4)** Some committees are liturgy, education, finance, evangelization, and peace and justice.

**(5)** The pastor at St. Mary's tries to keep the church open at all times to everyone in order to keep the church a place of activity. He also tries to encourage participation by sponsoring activities such as trips.

**(6)** A few specific activities are trips, breakfasts, movies, and ministries to people with special problems.

**(7)** Words to Know: *territorial parish* (one whose members are assigned by geographical boundaries); *non-territorial parish* (one whose members are determined by other factors such as people who all work in a certain area); *co-pastor* (associate pastor forming part of a team); *parish council* (lay and religious leaders of a parish trained to develop structures that allow for shared decision-making); *RCIA* (Rite of Christian Initiation of Adults).

## In Your World

**(1)** Focus on the variety of activities offered by the parish. Were students even aware that so many different things went on? Be sure students experience a range of activities.

**(2)** Obtain statistics from a parish or diocesan office. Have students give their own estimates or opinions about the makeup of the parish and then compare those views with the actual statistics.

## Scripture Search

The quarrels in these passages from Corinthians are over who should lead the Christian communities. Many people were expressing loyalty to a particular leader and that leader only. Paul responds by showing that Christ is the true leader of the Church, not anyone else. He warns against anyone boasting about his or her status, associating with the wrong people, and bringing a fellow Christian before the secular courts instead of before the Church. Paul emphasized that each person has his or her own unique gift and all these gifts reflect God in us. Together we all contribute to the unity and diversity of the Church.

## SECTION 3
**Text Questions** (Student text pages 135–140)

**Page 136**

**(16)** Reorganization was necessary in order to maintain consistency amongst all the parishes and to make sure that proper control was being exercised.

**Page 138**

**(17)** Answers will vary.

## SECTION 3 Checkpoint! (page 141)
### Review
**(1)** In the early Church bishops headed the Christian communities and were assisted by priests. Bishops performed all the important functions.

**(2)** Between 150 and 1535 a series of political changes made bishops lose and then regain their churches several times. Eventually the power of the bishop became narrower and the duties of bishop and pastor were separated.

**(3)** The "local church" refers to the diocese.

**(4)** Collegiality is Church leaders (bishops and the pope) working together as one body made up of equals.

**(5)** The bishop governs the local church, teaches, and governs with the pope.

**(6)** See Diocesan Curia, page 140, for these responses.

**(7)** Words to Know: *presbyter* (elder; refers to the priests in the early Church); *parochial* (referring to a parish); *local church* (the diocese); *diocese* (from a Greek word which means to keep house or govern, a territorial grouping of parishes); *collegiality* (bishops and the pope working together); *episcopus* (overseer, bishop); *coadjutor bishop* (bishop in line to succeed when a bishop dies or resigns); *dean* (a priest who acts as head of a group of parishes).

### In Your World
**(1)** Start with a map of your area. Outline the boundaries of your parish if it is territorial. Or get a diocesan map from your library or diocesan office. Use colored pins or magic marker to identify the individual parishes and any special buildings, colleges, or shrines contained within the diocese.

**(2)** Discuss the idea of a diocese as an extended family and each parish as an arm of that family. Be sure to acknowledge that sometimes the structure becomes more important than the thing it is structuring, but that Church structure is really for the service of the Christian community. Discuss the positive aspects of diocesan structure including interpersonal relationships, outreach, and recognized authority.

**5**

## Scripture Search

The bishop is concerned with every member of each parish in his diocese, just as the shepherd worries about every sheep in the flock. Bishops will devote time and care to all parishioners, especially if they are suffering. It is a joy for the bishop to care for a lost soul, just as it is for the shepherd to find the lost sheep.

## CHAPTER 5 Review (pages 142–143)

### Study

(1) Answers will vary.

(2) In a parish, every member must contribute. Parishioners don't just sit back and receive things from leaders, they must also give back to the parish.

(3) Each person in a parish has a unique contribution to make according to his or her gifts.

(4) Roles of pastors include leadership, administering sacraments, education, and counseling.

(5) Forms of lay ministry include teaching, outreach to the poor, fundraising, and evangelization.

(6) A parish can contribute through activities organized by the peace and justice committee, social programs, missions, food drives, and others.

(7) Parishes can minister to their members through counseling for singles, divorced, and unemployed, help for the elderly, programs for alienated church members, and so on.

(8) Shared leadership means that there is collaboration and that all members of a parish are able to take part in its organization.

(9) Committees mean that people become personally involved and must be trained. As a result they grow spiritually. Committees and joint programs foster community and unity. Their members and participants grow in understanding and profession of faith.

(10) Answers will vary. At St. Mary's there is constant activity and a wide appeal. The church has been made a part of everyday life.

(11) The bishop has authority over the pastors in his diocese. The pope has jurisdiction over bishops although they work together in governing the Church and diocese.

(12) Bishops used to have wider powers in the early centuries of Christian history. Later, duties of bishops and pastors were separated and the power of the pope grew.

(13) The vicar general exercises the power of the bishop in other diocesan regions as a representative and the chancellor prepares all the written documents for the diocese.

### Action

(1) Stress the interaction between the leader and the led. Show how parishioners are involved in the day-to-day life of the parish (even as secretaries and teachers).

(2) Focus on how the two parishes are the same and different; this is the concept of unity and diversity.

### Prayer

Stress the need for guidance in identifying our unique contribution to the Church. Our actions reflect God's will and the Spirit at work in us. Read the two Scripture passages aloud and write a prayer or service centered around the ideas contained in them.

# Experiencing the Image

**OVERVIEW:** The aim of this chapter is to introduce the students to parish, diocesan, and Church structure, and to facilitate their understanding of their history and role in the continued life of the Church.

**OBJECTIVES: The students will:**

- Discuss the concept of a parish by giving examples of what a parish does.
- Read about the function of each member of a parish and the contributions each makes to its vitality.
- Identify church leadership today and link it to the earliest beginnings of the Church.

**TIME FRAME: One to one-and-a-half hours.**

**MATERIALS: Bibles, any available diocesan maps and guides.**

**PROCEDURE:**

*Into:* Prayer—Begin class be reciting Psalm 40:1–11.

*Through:*

Activity One:

1. Ask students to volunteer definitions of a parish and the roles of its members.

2. Make a list of the way parishes might differ (see page 117) and use questions 1 and 2 to help.

3. Discuss the purpose of a parish in the religious life of its members and society as a whole. See questions 6–8 on page 123.

Activity Two:

1. Ask students to offer a description of a good leader. What qualities must he or she have, and how can these qualities be applied to Church leaders both religious and lay.

2. List the functions of a pastor. See how many the students can name and ask who else can serve in leadership roles in the church.

3. Name some activities your parish sponsors and have students come up with some activities or committees they would like to see—especially for youth. How do these activities contribute to the life of the Church?

Activity Three:

1. Have students identify the pope, their bishop, and their pastor and give the function of each.

2. On the board, have a student draw a diagram of Church authority by reading pages 136–139. Place parish, deanery, diocese, and the larger Church on the diagram.

3. Read over page 140 (Diocesan Curia) and ask students if they knew about any of these offices before.

*Beyond:* Suggest that students read "On This Rock," on page 118 and do the first part of activity 1 in Section 1, "In Your World," page 124.

*Prayer:* Close class with a prayer from Hebrews 2:12–13 which expresses faith in God declared in the congregation of the faithful.

Name: _____     Score: _____

## CHAPTER 5 QUIZ
# Experiencing the Image

Mark true (+) or false (o).

___ 1.   The parish is the Church in miniature.

___ 2.   The most important part of any parish is the church building itself.

___ 3.   Parishes reflect the values, needs, and problems of their parishioners.

___ 4.   The parish is first a people—a community.

___ 5.   A parish's main concern should be the quality of its sacramental life.

___ 6.   Good pastors don't need the help of lay people.

___ 7.   A parish's area of ministry should stay within its own boundaries.

___ 8.   All the structures of a parish should foster community and help to carry out its mission.

___ 9.   Parishes today include ordained and lay ministries.

___ 10.  In today's ideal parish the number of persons directly involved in parish life will be small.

___ 11.  A wide variety of new parish ministries have evolved since Vatican II.

___ 12.  The vitality of a parish is best measured by the number of people who attend Mass.

___ 13.  A good parish is identified by its structures.

___ 14.  The greatest compliment a pastor can receive is to be told his parish is "really active."

___ 15.  Parish life as we know it has always been a part of the Catholic Church.

___ 16.  The term "local church" refers to the diocese.

___ 17.  Each Apostle governed an individual church.

___ 18.  Bishops receive their authority from the pope.

___ 19.  Most bishops govern through a series of offices, tribunals, secretariats, and consultants.

___ 20.  The chief bishop of the Church is the pope.

# CHAPTER 5 QUIZ
Answer Key

| | |
|---|---|
| **1.** + | **11.** + |
| **2.** o | **12.** o |
| **3.** + | **13.** o |
| **4.** + | **14.** o |
| **5.** + | **15.** o |
| **6.** o | **16.** + |
| **7.** o | **17.** o |
| **8.** + | **18.** o |
| **9.** + | **19.** + |
| **10.** o | **20.** + |

**⑤**

## CHURCH ORGANIZATION

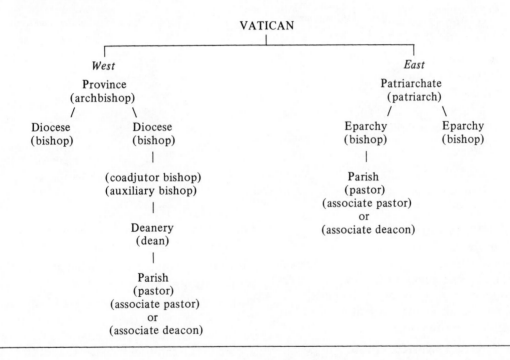

VATICAN

*West* — Province (archbishop)

Diocese (bishop) — Diocese (bishop)

(coadjutor bishop) (auxiliary bishop)

Deanery (dean)

Parish (pastor) (associate pastor) or (associate deacon)

*East* — Patriarchate (patriarch)

Eparchy (bishop) — Eparchy (bishop)

Parish (pastor) (associate pastor) or (associate deacon)

## ORGANIZATION OF THE ROMAN CURIA

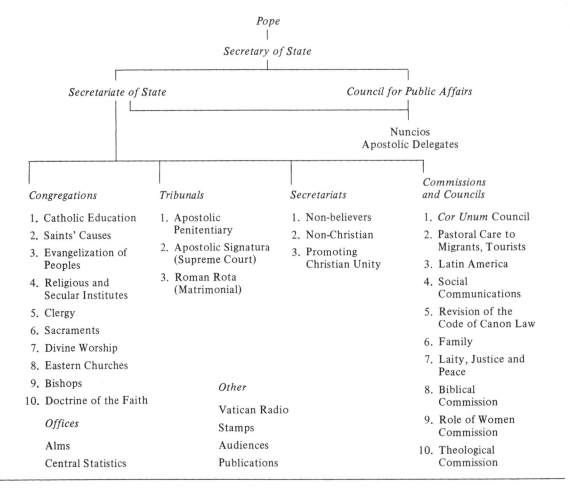

| | |
|---|---|
| Pope | |
| Secretary of State | |

| Secretariate of State | Council for Public Affairs |
|---|---|
| | Nuncios |
| | Apostolic Delegates |

**Congregations**
1. Catholic Education
2. Saints' Causes
3. Evangelization of Peoples
4. Religious and Secular Institutes
5. Clergy
6. Sacraments
7. Divine Worship
8. Eastern Churches
9. Bishops
10. Doctrine of the Faith

*Offices*

Alms

Central Statistics

**Tribunals**
1. Apostolic Penitentiary
2. Apostolic Signatura (Supreme Court)
3. Roman Rota (Matrimonial)

*Other*

Vatican Radio

Stamps

Audiences

Publications

**Secretariats**
1. Non-believers
2. Non-Christian
3. Promoting Christian Unity

**Commissions and Councils**
1. *Cor Unum* Council
2. Pastoral Care to Migrants, Tourists
3. Latin America
4. Social Communications
5. Revision of the Code of Canon Law
6. Family
7. Laity, Justice and Peace
8. Biblical Commission
9. Role of Women Commission
10. Theological Commission

## Skit on the Parish in Action

Holy Family Parish has probably one of the best developed Parish Councils in the Diocese of New Halifax. In September, President Janet Filmore conducted the meeting on the parish celebration of Thanksgiving. Present were all twelve members of the Council.

President: You're all prepared, I'm sure, to give your input—and the input of the people you represent—regarding our upcoming Thanksgiving celebration. We'll start with you, Father Gene.

Pastor Father Gene DiGeronimo: I'm wondering how much we can improve on last year's celebration. One thing that I received a lot of positive feedback on was the liturgy. There was so much parish involvement, from the youngest child to the oldest senior citizen. I'm hoping our liturgy will be able to involve everyone again this year. Of course, all the food and clothing we collected and gave to the local immigrant population not only brought a lot of publicity, but also gratitude from the people we served.

President: Thanks, Father. What are you planning for the liturgy? Father Phil? Bert?

Father Philip Peterson, Associate Pastor: When Bert and I met with the Liturgy Committee, they had some tentative plans. First, the Diocesan Liturgical Commission suggested several themes. The one we like is based on Paul's letter to the Colossians: "Christ's peace must reign in your hearts...Dedicate yourselves to thankfulness. Let the word of Christ, rich as it is, dwell in you" *(Colossians 3:15,16)*.

Bert Corrigan, Music Minister: There's a great deal of appropriate music. Something new we came up with is an entrance procession, representative of every group in the parish. Each group would place at the altar their offerings for peace in a spirit of gratitude.

President: How does this sound to you, Cora?

Cora (Mrs. Peter) Sarinskas, president of Holy Family's Social Justice Action Committee: That is right in line with what our committee had in mind. Since so much needs to be done to promote world peace and the plight of the homeless, we were planning to obtain pledges from our parish to work on the various national and diocesan programs addressing these concerns. Those who couldn't do that could write letters to their representatives and pray. Also, we thought of offering food to the aged confined to their homes and to families whose wage-earners have been laid off. We also want to enlist workers to do home repairs in order to keep utility prices down—especially for those on fixed incomes.

President: How would the schools respond to this, Sister Mary Grace and George?

Sister Mary Grace Kovach, principal of Holy Family Parish School: The children look forward to the yearly collection of food for the poor. Some of their own families may be recipients, so they will be motivated to get donations from merchants and parish families. Our School and Home Association was considering a family-to-the-aged ministry where a family in strong financial circumstances could personally invite an elderly person or couple to their Thanksgiving feast. This could be promoted in the parish bulletin, through the schools, and by posters. Even one Sunday could be set aside to explain the program at each Mass.

George Heilman, principal of the Parish School of Religion: Our faculty would support that, I know, because we were hoping to find a way of relieving the loneliness and financial burdens of our elderly parishioners.

President: We seem to have some consensus here. What does Youth Ministry say to all this? Sister Doris?

Sister Doris Velazques, Youth Minister: We would have no trouble getting the support of our youth groups. Discussion of these activities could form the agenda for our next meeting. We could get volunteers for doing posters, making pledge cards, and signing up pledges at each Mass until Thanksgiving.

President: Reverend Mr. Vincent, since your ministry to the elderly of the parish brings you into close contact with our senior citizens, can you offer any suggestions?

Rev. Mr. Arthur Vincent, parish deacon: I know that some of our seniors would like to participate in the liturgy but need transportation, and those who cannot get to church would like to participate in some way. Maybe we could arrange for a shut-in TV liturgy. Maybe our Reach-Out Committee could arrange transportation. I hope the Eucharistic Ministers will be able to get around to home-bound seniors after the parish liturgy. We could also see that they get a program booklet.

President: Sister Patricia, how can this fit into the parish's Religious Education program?

Sister Patricia Woodley, Director of Religious Education: It's fantastic! I see it as a golden opportunity to promote adult education and bring in people looking for a chance to get involved in the parish community.

President: Jake, what is your response?

Jake Jackson, college student and catechist in the PSR program: Really, Mr. Filmore, I think a lot of kids home for Thanksgiving would be glad for the opportunity to get involved in the celebration. I commute to school so I can teach in the PSR program, but those away would feel more a part of the parish community if they were invited.

President: And you, Jeanette, do you think we should be doing anything else to involve the parish?

Jeanette Colorone, a member of the Young Adult Group and also a minister of the Word: Well, Joe, you and I can participate through our ministries. I'm sure all the other ministers will want to take part as well. Could the Religious Education Office offer a simple but coordinated program—something in print that could be mailed to each household, with suggestions for what to do in preparation for the parish celebration, with volunteer forms that could be dropped into the collection basket on Sundays?

President: That's a great idea, Jeannette. Are we all ready now to line up the celebration program?

List the leadership positions in the parish and their function. What skills did the president exercise in the meeting?

How did the various parish models emerge through the meeting, especially community, institution, herald, servant, sacrament?

## Parish Bulletin Study

Each local Church (diocese) carries out Christ's three-fold mission of...

- Proclaiming the Good News *(Message)*
- Building community, especially through liturgy and prayer experiences *(Community)*
- Relieving human distress *(Service)*. Likewise each parish (a Christian community within a specific geographic area) attempts to carry out this mission through various opportunities and activities. The parish bulletin often announces such opportunities to the parishioners. Study your parish bulletin carefully and answer the following questions:

1. What opportunities are available for learning about the faith (message), for studying it more deeply, and for proclaiming it to others? (e.g. classes, Bible study groups, Catechumenate program)

2. What opportunities are available for growth in holiness and spiritual living? (e.g. Mass, sacraments, prayer groups, spiritual direction and/or personal counseling)

3. What provisions are made for teenagers; young adults; singles, widowed, divorced, or separated; married couples; families; senior citizens and the aged; the handicapped and retarded; and the needy, lonely, and sick.

4. Are there any other needs (physical or spiritual) for which your parish provides support? (e.g. AA groups, self-help groups)

5. What would make a person (or family) want to take a parish bulletin, read it, and even post it for reference? Attach a copy of your parish bulletin.

## Bishops Are Like That

1. On the day of his consecration as bishop, December 8, 1602, Francis de Sales said: "It was that morning that God took me away from myself, to make me his own and to give me in turn to my people." He immediately had his own confessional moved out to the door of the cathedral so that the poor and invalids wouldn't be embarrassed to come to him. He loved to teach catechism to the children right in the cathedral, to sit with them, talk, tell stories, and bring them to love God. To his priests he advised, "Above all, take care not to be rough with penitents. In the kingdom of grace, gentleness alone is in place."

2. When Augustine, still a young man searching for truth, wanted to talk to Bishop Ambrose of Milan, he related: "I was prevented from having an intimate conversation with him by the crowds of people, all of whom had some business with him and to whose infirmities he was a servant." After being converted by Ambrose, Augustine became a bishop in Africa. He told his people, "I am a Christian with you, and a bishop for you; what I am with you consoles me, what I am for you frightens me." To combat a raging heresy that was causing violence in his diocese, Augustine made huge posters for the streets and buildings, with slogans about the true Faith.

3. Charles Borromeo, seventeenth-century Bishop of Milan, lived in a grand palace which was open continually to give hospitality to guests traveling from northern Europe to Rome. His guests were treated royally, and each week the bishop entertained beggars and ate with them. The table he used is still preserved in Rome. He himself slept on a hard bed and ate hardly more than soup.

4. In 1954, when Archbishop Montini, later Pope Paul VI, approached Milan to become its 140th bishop, he stopped the car, knelt down on the ground, and after saying a short prayer kissed the earth of his church, the church of Milan. The next day it was biting cold and a driving sleet, but the archbishop chose an open car for the parade: "I want the people to see me," he said. Two days later he visited two older ladies in their apartment because they had sent a note saying they were sick and could not attend the Mass of installation. Montini also visited the factories and the mines to speak to the workers. He spent his first Christmas as a bishop in a tin shanty town and took the mayor of Milan with him. He wanted parish churches to be more than houses of prayer; parishes should have children's homes, a sports field, a movie theater, a recreation center, a library. The Archbishop had eight chapels built in the center of the city apartment complexes. Every Epiphany he entertained foreign students because he knew how homesick they could be.

## Elements of a Diocese

Before a local church is "mature," it is called a *mission territory* and usually included as part of a local church already formed. Until recently, the entire state of North Carolina was one local

Copyright © Glencoe, Macmillan/McGraw-Hill

church—Raleigh. Now it is two—Raleigh and Charlotte.

A local area is ready to be known officially as a diocese when:

1. There are sufficient lay people educated in their responsibilities as Catholic Christians and strong enough to mix with other members of society without losing their faith; a Catholic community of mutual encouragement and support in the Faith.

2. Priests from the local territory are able to care for the pastoral needs of the community.

3. The means to educate youth and adults in the Faith are available.

4. A local bishop is appointed. At the assignment of the bishop, the community officially becomes a local church. (Sometimes bishops are assigned to care for the needs of large mission areas as well.)

Three other signs of a healthy Catholic community are:

1. A sufficient number of vocations to the priesthood and the diaconate are present to care for all the pastoral needs of its own people: marriage counseling, education, confession, parishes, hospital ministry, youth guidance, adult education, and so on.

2. Vocations to the religious life—a sign of the community's appreciation of gospel values, and of deep family spirituality—are increasing.

3. The community—priests, religious, and laity—generously reaches out to other areas to evangelize.

## Exploring Family Images

Every family has its ups and downs.

What do you see as the greatest obstacles to harmony in your own family?

- Scarcity of money to accomplish family goals.
- Unwillingness of individual family members to sacrifice.
- Lack of time to be together.
- Failure to believe in Christ's presence and help.
- Personality differences.
- Poor communication.

- Disrespect of one another.
- Lack of prayer.
- Other.

What problems prevent your being able to experience your parish as an extended family?

- Noncaring parishioners.
- No activities for teens.
- Lack of truly spiritual opportunities.
- Poor leadership.
- Cliques or feuds among members.
- Not enough priests to meet the needs.
- Lack of faith among young people.
- Other.

**5**

## Getting to Know Your Parish and Diocese

1. What, from your experience, do you believe to be the real purpose of your parish?

2. How is *renewal* evident in your parish?

3. Which seems to be more important to you: "what" a parish is or "who" a parish is?

4. How would you describe an ideal parish? Is your parish like this? Why or why not?

Your Parish (Find the following information concerning your parish):

- Name and date of founding.
- County in which it is located.
- Names of parish priests.
- Religious community staffing the school.

Your Diocese (Consult your local Catholic Directory for this information.):

- Number of counties in the diocese.
- Percentage of the population in the diocese that is Catholic.
- Name of the bishop or archbishop.
- Names of auxiliary bishop(s).
- Number of parishes in the diocese.
- Number of Catholic elementary schools, high schools, colleges in the diocese.

How many dioceses are in your state?

What is the name of the present Holy Father?

## Plan Your Own Local Church (Imaginary News Release)

The Holy Father has asked all interested Catholics in the United States to submit plans for **A Model Local Church** to be newly set up in Appalachian territory or on Native American lands. Here is your chance to plan and shape the "local church community of your dreams"! Please give specific plans: size, geographic area, people (economic status, education, nationality), bishop qualifications, liturgy style, type of institutions, style of priests, types of religious communities, spiritual/social/ecumenical activities, patron saint, and design of cathedral.

**5**

## My Church

Father, help me to see the Church as the Christian community united in Christ; organized to obtain a common goal by means of prayer, reception of the sacraments, and the following of your will.

Let me experience the Church as Jesus, present today: teaching, governing, and sanctifying.

Father, help me to see the Church as the Body of Christ, working together for the good of the whole body, each member with a work to do.

Father, help me to see the Church as one, holy, catholic, and apostolic, and still my Church.

Let me experience the Church as both a divine and a human reality; as carrying on the life and work of Jesus, even though in constant need of renewal and reconciliation.

Father, help me to see the Church as both local and universal, governed by its bishops, united under the Vicar of Christ. My Church.

Let me experience the Church as both my neighbor's parish and mine, my neighbor and me, united in Christ Jesus: working with him; living according to his truths; loving as he loved; worshiping through him, with him, in him; carrying out your mission in the unique way you have entrusted to each of us. Let me see it all...as my Church.

## Additional Reading

Bausch, William J. *The Christian Parish: Whispers of the Risen Christ.* Fides/Clarendon, Notre Dame, 1980.

*Epistle to Diognetus.* In *Early Christian Writings. The Apostolic Fathers.* Translated by Maxwell Staniforth. New York: Penguin Books, 1968.

Lohse, Eduard. *The First Christians: Their Beginnings, Writings, and Beliefs.* Translated by M. Eugene Boring. Philadelphia: Fortress Press, 1983.

*The Rites of the Catholic Church as Revised by the Second Vatican Council.*

**CHAPTER 6**

# Rooted in Jesus, Formed by His Spirit

(Text pages 144–171)

## FOCUS
**Doctrinal:** The Church, a necessary and vital part of God's plan for our salvation, realizes Christ's life and mission on earth.

**Personal:** Am I open to the ways in which the Holy Spirit wants to work in my life?

## OBJECTIVES
**Cognitive:** (a) to recognize that the essential characteristics of the Catholic Church are rooted in the early Church; (b) to understand the Holy Spirit as the guide and power source of the Church.

**Affective:** (a) to grow in love for the Holy Spirit; (b) to be grateful for membership in the Church founded by Christ.

## Chapter 6 Outline

### SECTION 1
**Looking to Your Roots**

The Perils of Rootlessness

Christ's Family Tree

*On This Rock* (margin feature)

The Modern Question

Is Church Membership Necessary?

*Liberal and Conservative—Who Are They?* (text feature)

The Church Is Unnecessary?

The Church Is Unchangeable?

### SECTION 2
**Jesus, Founder of the Church**

What He Said, Did, and Was

*Communion of Saints* (margin feature)

The Role of the Apostles

After the Ascension

The Revelation of Pentecost

The Day of Pentecost

The Images of Pentecost

*Catching the Spirit* (text feature)

## SECTION 3
### Patterns in the Infant Church

Core Characteristics
*Kerygma*—Proclamation
*Koinonia*—Community
*Diakonia*—Service
*A People at Prayer* (margin feature)
*Leitourgia*—Worship
Additional Characteristics
Necessity of Church Membership
*Poverty and Wealth* (text feature)
The Church as Guardian of Revelation

**6**

## TEACHER'S RESOURCE 6A

### Historical Notes

In Judaism, the Torah was the sole source of unity. By reciting it and obeying it, the community was built up. For John and his followers, baptism became a symbol of unity; in Christian baptism, the individual is united to Jesus. Because of their faith in Jesus' resurrection and ongoing life in the Spirit, Christians continued to unite with Jesus as invisibly present through the Last Supper.

During the time of the Apostles, the Christian ritual of the shared meal was preceded by Jewish readings and prayers. The purpose of the meal was to recognize Christ's presence and to create fellowship and group unity. Between 400 and 600 distinct prayers which preceded the Eucharist were added as well as the practice of the offering. But the practice itself links all Christians to the Apostles and to Christ himself.

### Pedagogical Notes

1. Students often need encouragement to begin the study of history. Stress the relevance of seeing history as a living testimony to our vitality and a necessary part of our self-understanding.

2. Encourage students to discuss the views of other Christians and of non-Christians and how they fit into the global community of humankind. Be sure the approaches of these groups are clarified.

3. Focus on the biblical texts given as references for this chapter. The Scriptural material should heighten the reality of the events discussed here and bring them to life.

## TEACHER'S RESOURCE 6B

### Theological Notes

As Catholics, we believe that Jesus founded the Church. He may not have given us the visible organization that we have today, but he did give us our identity (disciples of Christ) and our mission (to baptize all the nations). In this sense, he is the founder of the Church. We are formed in his spirit.

If we look carefully at the Church as it began to develop during the days of Jesus' earthly ministry, we can identify what we might call its original charter. A charter is a document that defines the role and purpose of a group, and grants the group authority to fulfill this purpose. The Gospel is such a document for us. It outlines the goals of Jesus' mission and the mission of his followers, and it bestows upon the disciples of Jesus the authority of God—especially at Pentecost when the infant Church received the gift of God's Spirit.

According to our charter, the Christian Church is about one thing and one thing only: proclamation of the Good News that God's kingdom has broken into history. "Now is the time of fulfillment," Jesus told us in Mark 1:15. "The reign of God is at hand. Reform your lives and believe in the Gospel." Whatever else the Church says and does, and however it develops over the centuries, its mission remains as Jesus Christ established it. The Church stands for the kingdom of God.

Contemporary thinking about the Church takes this charter seriously. Theologians and bishops constantly remind us that being rooted in Jesus means being rooted in this proclamation of God's kingdom. This accounts for the fact that we are seeing a heavy emphasis placed on conversion these days ("Reform your lives"), as well as special attention to the two principal signs of God's kingdom which Jesus exhibited during his ministry: peace and justice.

Put simply, we cannot be the Church of Jesus Christ if we are not willing to accept his challenge to overcome sin in our lives, and if we turn our backs on the challenge to make peace and justice in our world.

In a sense, paying closer attention to our biblical charter suggests that "Church" is not really a noun, even though the term, grammatically speaking, names a "person, place or thing." If we follow our founder and draw life from the Spirit he and the Father sent, Church is a verb. It is an activity of spirit-filled people whose actions are directed toward completing the work of Jesus.

Like Jesus, we bring peace by healing broken lives and by giving people reason to hope. Like Jesus, we make justice by showing compassion toward the poor and all people on the fringes of society. None of these activities, of course, is possible until we let God's Spirit set us free from our sinful desires from our urge for self-indulgence and self-gratification. That's why Jesus included a call to conversion in the proclamation of God's kingdom.

This activity characterizes what it means to be church. We live as Christ's ambassadors in our world, as we rely on his promise that we will live forever with him in the world to come. We are Kingdom people.

**6**

# Reading Guide

1. On the reverse side of this page, trace your personal roots as a family member of the Catholic Church.

2. Did Jesus really found the Catholic Church?

   a. An answer requires _____.

   b. _____ claim the Church is not essential to salvation.

   c. _____ believe Jesus left us a blueprint of the Church.

   d. To "found" means _____

   e. The Church evolved from what Jesus said and did:

      (1) He _____

      (2) He _____

      (3) But it was by _____ and by _____ that Jesus founded the Church.

3. How were the Apostles prepared for their mission?

   a. Jesus chose _____ whom he _____ and _____ to baptize, preach, and heal.

   b. _____ was singled out as head.

   c. In Matthew 28:20, Jesus promised: _____

   d. The work of organizing the _____ began only after _____ left them.

4. What was the revelation of Pentecost?

   a. The Pentecost Event is recorded in _____ by _____.

   b. He describes it in the symbolic language of _____, and_____, _____, _____.

   c. Pentecost did not _____ the Church, but marked the moment when the Spirit's outpouring became _____ for the disciples.

5. What core patterns emerged in the infant Church?

   a. _____, b. _____,

   c. _____, d. _____.

   e. The _____ was the core of the Christian community.

   f. Other characteristics of the early Church were: _____, _____, _____, _____, _____, and _____.

6. To be saved, is it necessary to belong to the Church?

   a. For those who know God's plan of salvation, _____.

   b. Those _____, unacquainted with it, or who have not recognized it as the truth, will also find _____.

   c. Because of the indwelling of the _____, Christians ordinarily need not wait for _____ of the Church for reading and interpreting _____ and _____.

Name: _____    Score: _____

7. How do the Scriptures present the Spirit?

a. One basic difference between the Hebrew Scriptures and the New Testament is that while the former presents the Spirit as _____ the latter reveals him as _____.

b. In Acts, the time after the Ascension is clearly the Age _____.

c. In the Synoptics, the Spirit's role in Jesus' life is shown through _____ or _____. John's gospel presents the Spirit as _____.

d. Paul associates the Spirit with _____. He is distinct from _____ and _____.

e. For 2,000 years the Spirit has continued _____ the Church.

**6**

**Answer Key**

**Reading Guide**

1. Answers will vary.
2. Answers will vary.
   a. faith
   b. Liberal Protestants
   c. Fundamentalists
   d. to originate
   e. (1) preached that the kingdom of God had come to earth
      (2) demonstrated its arrival by performing miracles
      (3) who he was, his great act of redemption
3. a. helpers, instructed, sent out
   b. Peter
   c. "I am with you always until the end of the world."
   d. Church, Jesus
4. a. Acts 2, Luke
   b. noise, wind, fire, enthusiasm, proclamation
   c. start, a reality
5. a. *kerygma* or proclamation
   b. *koinonia* or community
   c. *diakonia* or service
   d. *leitourgia* or worship
   e. Eucharist
   f. authority, sense of mission, tradition, goods held in common, expectation of
      the Second Coming, a share in the Paschal mystery
6. a. it is necessary.
   b. of good will, salvation.
   c. Holy Spirit, official pronouncements, Scripture, Church Teaching.
7. a. ever present, personal.
   b. of the Holy Spirit.
   c. symbol, prophecy, Paraclete.
   d. Christ's glory, the Father, the Son
   e. to guide or direct

Name: _____ Score: _____

## CHAPTER 6 Test

### Rooted in Jesus, Formed by His Spirit

I. **Matching.** Write the letter of the best answer on the blank. There are extra answers.

a. charismatic
b. *diakonia*
c. eschatology
d. fundamentalist
e. *kerygma*

f. *koinonia*
g. *leitourgia*
h. Liberal
i. noise

j. roots
k. Scripture
l. Tradition
m. wind

___ 1. "Proclamation," the core action and message of the Gospel

___ 2. Ultra-conservative Christian, interprets Scripture literally

___ 3. Symbol of the Spirit, representing God's power

___ 4. "Work done by the people for the service of all," worship

___ 5. Body of revealed truth in oral and written form

___ 6. Term used to describe one's past, whether through personal relationships or national and cultural background

___ 7. Gifted by the Holy Spirit

___ 8. Theology that deals with the final things, especially the Second Coming of Christ

___ 9. "Service," the disciples' ministry to one another

___ 10. "Community," a group of Spirit-filled persons united in heart, mind, and worship

II. **Multiple Choice.** Write the letter of the best choice on the blank.

___ 1. Knowing our personal and Church roots (a) is a luxury, (b) is helpful to the curious, (c) gives perspective and wisdom.

___ 2. We know that Jesus really founded the Catholic Church (a) because of our faith in Jesus, (b) because the Gospels frequently present Jesus as its founder, (c) because the Apostles organized it while Jesus was with them.

___ 3. The Pentecost event, as told by Luke, is (a) exaggerated a bit, (b) highly symbolic, (c) an exact description of what happened.

___ 4. Core patterns in the infant Church did not include (a) liturgy, (b) service, (c) preaching, (d) the seven sacraments as we know them today.

___ 5. Authority, Tradition, a sense of mission, and an expectation of the Second Coming of Jesus were (a) present in the early Church, (b) absent, (c) not clear.

___ **6.** Membership in the Church is (a) optional, (b) unnecessary, (c) necessary for all, (d) necessary for those acquainted with God's plan for salvation.

___ **7.** The stumbling block to accepting Jesus as the Messiah came from (a) his not fulfilling the prophecies, (b) the crucifixion, (c) his political involvements.

___ **8.** Contemporary outpourings of the Holy Spirit are (a) few and far between, (b) clear and strong, (c) entirely missing.

___ **9.** Scripture references to the Holy Spirit are clearest in the (a) Hebrew Scriptures, (b) four Gospels, (c) Acts of the Apostles, (d) Book of Revelation.

___ **10.** One way of speaking of the Holy Spirit is to describe him as the (a) love, (b) knowledge, (c) gift between the Father and the Son.

**III. Completion.** Fill in the missing words. There are extra items: believe, Christ, Constitution, Decree, Easter, Pentecost, sanctify, save.

"The Holy Spirit was sent on the day of _____ in order that he might continually _____ the Church, and that those who _____ might have access through _____in one Spirit to the Father." _____ on the Church, 4

**IV. Essay.** Choose two.

1. How is the Holy Spirit active in the Church today?

2. Why can we say that Jesus founded the Catholic Church?

3. What aspects of the Holy Spirit appeal most to you? Why?

## CHAPTER 6 Test
## Rooted in Jesus, Formed by His Spirit

**I.**

1. e
2. d
3. m
4. g
5. l
6. j
7. a
8. c
9. b
10. f

**II.**

1. c
2. a
3. b
4. d
5. a
6. d
7. b
8. b
9. c
10. a

**III.** **Pentecost, sanctify, believe, Christ, Constitution**

**IV. Answers will vary.**

# CHAPTER 6

## SECTION 1
## Text Questions (Student text pages 144–151)

**Page 146**

(1) Answers will vary—in each there are important dates, people, fights, marriages/unions, moves, and compromises.

(2) No knowledge of your past would remove an important part of your identity and personal history. You would have very little sense of why you are where you are.

**Page 147**

(3) Learning about the history of the Church will help you find your own place in its continuing history which is being formed every day. You might identify with some figures from the past. Most people see history as memorizing dates or as being completely apart from themselves, when it is really a part of every person's identity.

(4) Answers will vary.

**Page 151**

(5) Answers will vary.

(6) Answers will vary.

(7) History will show us how people have dealt with these questions and how the Church has responded by forming answers. History provides us with the tools we need to confront and deal with questions.

## SECTION 1 Checkpoint! (page 152)
## Review

(1) Learning about history helps you discover the roots of your identity and the influences on you personal, social, and religious development.

(2) If we do not know about history, then we might make the same mistakes that were made before—with disastrous consequences. Knowing about our past will help us to avoid making those same mistakes.

(3) Knowledge of Church history shows us the progress of God's plan of salvation in the history of humanity (salvation history).

(4) It might seem from the biblical record that Jesus founded the organization now known as the Catholic Church, so someone might ask if indeed he founded it.

(5) Some say that the Church is unnecessary because all churches are created by human beings. No organization is needed to mediate our contact with God. Others say that Scripture must be followed to the letter and that there is no other authority.

(6) Words to Know: *genealogy* (study of history and descent of persons and families); *fundamentalist* (a conservative Christian who interprets all of Scripture literally); *verbatim* (word for word, literally).

## In Your World

**(1)** The aim of the activity is to integrate the parish into the history of the Church as a whole. Present the picture of the entire Church as a family and the parish as a branch of that family.

**(2)** The goal here is for students to appreciate the role that a faith community plays. You can expect a wide range of responses including those who say that their place of worship is not very important to them. Be prepared to discuss all types of responses.

## Scripture Search

These passages trace God's activity in the world from (a) the moment of creation which identifies God as the originator of all human history (Genesis 1), to (b) the initiation of the covenant with Abraham and the beginning of the choosing of a human "partner" who establishes God's holiness in the world (Genesis 12), to (c) the establishment of a covenant with an entire nation of the faithful, Israel, the Chosen People (Exodus 20), to (d) the birth of Jesus to fulfill the words of the Old Testament prophets, and finally to the baptism, miracles, death, and resurrection of Jesus. These passages represent all the stages of God's unfolding plan in history, through the Jewish people to the incarnation in Jesus. Those passages help us understand our bond with the Jewish people and the bond between the Jewish faith and its fulfillment in Jesus.

## SECTION 2

**Text Questions** (Student text pages 153–159)

### Page 154

**(8)** It means something is partially present but still evolving, like a caterpillar turning into a butterfly.

### Page 155

**(9)** Answers will vary.

**(10)** An illness or the death of a young person, poverty, or injustice are all events that might cause a test of faith.

**(11)** Jesus' words say that the mission of the Church is universal and is to be offered to all. It also says that Jesus is the head of the Church even if he is not physically present. The organization is best determined by the living faithful.

### Page 157

**(12)** Salvation history might mean the events which together make up the interaction between humanity and God and which have formed a part of the movement of humankind toward salvation. Other events which could be included are the entry of the Israelites into Canaan after the Exodus, the building of the Temple under King Solomon, the lives of the prophets, the Council of Trent, and Vatican II.

**(13)** Pentecost filled each apostle with the Spirit and gave each a gift to speak, teach, and heal. As a group, they received the power to act in Jesus' name.

### Page 159

**(14)** Transform means to take on a new shape. Events or people which may be named might include a friend, teacher, parent, the death or birth of someone, or falling in love.

**(15)** Some experiences might include falling in love or learning about something for the first time.

## SECTION 2 Checkpoint! (page 160)

### Review

**(1)** A founder originates something by proposing its basic vision, but does not necessarily organize the entire project, which continues to grow and develop even after the death of the founder.

**(2)** Jesus' actions which established the foundation of the Church included his preaching and his act of redemption.

**(3)** The Apostles reacted to the loss of Jesus by becoming scared and running away. They were humiliated and felt defeated.

**(4)** At Pentecost the Holy Spirit entered each apostle and they were given the power to teach, preach, establish the Church, and act in the name of Jesus.

**(5)** Luke used images because they reflected other events in history like what happened on Mount Sinai. Images capture the emotions, sights, and sounds of the event.

**(6)** Words to Know: *founder* (proposes the basic vision of a project but does not organize it completely); *Pentecost* (event at which the Apostles received the Holy Spirit and their commission to continue the work of Jesus); *salvation history* (the record of God in the world).

# In Your World

**(1)** The images include wind, fire, and different languages. Drawings or music should reflect the power of the event and its spirituality. Emphasize the range of emotions such as alienation, awe, fear, and adoration.

**(2)** Stress the confusion and fear of the Apostles. Encourage students to discuss the way they might have reacted and to present the scene in their own words.

## Scripture Search

**(1)** The Holy Spirit is described in these passages as counselor, ever present, dwelling with the Apostles, teachers, reminder of all that Jesus has done, and witness to Jesus. The Spirit is always with the faithful and true disciples of Jesus and acts as a mediator.

**(2)** Jesus performs miracles of healing which include the exorcism of a demon, healing of leprosy, paralysis, and epilepsy, and the feeding of thousands of hungry people with barely any food. The recipient of the miracle always expresses her or his faith in Jesus. Jesus' actions reveal his holiness and power, and his link to God.

# SECTION 3

## Text Questions (Student text pages 161–168)

### Page 163

**(16)** Answers will vary.

### Page 165

**(17)** All the characteristics apply in some sense. Religious communities use goods in common and the eschatological hope is still alive among all the faithful. People still suffer for their faith, and there is still a strong sense of mission.

**(18)** Again, all the models apply in some way: in its earliest form the Church was an institution; there have always been individual communities of believers; the sacramental focus is evident in the emphasis on the Eucharist; the apostles were heralds in their spreading of the Gospel; and many became servants by giving up their freedom or their lives for God's word.

### Page 166

**(19)** God can be everywhere and people may respond to that presence in different ways.

### Page 168

**(20)** One might respond that these documents need to be interpreted and the people who do the interpreting are living in a specific time and can make that document relevant for that time. Documents such as the Constitution and Scripture are living. They were not intended to be isolated from the movement of history.

## SECTION 3 Checkpoint! (page 169)

### Review

**(1)** *Kerygma:* the initial proclamation of salvation in Jesus—that proclamation is the core of our belief even today; *koinonia:* early community of faith—the local and worldwide communities of believers; *diakonia:* service in Jesus' name from the Apostles in ancient times and from both religious and lay members of the Church today; *leitourgia:* worship and the sacraments which knit together the faithful in the earliest small communities and today.

**(2)** The content of the Christian message is that God loves universally and unconditionally and establishes new relationships. Jesus reveals God's love and Jesus is Savior.

**(3)** Kerygma means proclamation or the proclamation of the Gospel message of salvation in Jesus.

**(4)** These can include *koinonia, diakonia, leitourgia, kerygma,* authority, sense of mission, tradition, goods held in common, eschatological hope, or share in the Paschal Mystery.

**(5)** The Catholic Church teaches that those who have not heard of its teachings can find salvation if they are of good will.

**(6)** The Church makes revelation important by continuing to interpret Scripture and making it relevant to people today.

**(7)** Words to Know: *kerygma* (proclamation of the Gospel message); *koinonia* (community of faith); *diakonia* (service); *leitourgia* (worship); *tradition* (body of revealed truth in oral and written form handed down from the Apostles); *eschatology* (part of theology dealing with final things); *magesterium* (teaching authority of the Church).

### In Your World

**(1)** Stress the different interpretations one might reach of the same passage. Explain that religious leaders and scholars who interpret Scripture are specially trained to do so. We must always be aware of the original intention of a passage or document and keep that in balance with a new interpretation. The Genesis passage represents a test of faith and demonstrates the need to have complete faith in God. It might be applied to someone who is about to make a decision about entering religious life.

(2) Some images might include a megaphone for proclamation, clasped hands for community, a chalice for worship, or a family tree for tradition.

## Scripture Search
(1) *Kerygma (Acts 2:22–39); Koinonia (Acts 2:42); Diakonia (Acts 6:3); Leitourgia (Acts 2:46).*

(2) The images used in these passages include natural disasters such as earthquakes, false prophets, rumors, wars, and a great prince. Perhaps the Apostles were frightened when they heard these descriptions, or convinced of who Jesus was. These passages show us the power of God over us and the dramatic changes that will precede the parousia.

## CHAPTER 6 Review (pages 170–171)
### Study
(1) The Catholic Church is the family of believers who are related in faith.

(2) Individually, knowledge of the past allows a person to have a sense of rootedness, benefiting from its wisdom and mistakes. As a Church, knowledge of the past can help a person assume a role in society, following in the footsteps of their ancestors.

(3) People might ask if Jesus founded the Church because of the changes the Church has experienced over the years.

(4) One reason for rejecting the need for Church membership is the assertion that Jesus never founded a Church. The other might be an unfortunate experience with a particular person that proves alienating.

(5) Jesus did not organize the Church but he founded it by who he was and what he did.

(6) Jesus' actions were for the whole world. His acts, including his death and resurrection extend to all people everywhere.

(7) The work of organizing the Church began right after Jesus' death with the Apostles, and especially at Pentecost when the Apostles received the Holy Spirit.

(8) The role of the Spirit is to enlighten us to Jesus' true identity and empower us to transform the world.

(9) Some of the experiences at Pentecost were speaking in tongues, preaching, and healing.

(10) Luke used images to capture the Pentecost event. Through images, he captured the emotions, sights, and sounds of the event.

(11) The core characteristics have lasted through time and still characterize the Church. They reflect our continuity throughout history.

(12) Tradition is the body of revealed truth handed down from the Apostles in doctrine and teaching.

(13) Church membership is necessary for those who are acquainted with God's plan for salvation and who clearly understand and recognize its truth.

(14) All Church members reflect the Spirit in them and offer insights into the meaning of Scripture.

### Action
(1) Stress the growth that goes on beneath the soil before the plant is even visible, and the slow progress it makes towards maturity. Also focus on the daily care and nurturing the plant needs. If a weed grows with the plant or part of the plant dies, these events can also be used as symbols of the growth of the Church.

(2) As with earlier activities, encourage students to express a range of emotions and to bring to the surface the rapid changes that occurred during the first 50 days of the Church's existence.

### Prayer
Stress the role of the Spirit daily as a comfort, counselor, and teacher. We often feel the Spirit is a stranger to us. We may not feel close to the Spirit as we do to Jesus, but God sent the Spirit to us to stay with us after the resurrection.

# Rooted in Jesus, Formed by His Spirit

**OVERVIEW: In this chapter, students will discuss the importance of feeling a part of the Church's history and will learn about the roots of the Church in the events of Pentecost.**

**OBJECTIVES: The students will:**

- Discuss the meaning of their own personal histories and their link to that of the Church.

- Learn about the event which formed the foundation of the Church.

- In small groups, examine characteristics of the Church and show how they are reflected in today's Church.

**TIME FRAME: One to one-and-a-half hours.**

**MATERIALS: Bibles, paper and pens, poster board and markers.**

**PROCEDURE:**

**6**

*Into:* Prayer—Begin class with the prayer cited in the Prayer section of this chapter (page 171).

***Through:***

Activity One:

1. Have each student draw a small family tree including grandparents, parents, and their own generation.

2. Now discuss how one's past adds to one's present and future. Use questions 1 and 2 on page 146 as a guide for discussion.

3. Ask why the Church is a part of each student's family tree and what role it plays in their lives. Follow up by discussing the importance of knowing the history of the Church.

Activity Two:

1. Ask students to name one thing Jesus did to "found" the Church and one thing the Apostles did. Define the term "founder."

2. Describe briefly the events around the crucifixion. Have each student say how they would have reacted and why. Use questions 9–11 on page 155 to encourage discussion.

3. Put the images from Pentecost listed on page 157 on the board or on poster board. Have students say what might be represented by each. Then read the scriptural account of Pentecost and discuss its role in the life of the Church.

Activity Three:

1. Have each student name a characteristic about themselves. Then have the class try to name some that apply to the Church.

2. List the four core characteristics (pages 162–163) on the board with their one-word definitions. Briefly explain each one.

3. Take a vote. Is Church membership necessary for salvation? Record the results of your poll.  Now read the short paragraph on page 165–166 to clarify the Church's position on this question.  Discuss question 19.

*Beyond:* suggest that students read "Catching the Spirit" on page 158 and Acts 1–6. Encourage them to try activity 1 from "Action," page 171.

*Prayer:* Close class with the hymn "Come Holy Ghost," found in most missals, which focuses on the Holy Spirit.

# Patterns In the Infant Church

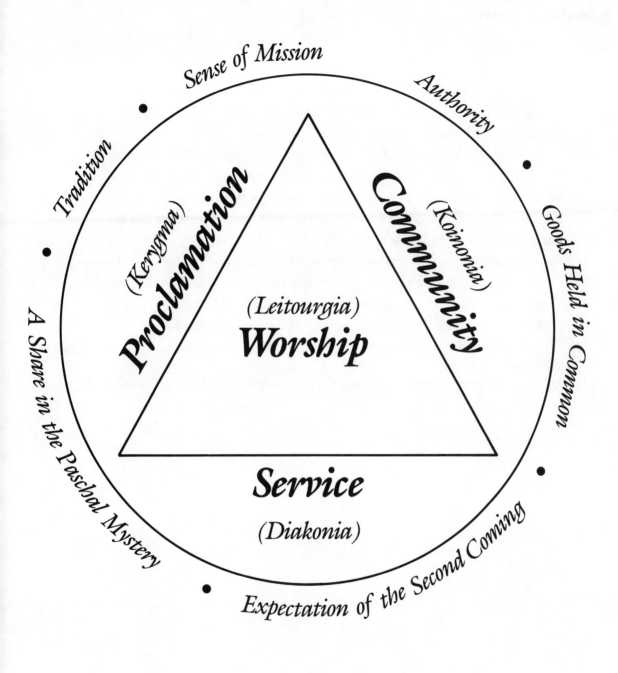

Name: _____    Score: _____

**CHAPTER 6 QUIZ**
# Rooted in Jesus, Formed by His Spirit

Mark true (+) or false (o).

___ **1.** Knowing one's roots helps one to live more fully and meaningfully.

___ **2.** The Church has survived for nearly 2,000 years because it is Spirit-filled.

___ **3.** It takes faith to accept Jesus as the founder of the Church.

___ **4.** The Apostles were loyal to Christ all through his passion.

___ **5.** They expected Jesus' resurrection and waited for it with joy.

___ **6.** Their actions on Pentecost were hardly different from what they had always been.

___ **7.** Jesus left the organization and growth of his Church to his followers.

___ **8.** Paul was chosen to replace Judas and restore the number of Apostles to twelve.

___ **9.** The Pentecost event in Acts is highly symbolic.

___ **10.** The Church was always characterized by preaching, community, service, and worship.

___ **11.** The Church's authority structure emerged only after the original Apostles were dead.

___ **12.** The New Testament writings shaped the first generation of Christians.

___ **13.** Christ's Second Coming was eagerly awaited by the first Christians.

___ **14.** Those who know God's plan for salvation through the Church have an obligation to become members.

___ **15.** An authentic interpretation of Christ's teachings is guaranteed through the Church.

# CHAPTER 6 QUIZ
Answer Key

1. +
2. +
3. +
4. o
5. o
6. o
7. +
8. o
9. +
10. +
11. o
12. o
13. +
14. +
15. +

## Carrying On

Professor Duane Wang Li, a gifted scientist, spent his life searching for a cure for cancer. One day he confided to his class of bright post-graduate students that he had made the breakthrough. There would have to be more research, but he was sure his investigation had led to a definite cure. Unfortunately, a few days later, the professor died of a heart attack.

After the funeral, his class—some of whom had heard him teach day in and day out for years—and several of his colleagues got together and formed a scientific team for the purpose of gathering the doctor's notes, carrying on his work, and making his contribution available to the world.

Form a group with other members of the class. Imagine that you are members of the team. Discuss and note down answers to the following questions.

1. How could you get together an authentic record of Professor Li's thoughts, teaching, and experiments?

2. What would be necessary to carry on his work and bring it to completion?

3. How could the results be shared with the world?

4. What possible problems do you think the team might run into?

## Summary of Acts 1 and 2
Chapter 1 Acts—*True or False*

___ 1. The writer indicates that he has written of Jesus before.

___ 2. Jesus first instructed the Apostles through the Holy Spirit.

___ 3. For forty days after the crucifixion, Jesus gave proof that he was alive and well on numerous occasions.

___ 4. The Apostles had been instructed to go to Galilee until the descent of the Holy Spirit.

___ 5. There was a distinct difference between the Baptism of John and the Baptism of Jesus.

___ 6. The Apostles by this time had given up any concern about being worldly rulers and understood fully that God's kingdom is not of this world.

___ 7. Jesus intended the Apostles to witness to him to the ends of the earth.

___ 8. Jesus made it clear that he and the Apostles were subject to the plan of the Father.

___ 9. Jesus' Ascension was made in a cloud of Mystery.

___ 10. After the Ascension, the Apostles returned to Jerusalem and gathered in the upper room.

___ 11. The names of the Apostles are clearly stated in Acts (1:13).

___ 12. Even before Pentecost the Apostles gathered together for group prayer with those who had associated with Jesus (1:14).

___ 13. Paul is the spokesman for the Apostles.

___ 14. One of the qualifications of the successor of Judas was that he be a man who had been with the Apostles during the whole time that they were with Jesus (1:21–22).

___ 15. The election of the man to replace Judas was done in the spirit of political rivalry.

Chapter 2 Acts

___ 1. The Holy Spirit came upon the early Christian community when they were gathered in one place (2:1–2).

___ 2. Those present for the First Pentecost saw visible signs of the coming of the Holy Spirit (2:2–3).

___ 3. According to Luke, just after the descent of the Holy Spirit, each person began to speak other languages (2:4).

___ 4. At the time of Pentecost, only the Jews living in Jerusalem heard the sound of the Spirit (2:5).

___ 5. The Jews visiting Jerusalem were amazed that Galileans could speak so many languages (2:7).

___ 6. Everyone was amazed and understood and accepted everything that was happening (2:13).

___ 7. The first sermon to the early believers was delivered by John (2:14).

___ 8. The whole interpretation of Pentecost is based on the words of the prophet Joel, of David, and of Jesus (2:14–37).

___ 9. Peter indicated right after Pentecost that the Good News was meant for all peoples in all places (2:39).

___ 10. The essentials for becoming a Christian were conversion and baptism (2:38).

___ 11. The justice of God is clearly indicated in the sermon of Peter (2:40).

___ 12. Several thousand people accepted the testimony of Peter and were baptized (2:41).

___ 13. Acceptance of Peter's testimony resulted in a change in the believer's whole way of life (2:42).

___ 14. Signs and wonders became common experiences in the Christian community (2:43).

___ 15. The early believers were despised by many people; they shared everything they had with one another and with the poor (2:45–47).

___ 16. Friendship and fellowship characterized the first Christian community (2:43–47).

___ 17. After the coming of the Holy Spirit, the Early Christians never went to the temple (2:45).

## Summary of Acts 1 and 2
Answer Key

1. +
2. o
3. +
4. o
5. +
6. o
7. +
8. +
9. +
10. +
11. +
12. +
13. o
14. +
15. o

**Chapter 2 Acts**

1. +
2. +
3. +
4. o
5. +
6. o
7. o
8. +
9. o
10. +
11. +
12. +
13. +
14. +
15. o
16. +
17. o

## Examples of Early Church Characteristics from the Epistles

| | |
|---|---|
| *Kerygma* (Message) | Romans 15:15–17 |
| *Koinonia* (Community) | 2 Corinthians 9:12–15 |
| *Diakonia* (Service) | 2 Corinthians 8:1–15 |
| *Leitourgia* (Worship) | James 5:13–16 |

## The Church's Mission

Jesus had a specific, three-fold mission to:

1. Teach truth (religious).

2. Shepherd people (help, guide).

3. Sanctify (make them like their Father).

   The Church continues this mission by:

1. Witnessing and teaching.

2. Building a true community of holy people in love (sanctifying).

3. Serving the needs of all people.

   Every member, according to his or her gifts from the Holy Spirit, takes part in this mission:

1. Permanent gifts, always present because so essential, go to certain members:

   • To preach in the name of Jesus

   • To administer sacraments

   • To offer sacrifice

   • To guide to holiness

   • Given to those in Orders.

2. Stable gifts, lasting for some time or contributing significantly: ministries.

3. Occasional gifts: services.

## Prayer Service to the Holy Spirit

Instruction: Assign a prayer leader to read aloud the introduction. Assign one person the part of first reader, and one person to be the second reader. Divide the class into two groups: one to read side 1, the other to read side 2.

*Introduction:* The Spirit of God is the breath, the life force of God. On Pentecost, God breathed mightily into the dormant human race, stifled by sin and selfishness. When we open to this breath, this power, we begin to expand, breathe again, grow beyond our limitations, and share something of God's infinite life, power, and vision.

## Hymn to the Holy Spirit

*First Reading:* The first Christians were a cautious, bewildered group, afraid to venture beyond the threshold of the upper room. How well they represent us—cautious, narrow, confused. But God's Spirit rushed in upon them and they burst out of the room to spread the news of Jesus. God's Spirit freed them and opened up new worlds to them. Let us listen to the story again. [Read Acts 2:1–1 1.]

*Response to the Reading:* In silence, ask the Lord to send the Holy Spirit to you …

*Together:* Come, Holy spirit, fill the hearts of your faithful, and kindle in them the fire of your love. Send forth your Spirit and we shall be created, and you shall renew the face of the earth.

*Second Reading:* Let us look at what the spirit did by his coming to the first Christians. [Read Acts 8:35–40, 11:1–8.]

*Response to the Reading:* (Recite, alternating sides.)

Side I.   Lord, you have made so many things! How wisely you made them all. The earth is filled with your creatures.

Side II.   There is the ocean, large and wide, where countless creatures live, large and small alike.

Side I.   All of them depend on you to give them food when they need it. You give it to them, and they eat it; You provide food, and they are satisfied.

Side II.   When you turn away, they are afraid, when you take away your breath, they die and return to the dust from which they came.

Side I.   But when you give them breath, they are created; you give new life to the earth.

## Prayers of Petition

*All:* Give me, Lord, the gift of **wisdom.**

*First Reader:* That I may be able to look at the values my society, my family, my school, and my peers are offering me, and when they differ, discern which are true.

*All:* Give me, Lord, the gift of **knowledge.**

*Second Reader:* That I may learn all I must know in order to love and serve you, and come to you.

*All:* Give me, Lord, the gift of **understanding.**

6

*Third Reader:* That I may see the persons, things, and events in my everyday life as you see them, in order that they may help me to grow in love for you and others.

*All:* Give me, Lord, the gift of **counsel.**

*Fourth Reader:* That I may always lead my friends, by word and example, along a path that is good for them and pleasing to you.

*All:* We pray you, O Holy Spirit, to direct our actions by your holy inspiration and carry them on by your gracious help, that every prayer and work of ours may always begin with you and by you be happily completed. We ask this through Jesus, our Lord, Amen.

**❻**

## Additional Reading

Chadwick, Henry. *The Early Church.*

Cross, F. L. and E. A. Livingstone, eds. *The Oxford Dictionary of the Christian Church.* New York: Oxford University Press, 1983.

*The Didache.* In *Early Christian Writings.*

Lohse, Eduard. *The First Christians.*

**CHAPTER 7**

# INDEPENDENCE IN THE SPIRIT: THE FIRST CENTURY

(text pages 172–201)

## FOCUS

**Doctrinal:** Under the guidance of the Holy Spirit, Christianity emerged from its Jewish cultural framework and spread throughout the Roman Empire. Amid persecution it developed new ministries and structures, and preserved its doctrinal heritage in writing.

**Personal:** How can an understanding of my Christian roots and heritage help me to be a better Christian today?

## OBJECTIVES

**Cognitive:** (a) to understand how Christianity separated from Judaism and became Gentile-oriented; (b) to realize that today's New Testament writings and basic Church structures were already part of first-century Christianity; (c) to see the importance of Peter and Paul in the early Church.

**Affective:** (a) to appreciate God's loving providence even when it works through human persecution and suffering; (b) to admire and love the Christian heroes of the first century; (c) to accept the Church as ever changing and yet changeless.

## Chapter 7 Outline

### SECTION 1
**The Church After Pentecost**

Acts of the Apostles

Events in Jerusalem Before Stephen's Death

*Simon the Magician* (text feature)

The Witness of Stephen

*On This Rock* (margin feature)

### SECTION 2
**The Missions of Paul and Peter**

Saul's Vocation and Mission

*Paul of Tarsus—An Autobiography* (text feature)

The Council of Jerusalem

Consequences of the Council

The Church's Loss of Privileges

*Communion of Saints* (margin feature)

The Spirit Acts in Peter

## SECTION 3
**Ends and Beginnings**

**❼**

# TEACHER'S RESOURCE 7A

## Historical Notes

Christianity developed from a small number of hesitant followers into the faith of nearly a billion people worldwide. Our knowledge of the early Church comes from the four Gospels, the letters of the Apostles, and the writings of the Apostolic Fathers, the Jewish historian Josephus, and the many archaeological finds from the Holy Land and the areas surrounding it. It is important to bear in mind the diversity of the early followers of Christ. They came from Palestinian Jewish communities, Hellenistic (Greek) Jewish areas, and the Gentile community. There were differences in language and culture. This chapter traces the spread of Christianity to the Gentile world, the reasons for its eventual split from Judaism, and its establishment as an independent religious tradition.

## Pedagogical Notes

1. It will be important for all students to have copies of the Bible (preferably *Benziger's New American Bible with Revised New Testament*) to refer to throughout this chapter.

2. The following are some of the values to be gained from studying Christian history which may enhance your presentation of the text material: (a) it gives insight and appreciation in the values of the Church; (b) it shows how we are the product of the past and that no total break with our heritage is ever possible; (c) it helps us to realize that there are no quick and easy solutions to problems; (d) it points out both the greatness and the limitations of the past; (e) it shows that basics in the Church do not change; and (f) it emphasizes the mystery of the Church as the Bride of Christ.

# TEACHER'S RESOURCE 7B

## Theological Notes

From time to time, we hear about religious groups that try to recreate the spirit of early Christianity by returning to what they consider the "golden age" of the Church—the first generation of Christianity. For these people, the Acts of the Apostles represent this pristine Church. It recalls an age of simple faith before Christianity became complicated by all the institutional, political, and doctrinal developments of the Middle Ages.

It is, of course, always important for us to remember our humble beginnings. It is even exciting to enter into the spirit of missionary zeal that marked the first century of the Church's life. Yet, we have to be careful not to romanticize the early Church or idealize it. This kind of uncritical thinking about our past can lead to a dangerous nostalgia for the "good old days." It's dangerous for two reasons.

First, nostalgic thinking about the Church implies that something was lost as soon as the Christian community found it necessary to adapt to the complexities of life in the Roman Empire after the fall of Rome in the fifth century. The Church was shaped by its history. It became less "spiritual" and more "secular." Many sixteenth- and seventeenth-century reformers seemed to feel this way. So do modern Evangelical and Fundamentalist Christians. It's as if the only "true" Church is the Church without a history.

The second reason that nostalgia for the Church of the first century can be dangerous is that a romantic understanding like this tends to create the image of a perfect Christian community. "If only we could return to the Church of Paul and Peter," the romantics seem to be saying, "we could reclaim the gifts of the Spirit and once again preach the pure Gospel in Jesus' name." The problem with this Alice in Wonderland scenario is that it does not agree with the Biblical testimony about the first century.

The early Church was far from perfect. There were people like Ananias and his wife Sapphira who cheated on their tithe (Acts 5: 1–11). The great preacher Paul could not convince the Greeks in Lystra that he wasn't a god (Acts 14:8–18). In fact, perhaps the greatest threat to unity and survival that the Church ever faced occurred in the first century. Acts 15 records the story of a major controversy between Paul and Peter (Galatians 2 tells the same story much more graphically!).

In addition, Paul frequently had to assert his authority over those who were preaching a less than "pure" gospel (Galatians 1:6–10). This suggests that the first generation of believers faced many of the same problems we encounter today: human greed, misunderstanding, differences of opinion, and external threats to the integrity of the Gospel proclamation. This is hardly a romantic situation!

As you teach this section remember: the only Church we have is the Church we have now. We can certainly work to change it as the Holy Spirit directs us, but we cannot pretend that it doesn't exist by wishing that our growth had been arrested in the first, thirteenth, nineteenth, or any other century. To do so would be to entertain a fantasy that dilutes the Church and diminishes our

responsibility to find contemporary solutions for contemporary problems. Nostalgic Christians have little energy for this sort of hard work.

The Acts of the Apostles should give us courage to face the present and the future with faith and hope. It should not be used as the model of a "substitute Church" for the twentieth and twenty-first century community of Christian disciples.

### The Church and I

# *Myself*     *The Church*

## *Infancy*

| *Myself* | *The Church* |
|---|---|
| 1. Birth | 1. Pentecost |
| 2. Rapid growth | 2. First century: 3,000 members to millions of members |
| 3. Dependence on the love and service of others | 3. Apostles spent themselves, martyrs witnessed by their deaths |

## *Childhood*

| *Myself* | *The Church* |
|---|---|
| 4. Constant questioning | 4. Heresies |
| 5. Exploring the real world | 5. Search for truth, Fathers and Doctors of the Church |
| 6. Need for education and discipline | 6. Church Councils |
| 7. Willingness to accept a Father's love | 7. Age of Faith |

## *Adolescence*

| *Myself* | *The Church* |
|---|---|
| 8. Rebellion against authority and injustice | 8. Protestant Reformation |
| 9. Intense search for identity | 9. Council of Trent, the Counter Reformation |

## *Adulthood*

| *Myself* | *The Church* |
|---|---|
| 10. Acceptance of responsibility | 10. Good papal leadership |
| 11. Concern for others in need | 11. Social services; Catholic schools, hospitals, orphanages, nursing homes |
| 12. Ability to improve oneself | 12. Vatican Council I |
| 13. Ability to accept differences and yet remain unshaken | 13. Vatican Council II, the ecumenical movement |

# Time Line A.D. 30–A.D. 100

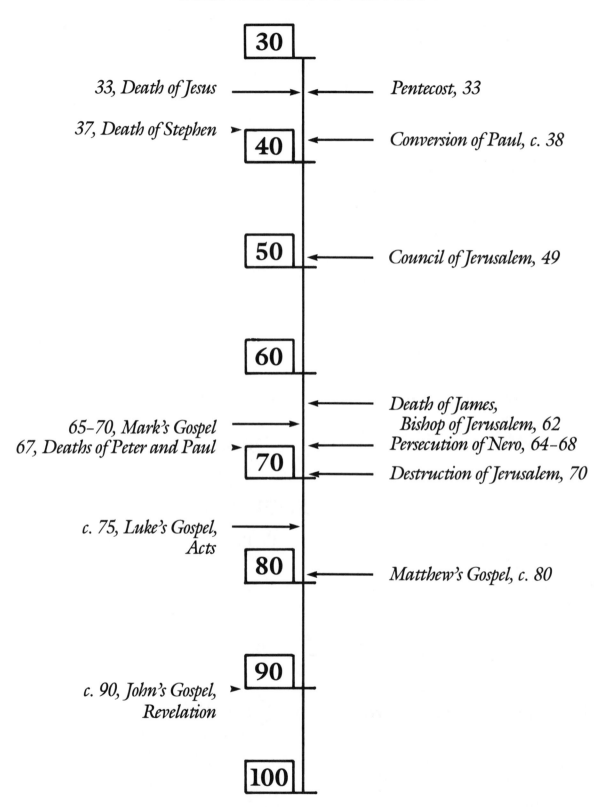

30

*33, Death of Jesus* ⟶ ⟵ *Pentecost, 33*

*37, Death of Stephen* ►

40

⟵ *Conversion of Paul, c. 38*

50

⟵ *Council of Jerusalem, 49*

60

⟵ *Death of James,
Bishop of Jerusalem, 62*

*65–70, Mark's Gospel* ⟶
*67, Deaths of Peter and Paul* ►

70

⟵ *Persecution of Nero, 64–68*

⟵ *Destruction of Jerusalem, 70*

*c. 75, Luke's Gospel,
Acts* ⟶

80

⟵ *Matthew's Gospel, c. 80*

90

*c. 90, John's Gospel,
Revelation* ►

100

# Twin Pillars of the Early Church

I.  **Directions:** Classify each of the following statements by placing the
    correct letter(s) on the line:

PE = Peter, PA = Paul, B = Both, N = Neither

___ **1.**  Jewish by birth

___ **2.**  An apostle

___ **3.**  Made three great missionary journeys

___ **4.**  Was martyred in Rome

___ **5.**  Labored at a trade

___ **6.**  Trained as a rabbi

___ **7.**  Knew the historical Jesus

___ **8.**  Tricultural, trilingual

___ **9.**  Died, like Jesus, by crucifixion

___ **10.** Preached the first sermon on Pentecost and converted thousands

___ **11.** Wrote a gospel

___ **12.** Belonged to the pharisees

___ **13.** Played a prominent role in Acts

___ **14.** Worked miracles

___ **15.** Suffered arrest and imprisonment several times

___ **16.** Persecuted the followers of Christ

___ **17.** Baptized the first Gentile converts

___ **18.** Had a conversion experience

___ **19.** Labored in the Church at Antioch

___ **20.** Believed that Gentiles were not bound to observe the Jewish law of
           circumcision and other Jewish customs

___ **21.** Called the Apostle of the Gentiles

___ **22.** Condemned Ananias and Sapphira for lying to the community about
           their possessions

___ **23.** Ordained ministers to take care of the Churches

___ **24.** Assumed general responsibility for the entire Church

___ **25.** Lived to see the destruction of Jerusalem

___ **26.** His epistles are part of the New Testament

___ **27.** Was taught by Gamaliel

___ **28.** Participated in the Pentecost event in Jerusalem

___ **29.** Lived to witness the Lord's Second Coming

___ **30.** Wrote more epistles than any other New Testament author

___ **31.** Preached in the Jewish synagogues

___ **32.** Was entrusted with preaching the Gospel to the uncircumcised

___ **33.** Had three years of instruction and training from Jesus

Name: _____ Score: _____

___ **34.** Denied Jesus by word or action

___ **35.** The dominant figure in Acts and the early Church

**II.** After checking your answers to Part I, give an oral summary of each of the four categories of answers. Begin with Peter.

**III.** Add any new items that you know to the above list.

**7**

# Twin Pillars of the Early Church
**Answer Key**

## I.

1. B
2. B
3. PA
4. B
5. B
6. PA
7. PE
8. PA
9. PE
10. PE
11. N
12 PA
13. B
14. B
15. B
16. PA
17. PE
18. B
19. B
20. B
21. PA
22. PE
23. B
24. PE
25. N
26. B
27. PA
28. PE
29. N
30. PA
31. B
32. PA
33. PE
34. B
35. PE

**II. Answers will vary.**

**III. Answers will vary.**

Name: _____     Score: _____

## CHAPTER 7 Test

## Independence in the Spirit: The First Century

I.  **True or false.** If the statement is true, place a plus sign (+) on the line. If it is false, place a zero (o).

___ **1.** Persecution was a part of Christianity from the beginning.

___ **2.** The destruction of Jerusalem increased anti-Christian persecution.

___ **3.** Peter's move to Rome helped shift the center of Christianity to the West.

___ **4.** From the beginning, Christians were isolated from the Jewish communities.

___ **5.** Antioch was the Mother Church of Christianity.

___ **6.** Paul turned to the Gentiles only after being rejected by the Jews.

___ **7.** From the moment it began, Christianity was persecuted by the Romans.

___ **8.** Stephen's death resulted in the spread of Christianity outside of Jerusalem.

___ **9.** Acts gives a complete account of the events in the early Church.

___ **10.** Miracles were a frequent occurrence in the early Church.

II.  **Cause-result.** In each set of two items, one is the cause of the other. Place a **C** in front of the item which is the cause and an **R** in front of the result.

**1.** ___ Christianity's break from Judaism    ___ Persecution by the Empire

**2.** ___ Council of Jerusalem    ___ Dispute over Gentile circumcision

**3.** ___ Christians persecuted    ___ Stephen's death

**4.** ___ Vision of Peter    ___ Baptism of Cornelius

**5.** ___ Turning to the Gentile    ___ Persecution by the Jews

III.  **Multiple choice.** Place the letter of the best answer on the line.?

___ **1.** The first Christian martyr was (a) Barnabas, (b) Paul, (c) Peter, (d) Stephen.

___ **2.** The first Christian community was (a) Antioch, (b) Ephesus, (c) Jerusalem, (d) Rome.

___ **3.** The first Gentile convert was (a) Cornelius, (b) Gamaliel, (c) Josephus, (d) Sapphira.

___ **4.** The author of Acts was (a) John, (b) Luke, (c) Mark, (d) Paul.

___ **5.** Opened the Church to Gentiles without binding them to the Mosaic Law: (a) Acts, (b) Council of Jerusalem, (c) fall of Jerusalem, (d) death of Peter and Paul.

**IV. Chronology.** In each set of two items, place a one (1) in front of the item which occurred first and a two (2) in front of the item which occurred second.

1. ___ Conversion of Paul          ___ Death of Stephen
2. ___ Leadership of Paul          ___ Leadership of Peter
3. ___ Council of Jerusalem        ___ Writing of New Testament
4. ___ Deaths of Peter and Paul    ___ Destruction of Jerusalem
5. ___ Acts of the Apostles was written   ___ Epistles of Paul were written

**V. Essay.** Answer any two.

1. Explain three of the major events on which the spread of Christianity hinged and tell why each was important.

2. In what ways did the leadership of Peter and Paul complement each other? Were both needed by the Infant Church?

3. How does first-century Christianity resemble twentieth-century Christianity? In what ways is it different? Which is more appealing to you and why?

4. At the close of the first century, what achievements could Christianity claim? What problems did it still face?

## CHAPTER 7 Test
### Independence in the Spirit: The First Century

**I.**

1. +
2. +
3. +
4. o
5. o
6. +
7. o
8. +
9. o
10. +

**II.**

1. C   R
2. R   C
3. R   C
4. C   R
5. R   C

**III.**

1. d
2. c
3. a
4. b
5. b

**IV.**

1. 2   1
2. 2   1
3. 1   2
4. 1   2
5. 2   1

**V.**

Answers will vary.

# CHAPTER 7

## SECTION 1
### Text Questions (Student text pages 173–179)

**Page 175**

(1) Answers might include letters, family trees, diaries, birth certificates, marriage certificates, and interviews.

(2) Church history is sacred history which is based on revealed Scripture. It is the history of the creation and saving of humanity, not of one event or of a temporary government or institution.

**Page 176**

(3) Answers will vary. Have students justify their answers.

(4) There was tension because there was fear of the Romans, disbelief in the message, and the authority of the Jewish officials was threatened.

**Page 179**

(5) Answers will vary. People are afraid of what is new and they are afraid of change. We always feel more comfortable with what we know and what is comfortable.

(6) In both accounts there is the rage of the crowd, neither Jesus nor Stephen resists their captors, both seek solace in God, and ask God to forgive the crowd.

(7) Simon Magus's failure would show them that God's power cannot be bought or sold. It is a gift to those who have faith.

## SECTION 1 Checkpoint! (page 180)
### Review

(1) A stylized history is written to follow a certain design or purpose, not necessarily to flow in a natural pattern.

(2) The book of Acts covers the time from the Ascension to Paul's imprisonment in Rome, c. A.D. 33–62.

(3) Peter and John were arrested for their preaching and healing.

(4) Stephen debated with Jewish leaders, preached, and suffered martyrdom.

**(5)** Stephen's martyrdom resulted in increased persecution of Christians, and a movement away from Jerusalem. This led to more Gentile converts.

**(6)** Simon Magus was a magician living in Samaria who was baptized and then tried to buy the power of the Spirit from the Apostles.

**(7)** The Ethiopian's baptism shows that Christianity was ready to move out of Jerusalem and to focus on the Gentile community.

**(8)** Words to Know: *stylize* (to make something conform to a design); *circa* ("around" the time of a date given); *Antioch* (city in Syria and center of Gentile Christianity); *Sanhedrin* (ruling body of Judaism); *Stephen* (deacon, first martyr of Christianity who died in A.D. 36); *Simon Magus* (magician who tried to buy the power of the Spirit); *Samaria* (part of northeast Palestine).

## In Your World

**(1)** Have students write out a script or, if they are able, ad lib. Stress their interpretation of Paul's reactions and emotions. They might include surprise, disbelief, weakness, awe.

**(2)** Be sure to answer any questions students might have about Judaism and its beliefs and practices, or to consult someone who can supply answers. Clarify the Jewish attitude toward Jesus. See Additional Resources for this Chapter for references.

**(3)** Students might draw a series of pictures showing each stage of this event and use accompanying music. Capture the crowd's anger and Stephen's serenity.

## Scripture Search

**(1)** Acts 10 is the conversion of Cornelius. It takes place in Caesarea and involves Cornelius and Peter. God shows Peter not to discriminate or be prejudiced and to reward faith. God is not partial and the message of salvation is for all to hear.

**(2)** Use a map to locate the places mentioned in the passage chosen. The back pages of *Benziger's New American Bible* has maps of Paul's journeys.

## SECTION 2
## Text Questions (Student text pages 181–189)

### Page 182

**(8)** Changing a name signifies a new stage of one's life, a turning point.

### Page 187

**(9)** Answers will vary—some might have tried to compromise more or have taken the other side.

**(10)** Judaism and Christianity were permanently separated by the decision of the Council. Christianity expanded and became open to converts from all backgrounds. Judaism closed itself off and there was tension between the two faiths.

**(11)** Answers will vary. Most students will probably say they were not aware of how closely Judaism and Christianity are related. This knowledge is valuable because it forms the basis of future dialogue.

**(12)** Roman worship involved adoration of the Emperor as a god. This is against the monotheism of both Judaism and Christianity.

### Page 189

**(13)** All priests carry on Peter's preaching of the Word. We all participate in conversion and can all teach and defend the faith.

**(14)** Answers will vary—Peter was strong, committed, determined, and pious.

## SECTION 2 Checkpoint! (page 190)
## Review

**(1)** Paul's special mission was to the Gentiles.

**(2)** In Antioch, Greek converts to Christianity led to mixed communities of Jewish and Gentile followers of Jesus. The city served as a home base for Paul for several years.

**(3)** Paul and Barnabas visited Iconium, Lystra, Deve, Cyprus.

**(4)** There was a conflict over whether Gentile converts should be required to observe Mosaic Law and be circumcised.

**(5)** Paul's side was victorious at the Council, saying that Gentile converts did not have to follow Mosaic Law or be circumcised. This led to the permanent separation between Christianity and Judaism.

**(6)** Christians had been seen as a sect of Judaism and Judaism was tolerated by the Romans. They lost their exemption after they broke away from Judaism.

**(7)** Peter preached and converted many, cured the sick, and was imprisoned.

**(8)** Words to Know: *Saul/Paul* (Jewish leader converted from being a persecutor of the early Church to a supporter and missionary to the Gentiles); *Mosaic covenant* (the obligations of the Jews contained in the Old Testament); *Council of Jerusalem* (first Church council held to determine the status of Gentile converts); *Judaizer* (an early follower of Jesus who continued to observe Jewish Law and required others to do the same).

## In Your World

**(1)** Be sure the arguments used on both sides are clear so that students understand the importance of this dispute for the history of Christianity and its relationship with Judaism.

**(2)** Possible events to represent include the conversion of the thousands, the conversion of Cornelius, or Peter's escape from prison. Students should capture Peter's determination, strength, and faith.

## Scripture Search

**(1)** Exodus 22:1–15 covers rules for farmers in case of stolen or damaged goods. Exodus 22: 21–27 explains laws for treating strangers and guests, and also rules for lending money. Leviticus 19 includes laws regarding stealing, paying hired help, and judging fairly. It is clear that every conceivable aspect of daily life was addressed in the Mosaic Law, and that Scripture could be consulted not only as a source of spiritual help, but also as a source of legal help.

**(2)** Acts 3:1–11 recounts a healing by Peter of a lame man and 12:1–19 tells of Peter's miraculous escape from prison. The Spirit empowered Peter to heal the man. A modern parallel might include the faith of the persecuted in some countries or the work of Mother Teresa.

## SECTION 3
## Text Questions (Student text pages 191–198)

### Page 194

**(15)** Answers will vary—some families might not be able to stay together or might lose all their possessions.

**(16)** Answers will vary—do encourage honesty. This is a good time to discuss the issue of stereotypes and how damaging they are.

### Page 197

**(17)** The different Gospels give different pictures of early Christian communities. They contain varied viewpoints and images and fill out our history of the development of the faith community.

**(18)** A letter should be understandable to those who will read it. In order for it to be useful the language and images must be familiar.

**(19)** Today the Apostles might have struggled with the problems of poverty, homelessness, AIDS, and apathy.

## SECTION 3 Checkpoint! (page 199)

**(1)** The fall of Jerusalem, Jewish persecution, growing Gentile converts, and the martyrdom of Peter and Paul in Rome all contributed to the emergence of Rome as the center of Christianity.

**(2)** Josephus says that Jerusalem was blockaded so no food could get in, the Romans crucified many who tried to escape, and most people were massacred or sold into slavery.

**(3)** After the revolt, Christians separated themselves from Jews, conversion dropped off, and anti-Semitism grew.

**(4)** Jews depend on the writings contained in the Hebrew Bible and after the destruction of the Temple in Jerusalem, the written Scripture became the center of Jewish religious life.

**(5)** The four Gospels were written in different places and at different times. They differ in focus and emphasis, and were aimed at different audiences.

**(6)** Mark was directed at the Gentile community in Rome; Matthew was written for Syrian Jewish and Gentile Christians; and Luke was aimed at Greek Gentiles.

**(7)** Words to Know: *Jewish Revolt* (lasted from A.D. 66–70 and resulted in the destruction of Jerusalem); *Josephus* (Jewish historian who recorded the destruction of Jerusalem); *Temple* (center of Jewish worship, destroyed during the Revolt); *canon* (definitive list of books recognized by the Church as inspired); *anti-Semitism* (prejudice against Jewish people).

## In Your World

**(1)** Use the timeline given as a base and have students add some events not entered on it. Use encyclopedias and other time lines. Events and figures from history, art, and literature, can be included.

**(2)** Use a copy of *Gospel Parallels.* Try using a passage such as a healing (Matthew 8:1–4, Mark 1:40–45, or Luke 5:12–16) or a parable (Matthew 13:1–9, Mark 4:1–9, or Luke 6:4–8). Have three groups write out the passages on poster board. Put the passages side by side in order to compare them.

## Scripture Search

**(1)** Paul claims to be an apostle of Christ based on his experience of the risen Christ. He says he has been appointed by God and Jesus. Paul did experience Jesus as did the other apostles, just not during Jesus' earthly life.

**(2)** Answers will vary. Suggest that students choose some of the shorter epistles. Discuss reactions to the readings. What was surprising about the content of the letters? Note the practical sorts of advice given.

## CHAPTER 7 Review (pages 200–201)

### Study

**(1)** A.D. 30–62

**(2)** The history covered in Acts covers the emergence of the Church and its independence from Judaism, the movement of Christianity toward Rome, the rise in Gentile converts, and the writing of the Gospels.

**(3)** Peter preached salvation to the Sanhedrin.

**(4)** Stephen was martyred for showing Christianity's independence from Judaism.

**(5)** (a) A large part of the Christian community fled from Jerusalem; (b) Faith was opened to Samaritans and Gentiles.

**(6)** Paul went all over Asia Minor and Palestine, to Rome, and Greece. He was sent by the Spirit.

**(7)** (a) Whether or not Gentile converts had to follow the Mosaic Law; (b) Gentiles did not have to follow the Mosaic Law.

**(8)** Christianity became disassociated from Judaism.

**(9)** Paul says that God does not reject the Jews but they have been hardened. The Jewish people have a permanent gift of God.

**(10)** The Romans saw the tensions between Jews and Christians as squabbles among the members of one group.

**(11)** Peter baptized the first Gentile convert. Peter also moved from Jerusalem, preaching in both Antioch and Rome.

**(12)** After Jerusalem's destruction, Jewish worship shifted from the Temple to smaller synagogues. Priests were replaced by rabbis who taught the Law and focus shifted to study of Scripture.

**(13)** Mark—written c. A.D. 65—for Gentile community in Rome; Luke—c. A.D. 75—to the Gentiles in Greece; Matthew—c. A.D. 80—written for the Jewish Christians in Syria; John—c. A.D. 95—written for the community in Asia Minor near Ephesus.

**(14)** The Gospels focus on the life, mission, and death of Jesus. Paul's letters deal with concrete issues facing an already formed Christian community.

## Action

**(1)** Be sure every student is prepared to explain the reasons why they ranked the events as they did.

**(2)** See the Additional Resources section for references that can be used for this activity. Students should learn about the religious significance of the holidays (belief) and the way they are celebrated (practice).

**(3)** The illustrations might also be on the pattern of a medieval illumination and use the first letter of the name of the Gospel or the first letter of the first word. Display the artwork in your classroom.

## Prayer

Read one or more of the miracle stories listed in the text and discuss them. Why would prayer precede and follow such events? Encourage students to share their prayers with the class.

# Independence in the Spirit: The First Century

**OVERVIEW: The aim of this chapter is to clarify the events in the history of Christianity between the Ascension and Paul's martyrdom.**

**OBJECTIVES: The students will:**

- Talk about the concept of martyrdom and focus specifically on the martyrdom of Stephen.

- Read about Paul's conversion and its effect on the Church at the Council of Jerusalem.

- Plot the Church's shift away from Jerusalem on a map and place the origin of each Gospel on it.

**TIME FRAME: One to one-and-a-half hours.**

**MATERIALS: Markers, map, Bibles, paper and pens.**

**PROCEDURE:**

*Into:* Prayer—Begin class with a reading of the Beatitudes from Matthew 5:3–12.

*Through:*

Activity One:

1. Ask for definitions and examples of a martyr. Introduce the book of Acts as a type of historical accounting of the first 35 years of Christian history.

2. Read the account of Stephen's martyrdom from Acts 7:54–60. Ask for reaction. Use questions 5–6 on page 179 as a guide.

3. Ask if students can guess what will happen as a result of the impending split between Judaism and Christianity. Can they name any ancient cities where Christians lived?

Activity Two:

1. Who was Paul? What did he do? Read the account of his conversion in Acts 9:1–19. Present the idea of his mission to the Gentiles.

2. Ask for definitions of a council. What does compromise mean? Explain both sides of the controversy that led to the Council of Jerusalem. Describe the decision made and its implications.

3. Ask the class to describe the characteristics of the Apostles who continued to preach and heal during this time when they were threatened by both the Jewish and Roman communities. Use Peter as an example.

Activity Three:

1. What is anti-Semitism? Why does it exist? Discuss stereotypes that exist about Jews. Emphasize the close ties between Jews and Christians.

2. Describe the destruction of Jerusalem and its consequences. Compare it to the reunification of Germany.

3. Ask students what they know about the Gospels. Describe their differences and similarities. On a map point out some of cities mentioned as audiences for the Gospels and places where Christian communities grew.

**Beyond:** Encourage students to read "Communion of Saints," on page 188 and "Masada-Place of Martyrs," on page 193. Suggest that they do activity 2 from Section 1, "In Your World," page 180.

**Prayer:** Close class with a reading of the Beatitudes from Luke 6:20–26.

Name: _____     Score: _____

**CHAPTER 7 QUIZ**
# Independence in the Spirit: The First Century

Mark true (+) or false (o).

___ **1.** Acts gives a complete and detailed history of the first-century Church.

___ **2.** Before Stephen's death the early Christian community was characterized by unity and love.

___ **3.** Stephen's death was the result of the Romans' attempt to punish Christians.

___ **4.** When Christianity spread from Jerusalem, Antioch became an important Christian center.

___ **5.** Saul's vocation grew out of the early preaching of the Apostles.

___ **6.** Paul's special mission was to the Gentiles.

___ **7.** Much knowledge of Paul comes from his own writings.

___ **8.** The Council of Jerusalem dealt with the problem of Gentile converts.

___ **9.** Paul believed that God had abandoned the Jews because of their blindness.

___ **10.** Jerusalem was completely destroyed because the Romans opposed the spread of Christianity.

___ **11.** Peter was undisputed leader of the early Church.

___ **12.** Both Peter and Paul were martyred in Rome.

___ **13.** Luke's gospel was the first to be written.

___ **14.** The anti-Semitism aroused by Jewish persecution is reflected in parts of the New Testament.

___ **15.** Each of the Gospels reflects its author, the life situation, and the faith of the community.

# CHAPTER 7 QUIZ
Answer Key

1. o
2. +
3. o
4. +
5. o
6. +
7. +
8. +
9. o
10. o
11. +
12. +
13. o
14. +
15. +

7

Name: _____     Score: _____

# The Roman Empire and "The Way"
**(Can be used with Section 3, Ends and Beginnings)**

**I.**   Christianity and the Empire of the Caesars began at almost the same
time. In God's plan it was the "right time" for the God-man's coming.
Study each of the first-century situations given below and decide if it
would be a HELP or a HINDRANCE to the spread of Christianity. If it is a
HELP, put a plus sign (+) on the line. If it is a HINDRANCE, place a zero
(o) on the line. Be able to give a reason for each classification.

___ **1.**   The spiritual and moral values of the Empire were bankrupt.

___ **2.**   Roman government was strong and kept order.

___ **3.**   Greek was a unifying language in the Empire.

___ **4.**   There was a widespread practice of magic.

___ **5.**   For Gentiles, becoming a Christian meant changing one's personal
moral life.

___ **6.**   Jewish communities were scattered throughout the entire Empire.

___ **7.**   Jews were a conquered people, victims of prejudice.

___ **8.**   Christianity's early preachers were on fire with faith in the risen Lord.

___ **9.**   The *Pax Romana* (Roman Peace) gave the Empire 300 years of peace
and general prosperity.

___ **10.**   The Apostles, for the most part, were poor, uneducated fishermen.

___ **11.**   Thousands of Jews flocked regularly to Jerusalem for the celebration
of their most important religious festivals.

___ **12.**   Jewish synagogues were often used as centers of evangelization.

___ **13.**   Emperor worship was required of all non-Jews.

___ **14.**   Christianity proposed a value system in direct contrast to the pagan
society of Rome.

___ **15.**   Each Christian was considered a missionary.

___ **16.**   Social distinctions existed between Jews and Gentiles, free persons
and slaves.

___ **17.**   Jesus was a crucified rabbi and member of a despised minority group.

___ **18.**   Roman civilization was characterized by cruelty, idolatry,
superstition, and sensuous living.

___ **19.**   Roman roads were excellent, the first-century equivalent of our
turnpikes.

___ **20.**   Jews were exempt from emperor worship.

Name: _____ Score: _____

**II.** List the numbers of the HELPS and HINDRANCES in the boxes below.

Add any others that you can think of.

| HELPS | HINDRANCES |
| --- | --- |
| **1.** _____ | 1. _____ |
| **2.** _____ | 2. _____ |
| **3.** _____ | 3. _____ |

**III.** What does this analysis tell you about God's providence? Christianity?

## THE ROMAN EMPIRE AND "THE WAY"

Answer Key

**I.**

1. +
2. +
3. +
4. o
5. o
6. +
7. o
8. +
9. +
10. o
11. +
12. +
13. o
14. o
15. +
16. o
17. o
18. o
19. +
20. +

**II.**

HELPS: 1, 2, 3, 6, 8, 11, 12, 15, 19, 20
HINDRANCES: 4, 5, 7, 10, 13, 14, 16, 17, 18

**III.**

Answers will vary.

# An In-Depth Study of Act 1–9

*Acts of the Apostles:* The Spirit of the Church

This is not an easy assignment. It will take time and reflection. We belong to a Church that has a **past**. We come from a **tradition** begun by the people who actually lived and worked with Jesus Christ. It is their **spirit**, the spirit of the early Church that we wish to discover. In order to do this, read Chapters 1–9 of the Acts of the Apostles slowly, thoughtfully, and prayerfully. As you do so, answer the following questions.

1. Before Pentecost, Peter was rash, impulsive, fearful, doubting, disloyal, unsure of himself, and imprudent. After reading the first two or three chapters of Acts, how would you characterize Peter? What changed him?

2. The "New Way" began with Jesus and his small group of followers. How large did it grow by the end of Acts 9? (Give the numbers and the references.) How can you account for this rapid growth?

3. List three to five adjectives that you would use to describe these early Christians. For each adjective, give an example from Acts to prove your descriptive word and briefly describe the incident. Give the references.

4. Give two or three examples that prove that Jesus and the Holy Spirit were truly with these early Christians. Include the references.

5. Of all the people you read about in these chapters, which one would you most like to meet and talk to? Why did you choose this person? What questions would you ask?

6. Was the early Church structured in any way? If so, in what ways?

7. What incidents (give two) show that the early Christians were human—that they had weaknesses and faults too. Cite the references.

8. If you had to choose one characteristic of the Early Church that you think we in the modern Church should stress more, what characteristic would you choose and why?

9. After reading Chapters 1–9 thoughtfully, what **one** thing impressed you the most and why?

## Acts 7: Short Answers

*Note to Students:* Chapter 7 is one of the most important chapters in Acts because it contains an entire summary of salvation history. Before reading it, give yourself a pre-test, writing the answers on a sheet of notebook paper. Then read the first fifty verses very carefully, correcting any errors you might have.

1. The place where Abraham has his first encounter with Yahweh. (7:2) (**Mesopotamia**)

2. The first command God gave to Abraham. (7:3) (**Leave your country for a land I will give.**)

3. The place where Abraham went to live after the command. (7:4) (**Haran**)

4. The land where Abraham moved to after the death of his father. (7:5) (**Canaan**)

5. The number of children that Abraham had at this time. (7:5) (**None**)

6. The prophecy that God first gave to Abraham. (7:6–7) (**His children would be slaves for 400 years.**)

7. The ceremony which God gave to Abraham. It was to be the rite of initiation into the Jewish faith. (7:8) (**Circumcision**)

8. Abraham's son. (7:8) (**Isaac**)

9. The descendant of Abraham who had twelve sons who in turn gave their names to the twelve tribes of Israel. (7:8) (**Jacob**)

10. The son first sold into slavery. (7:9) (**Joseph**)

11. The office that this son held in Egypt after gaining the favor of Pharoah. (7:10) (**Governor**)

12. The places where famine struck at this time. (7:11) (**Egypt and Canaan**)

13. The place where all the descendants of Abraham went to live and where they eventually became slaves. (7:19) (**Egypt**)

14. The man who finally liberated the Hebrews from slavery and led them toward the Promised Land. (7:36) (**Moses**)

15. The place where Moses first encountered Yahweh. (7:30) (**Near Mount Sinai**)

16. What promise did Moses make to the Hebrews according to Stephen's testimony? (7:37) (**God will raise up a prophet like me.**)

17. The individual who made an idol for God's people to worship (7:40) (**Aaron**)

18. The kind of worship which replaced devotion to Yahweh. (7:42–43) (**Astrology**)

19. The person who finally led the Hebrews into the Promised Land. (7:45) (**Joshua**)

20. The item that the Hebrews carried with them in the desert and into the Promised Land. (7:44–45) (**Ark of the Covenant**)

21. The individual who first wanted to build a temple to Yahweh. (7:46) (**David**)

22. The individual who actually built the temple. (7:47) (**Solomon**)

23. Whom did Stephen accuse the Hebrews of resisting? (7:51 and 6:15) (**Sanhedrin**)

24. How did the Hebrews of old treat God's messengers? (7:52) (**Persecution**)

25. Who is God's righteous Servant to whom Stephen refers? (7:52) (**Christ**)

26. What was the reaction of the Council to Stephen's summary of their history? (7:54) (**Anger**)

27. What vision did Stephen have at this point? (7:55–56) (**The glory of God and Jesus at his right hand**)

28. How did the Council react when Stephen exclaimed that he had a vision of the Son of Man? (7:57) (**They refused to hear.**)

29. What method did they use to kill Stephen? (7:58) (**Stoning**)

30. Who was the most significant witness of Stephen's death? Notice that this is the first time he appears in the history of the Church. The Good News has been preached by the Apostles in Jerusalem and has spread to the surrounding districts. This man will become an *Apostle* through the gift of the Holy Spirit. (**Saul**)

31. What are Stephen's dying words? (7:60) (**"Lord, do not hold this sin against them."**)

## Review of the People in Acts

1. I am the person to whom Acts is addressed (1:1). (**Theophilus**)

2. I am known as the Spirit of Jesus and enlighten people to understand the Word (2:33).(**Holy Spirit**)

3. We are the group to whom Christ entrusted the Word and the Good News. We were sent to preach it (Ch. 1). (**Apostles**)

4. I am the shepherd King who proclaimed the resurrection of Jesus (2:31). (**David**)

5. We cured a man at the Temple in the name of Jesus (3:4). (**Peter and John**)

6. I am the high priest who was annoyed by these men who are followers of Jesus of Nazareth (4:6). (**Annas**)

7. We are the husband and wife who lied to the Holy Spirit (5:1). (**Ananias and Sapphira**)

8. We are a party of Jews who do not believe in the resurrection of the body and who are extremely jealous of the Apostles (5:17). (**Sadducees**)

9. I am the Pharisee who taught Paul and I advised the Sanhedrin to leave these followers of Jesus alone lest they find themselves fighting God (5:34). (**Gamaliel**)

10. We are the seven helpers who were chosen to distribute food and goods to the poor (6:7). (**Stephen and the other deacons**)

11. I am the deacon who became the first martyr (7:59). (**Stephen**)

12. I am the first to whom God was revealed in Mesopotamia (7:2). (**Abraham**)

13. My brothers were jealous of me and sold me into slavery in Egypt (7:9). (**Joseph**)

14. I am the one to whom God revealed the Ten Commandments on Mt. Sinai (7:30). (**Moses**)

15. I had the privilege of building a temple for Yahweh (7:47). (**Solomon**)

16. I approved the stoning of Stephen and went to great lengths to arrest Christians and throw them into prison (8:3). (**Saul/Paul**)

17. I practiced magic and tried to buy Peter's power to give the Holy Spirit to people (8:9). (**Simon Magus**)

18. I explained the passage about the Suffering Servant in Isaiah to an Ethiopian who was then baptized. (8:26–28). (**Philip**)

19. I baptized Paul of Tarsus (9:10–18). (**Ananias**)

20. My name means "encouragement." I sold all my land and gave the money to the Christian community. Later I befriended Paul and would become his companion in preaching the Word to the Gentiles (4:36, 9:27). (**Barnabas**)

21. During my life I made shirts and coats. Peter raised me from the dead (9:39–40). (**Dorcas**)

22. We are a group respected for our knowledge of the Law. Several times we brought the Apostles before us and warned them not to spread the Word (5:21–40). (**Sanhedrin**)

23. I am the king who had James, the brother of John, put to death by the sword (12:2) (**Herod**)

24. Peter and the others often came to my house where I gave them hospitality (12:12). (**Mary, Mother of John Mark**)

25. I was a magician in Cyprus. I opposed the work of Paul and was struck blind for a time (13:8). (**Elymas**)

26. I traveled with Paul and Barnabas for a time, but at Pamphylia decided to leave them and return to my mother's house in Jerusalem (12:25, 13:13). (**John Mark**)

27. We are the Jews who insist that all people believing in Jesus must be circumcised in the Jewish religion before they can be baptized (15:5). (**Pharisees**)

28. I am a woman of Philippi who worshiped God and he opened my mind to the teaching of Paul (16:14). (**Lydia**)

29. I was with Paul at Philippi when we were dragged before a Roman court, beaten, and thrown into prison (16:19). (**Silas**)

30. I was a man who offered my house in Thessalonica for Paul's use. As a result I was made to pay a fine (17:5–9). (**Jason**)

31. We were men of Athens who debated with Paul on the strange teachings he was spreading (17:18). (**Epicureans and Stoics**)

32. We heard Paul speak to the people of Athens about resurrection. Some people ridiculed him but we believed (17:34). (**Dionysius and Damaris**)

33. We were a husband and wife who were ordered to leave Rome because we were Jews (18:2). (**Aquila and Priscilla**)

34. I was the Roman governor in Achaia in Greece who could not understand why the Jews took such opposition to Paul (18 :12). (**Gallio**)

## Recreating the Destruction of Jerusalem

(1) Write a newspaper article, for publication in Rome, telling of this imperial victory. (2) Write one or a series of diary entries that a Jewish teenager trapped within Jerusalem might have made during this time. (3) Impersonate a Roman soldier taking part in the siege. Write a letter home to your sweetheart explaining what you are doing and how you feel about it. (4) Imagine you are a Jewish rebel leader inside Jerusalem. Make a speech encouraging the inhabitants to persevere in their resistance. (5) Imagine that you are a Jewish rebel who has lost heart and decided to leave Jerusalem during the siege. Write the note you would leave your family.

## Pretests

### I. For all of Church history, Chapters 7–11

1. How does the history of the Church concern you?

2. How and why did Christianity split from Judaism?

3. How did it Christianize the Roman Empire and survive its destruction?

4. Who were its heroes and heroines?

5. How were its beliefs and traditions developed and clarified?

6. How was its message carried to the whole world?

7. What problems did it face? How were they handled? How do they affect us today?

### II. For Chapter 7

1. Where do we go to discover what happened to the Church after Pentecost?

2. How did Roman rule help the spread of Christianity?

3. Why was acceptance of Jesus easier for non-Jews than for Jews?

4. Why did first-century Christianity need both a Peter and a Paul?

5. How was the Church at the close of the first century different from the Church on Pentecost?

6. Why is the Church a "mystery"?

7. Because the Church is also people, who do you already know will be true about its history?

### III. Make a list of the questions you think a concerned Christian might wish to know about Christianity.

## Why Study Church History

### History ...

- Gives us an identity.
- Fosters pride in our heritage.
- Provides models for imitation.

- Gives us courage in times of difficulty when we see the sufferings others have endured for the faith.

- Answers questions we might have.

- Gives us a reason for holding fast to our own faith.

- Lets us see that saints and sinners were always part of the Church and so we should not be surprised to find that this is still true.

- Helps us to see how God is faithful to his promises and how the Holy Spirit has guided the Church through the ages.

What others say:

- "Consciousness of the past alone can make us understand the present" (Herbert Luethy).

- "History must be our deliverer not only from the undue influence of other times, but from the undue influence of our own, from the tyranny of environment and the pressures of the air we breathe" (Lord Acton).

## The *Didache* or the Teachings of the Twelve Apostles

In 1873 the Orthodox Metropolitan of Constantinople made one of the most important patristic finds of the century: a manuscript that contained the instructions used in the early Church for catechizing the pagans. The original dates from about A.D. 90, with strong evidence for Egypt as the place of composition. The following outline of the *Didache,* with brief excerpts or a summary of content will give the flavor of this new addition to our information about early Christianity.

Part I, paragraphs 1–6, is the catechetical section. It deals with the high moral behavior suited to those who wish to become Christians.

1. The great commandment of love of God and neighbor … "Bless those who curse you; and pray for your enemies; besides, fast for those who persecute you … love those who hate you, in fact have no enemy." "Let your alms sweat in your hands until you find out to whom to give."

2. "Sacrifice your life as a proof of your love."

3. "Accept as blessings the casualties that befall you, assured that nothing happens without God."

4. "Share everything with your brother….Such is the Way of Life."

5. "The Way of Death is this: murders, adulteries …thefts, idolatries, magical acts … men who turn away from the needy….May you be preserved from all this."

6. "If you are able to bear the Lord's yoke in its entirety, you will be perfect; if you are not able, then do what you can."

Part II, paragraphs 7–10, is a ritual or liturgical summary. It explains the rite of baptism and prayers for the celebration of the Eucharist.

7. "Baptize in the name of the Father and of the Son and of the Holy Spirit in running water or other, or pour water on the head three times, in the name, etc." Baptism should be preceded by one to two days of fasting.

8. The Lord's prayer was to be included and recited three times daily.

9. Communion is only for the baptized and is both cup and bread.

10. "If anyone is holy, let him advance; if anyone is not, let him be converted."

Part III, paragraphs 11–16, outlines Church organization and life. It speaks of three classes of Church officials: (1) apostles (itinerant missionaries), (2) prophets (men speaking in ecstasy), and (3) teachers (catechists). There are rules for hospitality, Sunday observance, and an exhortation to take life seriously.

11. Regarding prophets: "If he stays three days or asks for money, he is a false prophet … if he teaches the truth but doesn't live up to it, he is a false prophet."

12. Regarding a visitor who stays: "Let him work for his living."

13. Give first fruits of bread, wine, oil, money, and cloth to the prophets and teachers or the poor.

14. "On the Lord's own day, assemble in common to break bread and offer thanks, but first confess your sins, so that your sacrifice may be pure. However, no one quarreling with his brother may join your meeting until they are reconciled.

15. "Elect for yourselves bishops and deacons … of gentle disposition, not attached to money, honest and well-tried."

16. Regarding the Parousia: "Be ready. You do not know the hour in which our Lord is coming."

"The Didache" in *Ancient Christian Writers*, No. 6 (Westminster, MD: The Newman Press, 1948), pp. 3–25.

## Discussion-Review Activities

1. Cardinal Suenens said: "There are a significant number of young people who say 'yes' to the Gospel and to Jesus Christ and 'no' to the Church." What did he mean? Why is this happening?

2. Cicero wrote: "The first law of history is to dread uttering falsehood; the next, not to fear stating the truth." What did he mean? Do you agree? How does this apply to your study of Church history?

3. Rome's pagan philosophy could be summarized in these several short statements: (a) eat, drink, and be merry, for tomorrow we die, (b) might makes right, (c) the end justifies the means, and (d) Caesar alone is lord and god. What statements would a Christian have to substitute?

4. What did Augustine mean when he said: "Christ we have not seen, but we have the Church; let us therefore believe in him."

5. How does Cicero's statement, "Not to know what took place before you were born is to remain forever a child," apply to your study of Church history?

6. Interview Peter and/or Paul about their greatest successes and failures.

7. If your own source of information about the beliefs of the early Christians were the Scripture passages below, how much would you know? How do these beliefs compare with the Apostles' Creed?

Matthew 28:19

1 Corinthians 8:6, 12:3, 15:3-4

Acts 3:6, 8:37

I Timothy 2:5, 3:16

2 Corinthians 4:14

2 Timothy 4:1

Ephesians 4:4–6

## Additional Reading

Conzelmann, H. and A. Lindemann. *Interpreting the New Testament: An Introduction to the Principles and Methods of New Testament Exegesis.* Peabody, MA: Hendrickson Pubs. , 1988.

de Lange, Nicholas. *Judaism.* New York: Oxford University Press, 1987.

May, Herbert G., ed. *Oxford Bible Atlas.* New York: Oxford University Press, 1984.

Ruether, Rosemary. *Faith and Fratricide: The Theological Roots of Anti-Semitism.* New York: Seabury Press, 1974.

Sandmel, Samuel. *The First Christian Century in Judaism and Christianity.* New York: Oxford University Press, 1969.

Strassfield, Michael. *The Jewish Holidays: A Guide and Commentary.* New York: Harper and Row, 1985.

Throckmorton, Burton H., ed. *Gospel Parallels: A Synopsis of the First Three Gospels.* New York: Thomas Nelson Inc., 1967.

**7**

**CHAPTER 8**

# From Persecution to Power: A.D. 100–800

(Text pages 202–231)

## FOCUS

**Doctrinal:** The early Church grew numerically and developed doctrinally in spite of external pressures from persecution and war and internal problems of heresy, imperial interference, and differences of opinion.

**Personal:** Do I recognize the working of the Spirit in the way the Church was able to face and overcome the challenges of the early centuries?

## OBJECTIVES

**Cognitive:** (a) to understand how Christianity moved from a despised, persecuted minority group to become the official religion of the whole Roman Empire; (b) to learn how monasticism, Christian writers, heresies, and the barbarians all enriched Christianity; (c) to realize that close Church-state ties and the rise of Islam created problems for the Church.

**Affective:** (a) to admire the great men and women of the past who gave their lives, gifts, and talents to Christ for his Church; (b) to grow in the ability to see problems as hidden opportunities from which good can come.

## Chapter 8 Outline

### SECTION 1
**The Big Picture**

The Earliest Opposition

Nero: The First Challenge

Bread of Christ

*On This Rock* (margin feature)

The Empire Versus the Church

*The Creed of the Catacombs* (text feature)

The Final Persecution

Christians in the Roman World

### SECTION 2
**From Persecution to Power**

Constantine's Conversion

A New Christian Lifestyle

*Communion of Saints* (margin feature)

Monasticism in the West

*Heresies and Councils: Problems and Solutions*
(text feature)

Disunity from Within

**8**

# TEACHER'S RESOURCE 8A

## Historical Notes

The period of time covered in this chapter traces monumental changes in Church structure and in Christian doctrine and practice. The shift from persecuted minority to recognized and official religion was accompanied by many other external and internal changes. Some of those changes and problems included the demand by the Frankish kings to have a say in the nomination and consecration of bishops. Later, the acquisition of lands by the pope made him a temporal as well as a spiritual leader. On the positive side, the Benedictine rule gave the Church its predominant form of monasticism which was self-supporting as well as closely linked to the Church. The stability of monastic communities weathered many political, social, and economic upheavals.

## Pedagogical Notes

1. Some discussion of the good and bad aspects of Christianity's rise to official state religion will put the problem of Church-state relationships into perspective. Some of those aspects include a rise in conversions (not always out of personal conviction), the emergence of the clergy as an elite class, the designation of Sunday as an official day of rest, and the division of Church responsibilities. There was also room for tension between the political leader (emperor) and spiritual leader (pope) concerning bishop appointments and theological opinions.

2. Focus on the appeal of a monastic lifestyle for those people who wish to dedicate their lives to prayer and to be somewhat removed from the pressures and temptations of everyday life. Show how these early communities realized the need for some conformity and regulation and for a link to the larger Church.

# TEACHER'S PREVIEW 8B

## Theological Notes

During its first 800 years, the Church's self-understanding and role in society changed more dramatically than in any other segment of its long history. The title of this chapter suggests just how radical the changes were: "From Persecution to Power." It is difficult for us to appreciate the turmoil of this era. Some thirty years before the end of the first century, the homeland of Jesus and the birthplace of Christianity was devastated by the Roman army of occupation. Jerusalem was destroyed; with its destruction, the focus of the Jesus movement shifted forever from Palestine to the Greco-Roman world in the West. Paul's missionary journeys had already established Christianity there, but as the first century drew to a close, the physical ties to the mother Church in Jerusalem were completely severed. This in itself presented challenges for the infant Church, but even more challenges were to come.

First there was the assault of heresy—false doctrines about the person and nature of Jesus that had to be confronted. There was persecution at the hands of the Romans that ended only in the year 313 when the emperor Constantine made Christianity legal. In the meantime, Church leaders were faced with the task of organizing the ministries and administration of a growing community of Christians who were separated from one another by great distances. Again, any one of these circumstances would have been more than enough for a young Church to deal with.

But then, the whole world literally came crashing down! In the middle of the fifth century, the Roman empire fell to the invading German tribes from the north. Once again, the process of integration and adaption in the face of new social and political circumstances had to begin all over for the Christian community. What was the difference between the Church of the fifth to eighth centuries and the Church that had to cope with the destruction of Jerusalem and Roman persecution earlier in its history? By the fifth century, Christianity was not only legal, but it was also becoming an influential and powerful force in Western society.

This new-found influence brought with it a whole new set of problems and challenges. Once Church leaders were accepted as respected leaders in society after the fall of the Roman Empire, the role of the Church in the day-to-day affairs of people was greatly enhanced. In the process, however, Christians had to remind themselves that their mission was primarily to proclaim the Gospel of Jesus Christ and announce the Good News of God's Kingdom—not to create and promote the agenda of any political entity.

For better or for worse, however, the Church did become involved in political affairs during the

Feudal period and it remained involved in them after the establishment of the Holy Roman Empire (800) and throughout the Middle Ages. As a result, it became increasingly difficult for Church leaders—who were often political statesmen as well—to maintain the kind of distance from the body politic that allowed them to critique the shortcomings of society in light of the Gospel.

While never completely losing sight of its religious mission, the Church was to grow rich and powerful. It slowly found itself investing in political agendas as well as in real estate. Naturally, abuses of power and wealth followed.

The years 100 to 800 demonstrated the dynamism, vitality, and adaptability of the Church, but this period was also the beginning of some serious soul-searching for Christians. To what extent should the Church involve itself in systems of governance? How close can people get to the seat of power without being distracted by the glamour of power? It would take a long time to work through these questions, but for contemporary American Christians who continue to debate the relationship of Church and state, these early years of Christian history are certainly instructive.

# Time Line A.D. 100–A.D. 800

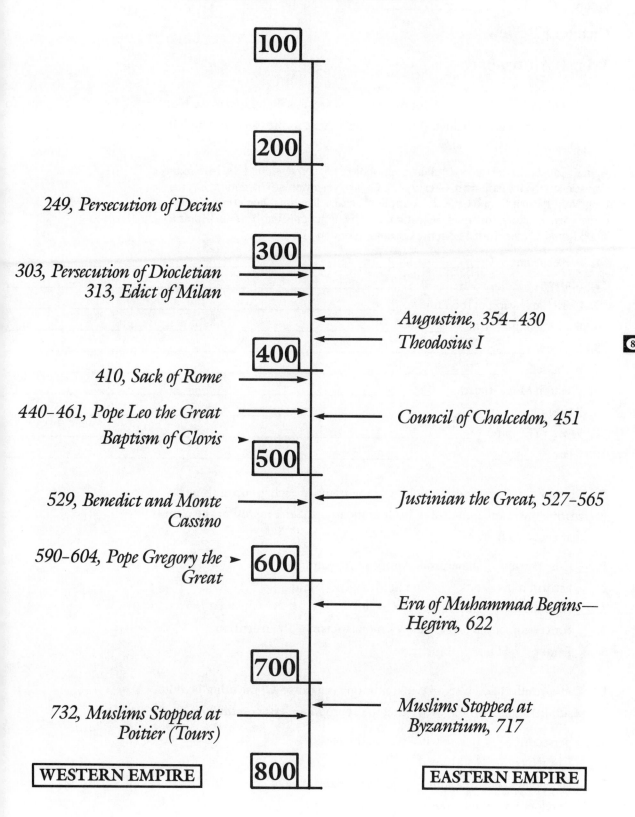

**100**

**200**

249, *Persecution of Decius* →

**300**

303, *Persecution of Diocletian* →
313, *Edict of Milan* →

← *Augustine, 354–430*
← *Theodosius I*

**400**

410, *Sack of Rome* →

440–461, *Pope Leo the Great* →     ← *Council of Chalcedon, 451*
*Baptism of Clovis* →

**500**

529, *Benedict and Monte* →     ← *Justinian the Great, 527–565*
*Cassino*

590–604, *Pope Gregory the* → **600**
*Great*

← *Era of Muhammad Begins—
Hegira, 622*

**700**

732, *Muslims Stopped at* →     ← *Muslims Stopped at
Poitier (Tours)*          *Byzantium, 717*

**800**

| WESTERN EMPIRE | | EASTERN EMPIRE |

8

157

Name: _____   Score: _____

## Chapter 8 Review

## Tying It All Together

I. **Classification:** Three of the following terms are closely related to each of the ten topics given below. Write each term next to the topic to which it is best related.

Agnes, Constantine, Franks, Muhammed, apologists, conversion of the barbarians, Gnosticism, Nero, Arianism, Gregory the Great, Nestorianism, Benedict, Decius, Holy War, Patriarchs and Church Councils, Caesaro, Papism, Diocletian, Huns, catacombs, Doctors, Justinian, Sebastian, Cecilia, Edict of Milan, Qu'ran (Koran), Theodosius, Clovis, Fathers, Monte Cassino, Work and Pray

1. Persecution: _____
2. Martyrs: _____
3. Christianization of the Empire: _____
4. Explained the Faith: _____
5. Heresies: _____
6. Barbarians: _____
7. Western Monasticism: _____
8. Eastern Empire: _____
9. Western Empire: _____
10. Islam: _____

II. **Chronology:** Show the chronology of the items in each group of three by writing the numbers **1–2–3** in front of the items. Let **1** represent the item that occurred first.

1. ___ Constantine ___ Ignatius of Antioch ___ Nero
2. ___ barbarian invasions ___ Edict of Milan ___ Islam
3. ___ Athanasius ___ Augustine ___ Gregory
4. ___ conversion of the barbarians ___ monasticism ___ persecution
5. ___ Franks ___ Huns ___ Muslims

III. **Cause-result:** In each set of two items, one is a cause (C) the other is the result (R). Identify them by writing the appropriate letter on the line.

1. ___ persecution ___ heroic witnesses to the faith
2. ___ Church councils and creeds ___ heresies
3. ___ acceptance of Christianity ___ Caesaro-Papism
4. ___ development of religious life ___ monasticism
5. ___ Alliance with the Franks ___ rise of the papacy

# Chapter 8 Review
## Tying It All Together
**Answer Key**

1. Decius, Diocletian, Nero
2. Agnes, Cecilia, Sebastian
3. Constantine, Edict of Milan, Theodosius
4. Apologists, Doctors, Fathers
5. Arianism, Gnosticism, Nestorianism
6. Clovis, Franks, Huns
7. Benedict, Monte Cassino, Work and Pray
8. Caesaro-papism, Justinian, Patriarchs, and Church Councils
9. catacombs, conversion of the barbarians, Gregory the Great
10. Holy War, Qu'ran (Koran), Muhammad

**II.**

1. 3    2    1
2. 2    1    3
3. 1    2    3
4. 3    2    1
5. 2    1    3

**III.**

1. C    R
2. R    C
3. C    R
4. R    C
5. C    R

Name: _____ Score: _____

## CHAPTER 8 Test
## From Persecution to Power: A.D. 100–800

**1. Multiple Choice:** Write the letter of the best answer on the line.

___ 1. Roman law stated: (a) "It is forbidden to be a Christian." (b) "The Christians are to be fed to the lions."

___ 2. Ignatius, Bishop of Antioch, (a) tried to escape persecution, (b) begged the Christians not to prevent his death.

___ 3. Decius and Diocletian tried to (a) punish Christians, (b) destroy Christianity.

___ 4. The catacombs were (a) Roman burial grounds, (b) used only by Christians.

___ 5. Martyrdom and persecution were constant (a) realities, (b) possibilities.

___ 6. Constantine (a) favored Christianity, (b) made his empire a Christian one.

___ 7. The Edict of Milan (a) stopped Christian persecution, (b) destroyed paganism.

___ 8. Monasticism originated in the (a) East, (b) West.

___ 9. Benedict (a) started monasticism, (b) humanized monasticism.

___ 10. Heresy raged most fiercely in the (a) East, (b) West.

___ 11. The great defender of Christ's divinity was (a) Athanasius, (b) Gregory.

___ 12. Saint Justin the martyr was the greatest of the (a) Apologists, (b) Fathers.

___ 13. The Church's first reaction to the barbarians was (a) conversion, (b) defense.

___ 14. The title "Servant of the Servants of God" was first used by (a) the emperor, (b) the pope.

___ 15. Eastern Christianity (a) resisted change, (b) welcomed change.

___ 16. Constantinople (a) bowed to Rome, (b) tried to rival Rome.

___ 17. Islam spread rapidly because of (a) its doctrines, (b) use of the sword.

___ 18. The fourth and fifth centuries were known as the (a) Age of Martyrs, (b) Age of Heresy.

___ 19. The barbarians were best assimilated in (a) the East, (b) the West.

___ 20. The greatest danger to Christianity was (a) barbarian invasions, (b) Islam.

**II. Incorrectly classified:** On the line, place the number of the item which does not belong.

___ 1. Roman emperors who persecuted Christianity: (1) Decius, (2) Diocletian, (3) Justinian, (4) Nero.

___ **2.** Christian martyrs: (1) Ignatius, (2) Augustine, (3) Cecilia, (4) Lawrence.

___ **3.** Main reasons for Roman persecution: (1) economic, (2) political, (3) religious, (4) superstitious.

___ **4.** Defended the faith: (1) apologists, (2) doctors, (3) hermits, (4) martyrs.

___ **5.** Associated with the Eastern empire: (1) Caesaro-papism, (2) theological controversies, (3) conversion of the barbarians, (4) battle against Islam.

___ **6.** Helped to Christianize the West: (1) policies of Constantine, (2) barbarian invasions, (3) Pope Gregory's policies, (4) monasticism.

___ **7.** Early heresies: (1) Arianism, (2) Gnosticism, (3) Nestorianism, (4) Islam.

___ **8.** The Church's defense against heresy: (1) catacombs, (2) Church councils, (3) formulation of creeds, (4) writings of the Fathers.

___ **9.** Church leaders: (1) Athanasius, (2) Benedict, (3) Gregory, (4) Justinian.

___ **10.** Effects of Islam: (1) alliance between the Franks and the papacy, (2) imperial persecution, (3) numerical losses to the Church, (4) religious wars.

**III. Essay:** Choose two.

**8**

1. How could each of the following have destroyed Christianity: (a) persecution, (b) heresy, (c) barbarian invasions, (d) Islam? What does the fact that Christianity survived and grew in spite of each, tell you about God's provident care of the Church?

2. As a Christian, would you have preferred to live your life in the eastern half of the Empire or in the western half? Give reasons for your choice.

3. What did each of the following contribute to Christianity? (a) the martyrs, (b) the apologists, (c) the fathers, (d) Church Councils, (e) Augustine, (f) Gregory the Great.

## CHAPTER 8 Test
## From Persecution to Power: 100–800

**I.**

1. a
2. b
3. b
4. a
5. b
6. a
7. a
8. a
9. b
10. a
11. a
12. a
13. b
14. b
15. a
16. b
17. b
18. b
19. b
20. b

**II.**

1. 3
2. 2
3. 1
4. 3
5. 3
6. 2
7. 4
8. 1
9. 4
10. 2

**III.**

Answers will vary.

# CHAPTER 8

## SECTION 1
### Text Questions (Student text pages 203–209)

**Page 205–206**

(1) Answers will vary. People hate and persecute those who are different than themselves out of fear and ignorance. Minority and religious groups experience hatred, oppression, and discrimination.

(2) Some modern martyrs might include the Chinese dissidents and students of June 1989, Eastern Europeans working toward democracy, or the Jesuits murdered in Central America in 1989.

(3) Answers will vary. Scapegoats are created so people will not have to take responsibility for their actions and so they will not have to face their problems or guilt.

(4) Ignatius uses the symbols of love being poured out (as blood or wine), and bread. These symbols remind his listeners of his faith.

**Page 206**

(5) Answers will vary. People might think that those who bought certificates "copped out" and abandoned their faith. Situations such as these provide real tests for faith.

**Page 209**

(6) Diocletian's laws might result in people losing jobs, breaking up families, or even death.

## SECTION 1 Checkpoint! (page 210)
### Review

(1) Some of the events contributing to the tapestry include persecution, division, acts of heroism and martyrdom, the growth of the Church, and heresy.

(2) Christians were accused of disrespect and treason for not worshiping the emperor. They were also accused of cannibalism.

(3) The emperors made scapegoats of the Christians for all that went wrong in the Empire— Christianity was outlawed and there were sporadic persecutions.

(4) At the end of the Age of Martyrs, Christianity had spread to Africa and Europe and many conversions had taken place. Many of the faithful

had also been killed, and many of the clergy imprisoned.

**(5)** Words to Know: *martyr* (someone who sacrifices his or her life for a principle or religious value); *Nero* (Roman emperor who began the first persecution of Christianity); *Diocletian* (Roman emperor who inaugurated the last and most far-reaching persecution); *scapegoat* (a person or thing blamed for the mistakes or crimes of others); *persecution* (when a person or group is harassed, injured, or oppressed).

## In Your World

**(1)** See the Additional Resources for references to the early accounts of the martyrs. The *Martyrdom of Polycarp* would be appropriate. Stress the reasons why these sometimes horrifying accounts were written down. These stories provided spiritual and physical strength to those undergoing the same thing. They are pictures of faith and a life lived and died in imitation of Christ.

**(2)** People place religious symbols such as crosses on graves as well as hands in prayer, or a Bible. These symbols may express the character of the deceased or the memories of those still living.

## Scripture Search

The early Church is described as everything from a scattered group of believers to small bands of more organized faithful. The Church is pictured as a loosely organized institution with clearly identified authority figures. There were obstacles from the Roman government and from Jews who felt threatened by the growing numbers of converts.

## SECTION 2
## Text Questions (Student text pages 211–219)

### Page 212

**(7)** Advantages were the end of persecutions and a higher status including the ability to own land, build churches, and raise money. Disadvantages include possible state interference into Church matters or the corruption that accompanies a growing bureaucracy.

**(8)** In the US, public education is secular, and no tax money is used to build or maintain Church properties. This keeps the two bodies, Church and state, financially separate.

### Page 213

**(9)** The solitary life is quiet and free from the distractions of regular daily life. The person can concentrate on his or her devotion.

**(10)** Vowed religious spend their lives in devotion to God, particularly in prayer and works of charity, so that they seem to be more holy than the average person. The advantage of a vowed life is that one can concentrate on cultivating a relationship with God. The disadvantages include a tendency to become too wrapped up in oneself and cut off from the world and people around. The secular, or lay, life may lead us to forget or delay the development of our spiritual life, but it also brings us into daily contact with others who share our world experience.

### Page 216

**(11)** Prayer and work combine spirituality and activity. They allow a person to make contributions on several levels by being self-sufficient and using one's physical gifts, and by prayer. A life of just prayer might lead a person to remain unaware of the problems of life for most people, and the challenges facing the world. A life of just work might result in a person ignoring their spiritual life.

**(12)** Answers will vary, but will probably include the religious orders represented in the school and parish.

### Page 219

**(13)** The Gnostic belief suggests that the body is evil and the soul is the good and holy part of us which is trapped in the body. Dualists do not believe that marriage or creation are divinely sanctioned because they encourage the joining of body and soul.

**(14)** Creeds provide short and easily understandable statements of doctrine and belief that can be used as part of worship.

**(15)** Heresies always exist. They represent controversy over issues that confront the Church at any given time. These issues threaten to divide the Church when different answers are suggested and some people or groups refuse to abide by the decisions made to resolve those problems.

**(16)** Answers will vary.

**(17)** Some controversial issues today include the question of the role of women in the Church

8

(including the ordination of women), divorce, contraception, and the shortage of priests.

## SECTION 2 Checkpoint! (page 220)

### Review

**(1)** During Constantine's reign persecutions ended, conversions increased, and Christianity was given legal and political rights and privileges.

**(2)** Christianity adapted by becoming a part of the political structure (it created divisions which matched political ones), by acquiring land and money, and by the development of monasticism.

**(3)** In the East monks led a solitary life of prayer and obedience to a superior.

**(4)** The purpose of a monastic lifestyle is to nourish one's relationship with God through prayer and work.

**(5)** Benedict's rules provided structure and adapted the monastic ideal to Western needs and the Western mentality.

**(6)** Heresy threatens from the inside and uses familiar ideas. Arianism claimed Jesus was not divine. The war of words that resulted led to the Council of Nicaea.

**(7)** Words to Know: *Constantine* (Roman emperor who created a climate favorable to Christianity); *Edict of Milan* (A.D. 313, ended Christian persecution by proclaiming liberty of worship in the Empire); *monasticism* (a way of life characterized by prayer, penance, and solitude, and later on the vows of chastity, poverty, and obedience); *heresy* (any deviation, distortion, or rejection of revealed truth or dogma); *Arianism* (a heresy which threatened the unity of the Church, it claimed that Jesus was not divine); *Nicene Creed* (the creed developed in response to Arianism which states that Jesus is divine); *apostates* (those who abandon their faith under persecution).

### In Your World

Be sure students address every aspect of daily life and discuss the balance that needs to be set up between prayer and work. The class must decide whether the order is self-sufficient or not, how its members serve the community (or whether they are cloistered), and who is in charge. Keep in mind that the goal of a monastic lifestyle is not suffering or hardship for its own sake, but a life devoted to God.

### Scripture Search

Genesis states that God created our bodies and our souls, and that everything that God created is good. Therefore we believe that, when used properly, our bodies reflect God's love for us. Our whole being is dedicated to God, and our task is to understand what God asks from us and to learn to discipline ourselves and to use our free will to grow spiritually in both body and soul.

## SECTION 3

### Text Questions (Student text pages 221–228)

#### Page 223

**(18)** One might find praise of martyrs, explanations of Christian beliefs, or attacks on heresies.

**(19)** Answers may include Cyprian, Ambrose, Gregory of Nyssa.

**(20)** Some characteristics might include faith, strength, determination, and compassion.

#### Page 226

**(21)** The benefits are encouraging conversion and not angering certain groups. The dangers are that misunderstandings about the nature of God might occur, and the action might be seen as an attempt to take over the temple by force.

**(22)** Close Church-state relationships can lead to pressure from one group on the other, or attempts to influence decisions or appointments.

#### Page 228

**(23)** Answers will vary.

## SECTION 3 Checkpoint! (page 229)

### Review

**(1)** The Apologists defended the faith, explained it, and responded to criticism.

**(2)** Doctors of the Church are pious and learned, they are usually highly educated and many have had successful careers.

**(3)** Rome's downfall was the result of barbarian invasions, and political and linguistic divisions.

**(4)** Gregory the Great reorganized the Church, reformed the liturgy, and began a missionary program.

(5) East and West were separated by internal problems, linguistic differences, cultural differences, and the questions of papal primacy.

(6) The spread of Islam meant that Muslims controlled political and religious life in many areas and pressured people to convert. Much geographical territory was lost to Islam, including the Holy Land.

(7) Words to Know: *apostolic fathers* (men who had known the Apostles or their disciples personally); *apologist* (one who writes or speaks in defense of the faith); *barbarian* (the name given to any non-Roman); *see* (the official center or authority of a bishop, a diocese); *Canon Law* (the body of Church laws); *Sacramentary* (book containing the prayers and directions for Mass, but not the Scripture readings).

## In Your World

(1) Encourage students to use a historical atlas and then to consult a contemporary one in order to see how geographical boundaries and names have changed.

(2) Note that the Qu'ran (Koran) is arranged from the longest chapter to the shortest. It was originally written in Arabic, a language from the same linguistic family as Hebrew. It is written and read from left to right. Muslims recognize the Hebrew Bible and New Testament as revealed and inspired. Choose a chapter from the Qu'ran (Koran) that discusses creation or the birth of Jesus. Discuss the particular style of the writing.

## Scripture Search

The disciples were fishermen, tax collectors, and other professions. Everyone's life prepares them for its challenges and gives them a special perspective. The education and lives of the groups discussed in the chapter provided them with insights into organization, education, the personality of the Apostles, or the most effective ways to meet the criticism of others.

## CHAPTER 8 Review (pages 230–231)

## Study

(1) Difficulties included persecution, intimidation, heresy, enemy invasions, and division.

(2) Christians were accused of treason and disrespect, and were made scapegoats for other social and economic problems of that time.

(3) Martyrs witnessed to their faith and served as examples and models of strength.

(4) The emperors felt threatened that Christians did not express loyalty to them and did not worship them as gods.

(5) The written accounts of the martyrs still serve as examples and act as witnesses of the struggle for the survival of the faith. That struggle is still going on all over the world.

(6) After the Edict of Milan, there was liberty of worship so that Church courts were recognized as valid, Christians were allowed to hold political office, and they were allowed to own and maintain public buildings for Church use.

(7) The purpose of monasticism is to nourish the relationship we have with God through solitude and prayer. Some thought that those who chose that lifestyle felt that they were superior to those who did not.

(8) In the East, monastic life was more solitary and withdrawn. In the West, there were structured communities all following a preset rule, and daily work was required.

(9) A heresy is an idea which is contrary to revealed Christian doctrine or teaching. The Church faced the challenge of heresies early on because the faith was developing and the search for truth led Christianity into new areas.

(10) Answers will vary and will be taken from the chart on page 215.

(11) The three groups show that, in the beginning, Christians were concerned with the legacy of the Apostles and their teachings. Then it became necessary to defend the faith against the criticisms of outsiders. Finally, full intellectual and spiritual expression was possible when the Church had gained legitimate status.

(12) Gregory organized the defense of Rome, ransomed captives, negotiated peace, provided relief for the destitute, and reformed the Sees of Italy. He also reorganized the Church, Canon Law, the Liturgy, and Church music.

(13) The struggle between East and West goes back to the Council of 381 and the Council of Chalcedon of 451 concerning Church primacy. The Eastern Church also became very closely connected to civil governments.

(14) Most of Christian Africa became Muslim within fifty years. Spain and France were in danger of falling. Christianity had to become better organized to face this threat.

## Action

(1) Encourage creativity here. Be sure to address the attitude of the martyr and all the circumstance surrounding their life and death. How does the martyr respond to threats or enticements to renounce the faith? What personal attachments will the person be giving up in his or her witness?

(2) Discuss the importance of symbols as visual representations of faith and beliefs that transcend culture and language. Students will need to consult books on Christian art or encyclopedia articles on the various symbols.

(3) Use the time line provided for the chapter as a base. Add other dates not included on the time line as necessary.

## Prayer

Encourage every student to try this. Most students probably do not pray on a daily basis. Discuss the value of daily prayer, even if done only for a short period. If any students have been on retreat, focus on the merits of that experience. Discuss the advantages and difficulties of each type of prayer. Sometimes the solitude can be just as distracting as prayer in public or community.

**8**

# From Persecution to Power: A.D. 100–800

**OVERVIEW:** The goal of this chapter is to introduce students to the events in the transition of Christianity from a persecuted minority group to a legitimate world power. It includes persecutions, the rise of monasticism, the threat of heresy, and the spread of Islam.

**OBJECTIVES: The students will:**

- Talk about early Christian martyrs and their legacy to the Church.

- Debate the pros and cons of (a) legitimizing Christianity, and (b) the monastic lifestyle.

- Discuss the effect of cultural difference on the unity of groups and focus on the tensions between East and West and the new threat to the Church from Islam.

**TIME FRAME: One to one-and-a-half hours.**

**MATERIALS: Map, time line, book on Christian art or symbols.**

**PROCEDURE:**

*Into:* Prayer—Begin class with the Nicene Creed which will come into focus in Sections 2 and 3.

*Through:*

Activity One:

1. Tell the story of Ignatius of Antioch and his fate. Use questions 1–4 on pages 205–206 to enhance discussion. Clarify the reasons for the persecution of Christians.

2. Set up the dilemma of buying or forging a certificate of compliance with the emperor or risking death. Let students explain the choice they would make if they were in such a situation.

3. Ask students what positive effects martyrdom had on the history of Christianity.

Activity Two:

1. Ask students to discuss how religion and politics are linked today. Make a list of advantages and disadvantages. Describe the changes that occurred to the status of Christianity under Constantine and Theodosius.

2. Ask students to describe a monastery or convent and its purpose. Do they think vowed religious are more holy than lay people? Why? What are the advantages and disadvantages of such a life?

3. What should any organization do when there is dissent from within? Discuss the ways in which dissent can be good and lead to positive change. Show how heresy led the Church to search for the Truth and to define its beliefs clearly in creeds. Look over the chart on page 215 with the class.

Activity Three:

1. Name some great Church figures. List them on the board and encourage students to contribute to the list.

8

2. Ask students how language and cultural differences can lead to disputes and misunderstandings. Use the differences between the Greek and Latin sides of the early Church as an example. Discuss the fall of Rome and the work of Gregory the Great to revitalize the Church.

3. Ask students what they know about Islam and its beliefs. Clarify any misunderstandings. Be sure it is clear that Islam is a monotheistic religion that accepts the Hebrew Bible and New Testament as revealed Scripture, although it also adds the Qu'ran (Koran) as the fulfillment of those earlier books.

*Beyond:* Suggest that students read "A Restless Heart," on page 224. Ask them to try the "Prayer" exercise on page 231.

*Prayer:* Close class with the reading of Gregory of Nyssa about the process or prayer given in "A People at Prayer," page 226.

8

Name: _____    Score: _____

## CHAPTER 8 QUIZ
# From Persecution to Power: A.D. 100–800

Mark true (+) or false (o).

___ 1. Christians in the Roman Empire underwent continuous persecution for nearly 300 years.

___ 2. The first persecution was under Emperor Decius.

___ 3. Martyrs came from every rank in Church and society.

___ 4. Persecution and the example of the martyrs often won converts to Christianity.

___ 5. By the third century, Christianity had spread throughout the empire.

___ 6. Persecution sometimes included exile, torture, imprisonment, loss of property, or death.

___ 7. Denying Christ was unheard of among the Christians.

___ 8. Constantine's favor of Christianity was linked to the military victory which made him emperor.

___ 9. The Edict of Milan brought a decline in the number of converts to Christianity.

___ 10. Constantine made Christianity the official religion of the empire.

___ 11. The first monks lived alone as hermits.

___ 12. Monasticism developed very slowly and was regarded as suspect.

___ 13. The Benedictine Rule was the basis of monastic life in the West.

___ 14. Western monasticism involved manual labor and intellectual pursuits as well as prayer.

___ 15. Most heresies centered around who Jesus was.

___ 16. Nothing good ever came from heresy.

___ 17. There were no heresies until the fourth and fifth centuries.

___ 18. The Eastern mind is not inclined to religious debate and theological distinctions.

___ 19. Arianism, which claimed that Jesus was not divine, was never officially condemned.

___ 20. Church councils often dealt with heresy.

___ 21. From the beginning the Church attracted men who explained and defended the Faith.

___ 22. Those who wrote or spoke in defense of the Faith were called Apologists.

___ 23. The title "Father" was given to individuals noted for holiness and learning.

___ 24. For centuries barbarian tribes were a political and military threat to the Roman Empire.

___ 25. The West was better able to defend itself against the barbarians than the East.

___ 26. The Huns were the first of the barbarian tribes to accept Christianity.

___ 27. Eastern Christianity was characterized by a close relationship with the state.

___ 28. Byzantine art and liturgy were ornate, extravagant, and magnificent.

___ 29. Islam's threat to Christianity was brief.

___ 30. Muhammad's religion was spread by the sword.

## CHAPTER 8 QUIZ
Answer Key

1. o
2. o
3. +
4. +
5. +
6. +
7. o
8. +
9. o
10. o
11. +
12. o
13. +
14. +
15. +
16. o
17. o
18. o
19. o
20. +
21. +
22. +
23. +
24. +
25. o
26. o
27. +
28. +
29. o
30. +

### Benedict's Rule of Life
(Can be used with Section 2, Monasticism in the West)

"In every aspect all shall follow the *Rule* as their guide: and let no one depart from it without good reason. Let no one in the monastery follow his own inclinations, or brazenly argue with his abbot ... The abbot, for his part, should do everything in the fear of the Lord and in obedience to the Rule, knowing that he will have to account to God for all his decisions.

"If a brother is insubordinate or disobedient, proud or a grumbler, or in any way acting contrary to the holy Rule and despising the orders of his seniors, let him according to the Lord's commandment, be privately warned twice by his seniors. If he does not improve, let him be publicly rebuked before them all. But if even then he does not correct himself, he should be excommunicated, if he understands how severe this penalty is. If, however, he is beyond conviction, he should be physically punished.

"The brothers shall take turns to wait on each other so that no one is excused from kitchen work, unless prevented by sickness or taken up with some vital business ... An hour before each meal the week's servers are to receive a cup of drink and a piece of bread over and above their ration, so that they can wait on their brothers without grumbling or undue fatigue.

"At the brothers' meal times there should always be reading ... There shall be complete silence at table, and no whispering or any voice except the reader's should be heard."

*Eerdman's Handbook to the History of Christianity* (Grand Rapids, MI: Wm. B. Eerdman's Publishing Company, 1977).

### Polycarp: Unshakable Fidelity
Polycarp (A.D. 69?–155?), Bishop of Smyrna, was in his late eighties when martyrdom beckoned. Ignatius of Antioch's advice still rang in his ears: "As God's athlete be sober; the stake is immortality and eternal life." Polycarp had been mysteriously forewarned of his coming death by fire and played the gracious host to the mystified officials who came to arrest him.

Even his judges tried to save the venerable bishop, arguing, "What harm is there in saying 'Lord Caesar' and offering a little incense?" Polycarp was unshakable: "For eighty-six years I have been Christ's servant, and he has never done me wrong. How can I now blaspheme my king?" Polycarp's execution took place in the amphitheater of Smyrna where the pagans had readied a huge pyre for "the teacher of Asia, the Father of the Christians, and the destroyer of our gods," as they called him. When the flames failed to consume Polycarp, the executioner used his dagger.

Members of the Christian community recorded the details of their bishop's trial and martyrdom in a letter sent to their sister churches as a source of inspiration and encouragement. It contains the first testimony that the relics of the martyrs were venerated and the first reference to a martyr's death as a birthday. The letter closed with the words, "It was thus that Blessed Polycarp suffered martyrdom. May we be privileged to follow in his footsteps and arrive at the Kingdom of Jesus Christ." The Church celebrates the Feast of Saint Polycarp on February 23.

## A Monk's Life

*A Contented Monk* "Our food is scanty, our garments rough; our drink is from the stream and our sleep often upon our book. Under our tired limbs there is but a hard mat; when sleep is sweetest we must rise at a bell's bidding … Self-will has no scope; there is no moment for idleness or dissipation … Everywhere peace, everywhere serenity, and a marvelous freedom from the tumult of the world. Such unity and concord is there among the brethren, that each thing seems to belong to all, and all to each … To put all in brief, no perfection expressed in the words of the Gospel or of the Apostles, or in the writings of the Fathers, or in the sayings of the monks of old, is lacking to our order and our way of life."

Ailred, *Speculum Caritatis*, 1.17. *Eerdman's Handbook to the History of Christianity* (Grand Rapids, MI: Wm. B. Eerdman's Publishing Company, 1977).

*A Discontented Monk:* "Everything here and in my nature are opposed to each other. I cannot endure the daily tasks. The sight of it all revolts me. I am tormented and crushed down by the length of the vigils; I often succumb to the manual labor. The food cleaves to my mouth, more bitter than wormwood. The rough clothing cuts through my skin and flesh down to my very bones. More than this, my will is always hankering after other things; it longs for the delights of the world and sighs unceasingly for its loves and affections and pleasures."

Walter Daniel's *Life of Ailred, Eerdman 's Handbook to the History of Christianity* (Grand Rapids, MI: Wm. B. Eerdman's Publishing Company, 1977).

If both accounts are true, why are they so contrary?

## Activities

1. Look up the details of the incident involving Saint Ambrose and the Emperor Theodosius at the Cathedral of Milan and tell the story to the class. What issue was at stake?

2. In northern Europe the Celtic monastic tradition inspired by Saint Columbanus had a strong emphasis on penance. Research the life of the saint and tell how he affected the Church.

3. Make a large chart on which you compare and contrast Islam and Christianity. Explain it to the class.

4. Pretend you are a Muslim and explain to a Christian why you are willing to die in a holy war and why you think he should join Islam even without being forced to do so.

## Additional Reading

Athanasius, *The Life and Affairs of Our Holy Father Antony.* Translated by Robert C. Gregg. *Classics of Western Spirituality.* New York: Paulist Press, 1980.

Brown, Peter. *Augustine of Hippo.* Berkeley: University of California Press, 1969.

Chadwick, Henry. *The Early Church.* Pelican History of the Church, vol. 1. New York: Penguin Books, 1967.

Frend, W.H.C. *The Rise of Christianity. Philadelphia: Fortress Press, 1985.*

_____. *Saints and Sinners in the Early Church: Differing and Conflicting Traditions in the First Six Centuries. Theology and Life Series II.* Wilmington, DE.: Michael Glazier, 1985.

Ignatius. Epistles. *In Early Christian Writings.* Translated by Maxwell Staniforth. New York: Penguin Books, 1968.

Jomier, Jacques. *How to Understand Islam.* Translated by John Bowden. New York: Crossroad, 1989.

Kelly, J.N.D. *Early Christian Doctrines.* Revised edition. New York: Harper and Row, 1978.

### CHAPTER 9

# Building Christendom: A.D. 800–1500

(Text pages 232–265)

## FOCUS

**Doctrinal:** In every age the Church's divine-human nature is reflected in the unfailing guidance of the Holy Spirit who works through both the strengths and the shortcomings of its human members.

**Personal:** Do I love the Church enough to try to make myself a better instrument of Christ's mission?

## OBJECTIVES

**Cognitive:** (a) to understand how the historical situation of feudalism both influenced the Church and weakened it; (b) to realize that medieval Christendom, for all its failures, was an age in which faith permeated every level and aspect of society; (c) to be able to see the human element in the Church without letting it overshadow or detract from the divine element.

**Affective:** (a) to appreciate the debt Christianity owes to the Church of the Middle Ages and to value what is positive and good in the Catholic heritage; (b) to desire and to take action for the reunion of Eastern and Western Christianity; (c) to grow in love for the Church and its members.

## Chapter 9 Outline

### SECTION 1
#### Looking Ahead

A Bright Light—Charlemagne

Problems and Solutions

Feudalism

Invasions

*Bernard: Bridge Between Two Eras* (text feature)

Reform

The Greek Schism

*On This Rock* (margin feature)

Pope Versus Emperors

The Era of Antipopes

The Great Insult

### SECTION 2
#### Crusades, Orders, and Pilgrims

On the March for God

The Flowering of Christendom

God's Mendicants

Franciscans

# TEACHER'S RESOURCE 9A

## Historical Notes

Despite his personal shortcomings, Charlemagne was responsible for a cultural and intellectual rebirth which resulted in the flourishing of schools and the arts. He was also responsible for forced conversions which had long-lasting and adverse affects on German Catholicism. The rise of feudalism led to increased wealth for the Church and the continued struggle between emperors and popes. The split between East and West was followed by the weakening of the Eastern Empire and a new focus on the West where Christianity was characterized by both piety and corruption. The centuries that followed exhibited both significant developments in the arts (architecture) and in education. Most universities were under papal charter. The Great Western Schism mirrored the breakdown of Christendom in Europe and shifting political situations.

## Pedagogical Notes

1. In dealing with the excesses of the Inquisition, explain that the use of torture to extract confessions of guilt, and death by burning at the stake, were acceptable practices of the day. Certainly this does not condone the excesses themselves, but will help to put them into a historical perspective.

2. In studying the decline of the fourteenth- to fifteenth-century papacy and the scandal of the Renaissance popes, stress the fact that the Holy Spirit's continual guidance is evident in the fact that no pope, however corrupt, ever tampered with basic Church doctrines or teachings.

# TEACHER'S RESOURCE 9B

## Theological Notes

In the last chapter, students learned about the Church's growth from a persecuted minority to a powerful majority. As we turn now to a consideration of the increasingly influential role the Church played in the political affairs of Europe between 800 and 1500, the classic text of H. Richard Niebuhr, *Christ and Culture* (Harper, 1951), may help clarify some of the issues raised by this period of Church history called "Christendom."

Niebuhr offers a theological perspective for considering the implications of Church power in the processes of civil governance, but he pushes the issue back to the broader and more foundational question of the relationship between Christ (and, therefore, the Body of Christ) and culture (which would include political systems as one of the products of culture). Niebuhr's question comes down to this: "To what extent, if any, are the goals, values, and concerns of the Christian community consistent with those of the cultures in which the Christian message is preached?"

Niebuhr suggests that, over the centuries, Christians have given five different answers to this question. What is particularly interesting and useful in the survey of these five answers is the fact that all of them continue to affect twentieth-century thinking about the Church's place in society.

1. *Christ Against Culture:* This response pits Christ against the world (the Church against state). It stresses the opposition of the Gospel to the affairs of the body politic. To be holy, one would do well to avoid the world and its concerns altogether. Radical Christian Fundamentalists today are attracted to this response, as were most Christians before the fifth century.

2. *The Christ of Culture:* Just the opposite of the first response above, Christ is understood as the ideal human who legitimizes "Christian culture." He blesses the works and institutions of Christian people. He helps them prosper. This is the response of American Christians like Robert Schuller (the Crystal Cathedral in Garden Grove, California). For those who take this approach, the Sunday service pays more attention to the success stories of people and to their heroic deeds than to prayer and preaching of the Scriptures.

3. *Christ Above Culture:* This third response tries to synthesize the first two. Because Jesus was human, linked historically to Jewish culture (and through Christendom, to western culture), Jesus is seen as present and active in Christian culture (primarily through the institutional Church). Yet, Jesus also points us beyond culture—to the kingdom of God. This

has been the typical approach of the Roman Catholic Church, particularly during the period of history discussed in Chapter 9.

4. *Christ in Culture in Paradox:* This is the response of many of the more conservative Reformation Churches. While Christians must live **in** the world and even get involved in the works of its cultures, no worldly wisdom or institutions can lead us to salvation. The world is sinful; this means that believers will always experience tension in their dealings with "the works of man." We cannot and should not turn our backs on this life, but in reality, the only life that counts is the next life. Modern televangelists who preach about the need to make America more Christian are contemporary examples of this approach.

5. *Christ, the Transformer of Culture:* Sometimes called the "conversionist response," this last approach sees the Christian as "leaven" in the world. Proponents are positive and optimistic about the world. They are at peace with human institutions, but they also recognize the need to challenge sinful society with the Gospel of Jesus Christ. Many of the documents of Vatican II, particularly the "Pastoral Constitution on the Church in the Modern World," seem to be moving contemporary Catholicism more in the direction of this response than evident in the past (see response #3 above). A number of mainline Protestant denominations are also taking this approach rather than the one that characterized the Reformation in the sixteenth century (see response #4 above.)

Any evaluation of Christendom (800–1500), whether positive or negative, is likely to be made in light of one's understanding of the relationship between Christ and culture as outlined above. Our opinion about the proper role of the Church in **modern** society will probably also be based on how we view this relationship.

**9**

# Time Line A.D. 800–1500

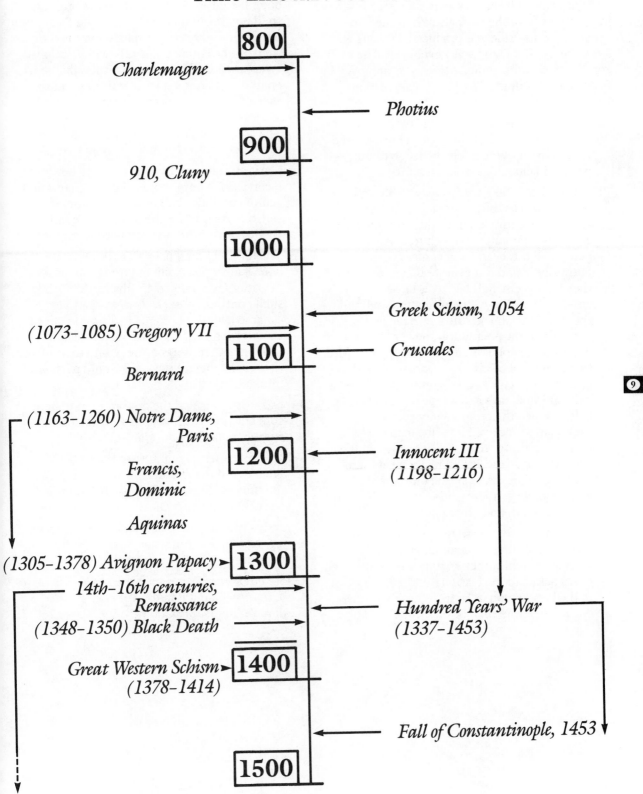

Charlemagne

Photius

900

910, Cluny

1000

Greek Schism, 1054

(1073–1085) Gregory VII

1100 Crusades

Bernard

(1163–1260) Notre Dame, Paris

1200 Innocent III (1198–1216)

Francis, Dominic

Aquinas

(1305–1378) Avignon Papacy 1300

14th–16th centuries, Renaissance

(1348–1350) Black Death

Hundred Years' War (1337–1453)

Great Western Schism 1400 (1378–1414)

Fall of Constantinople, 1453

1500

# The Rule of St. Francis

The original Rule of Francis consisted in a few instructions from the Gospels. When the Order expanded, a new rule was produced, but this was felt to be too strict, and was never used. The final version of the rule, quoted below, was approved by Pope Honorius III in 1223, three years before Francis's death.

1. This is the rule and way of life of the Brothers Minor: to observe the holy gospel of our Lord Jesus Christ, living in obedience, without personal belongings and in chastity.

2. If any wish to take up this way of life and join our brothers ... the provincial ministers shall carefully examine them in the Catholic faith and the sacraments of the church. And if they believe all these, and will confess them faithfully ... and if they have no wives, or if they have them and the wives have already entered a convent ... the ministers shall tell them ... to go and sell all they have and give it carefully to the poor. But if they are not able to do this, their good intention is enough ... After that they shall be given the garments of the probationers: two gowns without hoods and a belt, and stockings and a cape reaching the belt ... When the probationary year is over, they shall be received into obedience, promising always to observe this way of life and the rule ... those who really need them may wear shoes. And all the brothers shall wear humble garments, and may repair them with sackcloth and other remnants.

3. The clerical brothers shall perform the divine service according to the order of the holy Roman church ... they shall fast from the feast of All Saints to the Nativity of the Lord; but as to the holy season of Lent ... those who fast during this time shall be blessed of the Lord, and those who do not wish to fast shall not be bound to do so. At other times the brothers shall not be bound to fast except on Friday; but when there is a compelling reason the brothers shall not be bound to observe a physical fast.... When they go into the world, they shall not quarrel, nor contend with words, nor judge each other. But let them be gentle, peaceable, modest, merciful, and humble, as is fitting. They ought not to ride, except when infirmity or necessity clearly compels them to do so.

4. I strictly command all the brothers never to receive coins or money.... The ministers and guardians alone shall make provision, through spiritual friends, for the needs of the infirm and for other brothers who need clothing.

6. The brothers shall possess nothing, neither a house, nor a place, nor anything. But as pilgrims and strangers in this world ... they shall continually seek alms, and not be ashamed, for the Lord made himself poor in this world for us.... And if any of them fall sick, the other brothers are bound to minister to them as they themselves would wish to be ministered to.

11. I strictly charge all the brethren not to hold conversation with women so as to arouse suspicion, nor to take counsel with them.

What similarities do you find in the Rule of Francis and the religious rules of today? What differences? Should religious communities today have stricter rules?

Does this rule seem too demanding of the friars? If so, in what way? In what ways does the community care for its members?

Quoted in *Eerdman's Handbook to the History of Christianity* (Grand Rapids, MI: Wm. B. Eerdman's Publishing Company 1977), pp. 266–7.

## CHAPTER 9  Test

## Building Christendom: A.D. 800–1500

I.  **Matching:** Place the letter of the best answer on the blank. There are extra terms.

a. Alexander VI  
b. Avignon  
c. Canterbury  
d. Catherine of Siena  
e. Charlemagne  
f. Cluny  
g. Dominic  
h. Francis  
i. Gregory VII  
j. Innocent III  
k. Joan of Arc  
l. Michael Cerularius  
m. Savonarola  
n. Thomas à Becket  
o. Thomas à Kempis  
p. Thomas Aquinas  
q. Urban VI  

___ **1.** Intellectual giant whose writings reconciled faith and reason

___ **2.** Imposed Christianity as the state religion of the West

___ **3.** Led the eleventh-century reform of the Church

___ **4.** Represents the Church at the height of its temporal power

___ **5.** Drew the Eastern Church into schism

___ **6.** Led the tenth-century monastic reform

___ **7.** Restored the Church's ideals of poverty and humility

___ **8.** His order was founded to fight heresy

___ **9.** A famous place of pilgrimage

___ **10.** For seventy years the residence of the Holy Father

___ **11.** Pope whose election caused the Great Western Schism

___ **12.** Pleaded with the Holy Father to return to Rome from Avignon, France

___ **13.** Heroine of the Hundred Years' War

___ **14.** Author of *Imitation of Christ*

___ **15.** Martyred for his defense of the English Church

**9**

II. **Modified true or false.** If the statement is true, place a plus sign (+) on the line. If it is false, replace the *italicized* words with the correct answer.

_____ 1. Temporal power *corrupted* the papacy.

_____ 2. *The Renaissance* was an intellectual movement that strove to reconcile faith and reason.

_____ 3. The greatest damage to the image of the papacy was caused by the *"Babylonian Captivity."*

_____ 4. *Crusades* were popular journeys undertaken for social as well as religious reasons.

_____ 5. *Friars* were religious who modeled their lives on the gospel without retiring from the world.

_____ 6. *Feudalism* is the appointment of bishops and abbots by the temporal ruler, and giving them the insignia of their religious office.

_____ 7. The separation of the Eastern and Western Church in 1054 is known as the *Great Western Schism.*

_____ 8. "The Poor Man's Bible" was a nickname given to the medieval *cathedral.*

_____ 9. *Bernard* was both a contemplative monk and the twelfth-century's most active man of affairs.

_____ 10. All of fourteenth-century Europe was ravaged and laid waste by the *Cathari.*

III. **Essay:** Choose two.

1. List and explain three strengths of medieval Christendom.

2. Give three events which signaled the decline of Christendom and explain how each weakened the Church.

3. How did each of these persons love and build up the Church: Charlemagne, Bernard, Francis of Assisi, Thomas Aquinas, and Catherine of Siena.

# CHAPTER 9 Test
## Building Christendom: A.D. 800–1500

**I.**

1. p
2. e
3. i
4. j
5. l
6. f
7. h
8. g
9. c
10. b
11. q
12. d
13. k
14. o
15. n

**II.**

1. +
2. Scholasticism
3. Great Western Schism
4. pilgrimages
5. +
6. lay investiture
7. Greek Schism
8. +
9. +
10. Black Death

**III.**

Answers will vary.

# CHAPTER 9

## SECTION 1
## Text Questions (Student text pages 233–243)

**Page 235**

(1) Some problems might include law enforcement, developing a legal system that would be fair to all members of society, or determining the status of Catholicism if the state is pluralistic.

(2) Charlemagne's policies may have confused secular and religious authority. By giving the Church more secular power, he may also have given it more enemies.

(3) Charlemagne allowed his personal likes and dislikes to play a role in his choice of Church leaders. He chose them to suit his own purposes, not always those of the Church.

**Page 238**

(4) People are often wary and distrustful of changes and reforms. They don't like what is not familiar to them or they fear they will not benefit from change.

(5) The Cluniac reforms gave the monks more integrity and independence. They could attend to spiritual matters, and not become involved in political intrigue.

(6) Today the Church is working to increase the role and involvement of the laity, simplify sacramental rites, become more involved in issues of social justice, and revise Canon law.

**Page 239**

(7) Answers will vary.

**Page 243**

(8) Today there are conflicts over the use of tax money to maintain parochial schools, and the prohibition of prayer in public schools.

(9) Answers will vary.

## SECTION 1 Checkpoint! (page 244)
## Review
(1) Charlemagne regulated attendance at Church, tithing, alms, and baptism. He also created dioceses, seminaries, and libraries.

(2) Lay investiture is the process by which temporal rulers appoint bishops and abbots and give them the insignia of their religious office. As a result, people were sometimes able to buy their way into religious offices, relatives of state officials might be given preference, or clergy might even marry in order to keep benefits in the family.

(3) Bernard balanced the feudal world and monastic life. He stressed poverty and contemplation, and fought heresy, yet also encouraged the Crusades.

(4) The schism of 1054 was caused by centuries of slowly drifting apart in language, customs, and mentality, as well as by theological differences and scandals. Specifically the *filioque,* issue of papal primacy, and iconoclastic controversy contributed to the split.

(5) Gregory VII deposed the German Emperor and freed his servants. It didn't work because the emperor later deposed Gregory.

(6) Thomas à Becket was murdered because he did not believe the government could tax Church property and Henry II wanted to get rid of him.

(7) Words to Know: *Charlemagne* (first non-Roman emperor of the West; imposed Christianity as the state religion); *"filioque"* (clause added to the creed by Charlemagne stating that the Holy Spirit proceeded from the Father and the Son); *lay investiture* (the appointment of bishops by temporal leaders); *simony* (buying and selling of Church offices); *Cluny* (Abbey which led the movement for reform by guaranteeing monks the right to elect their own abbot); *schism* (formal split or division of a Church body into two); *papal bull* (official document, edict, or decree issued by the pope); *antipope* (person pretending to be pope); *Thomas à Becket* (Archbishop of Canterbury murdered for opposing Henry II's policies).

## In Your World

(1) Note the domed shape of the building and its similarity to the dome found on all mosques. This is a distinguishing feature of Eastern architecture. Encourage students to find the differences noted in this section such as the lack of the *filioque,* the use of icons, and the language.

(2) Focus on some of the reforms mentioned earlier in the section. What is the value of reform, and when does it become a way of easing requirements people perceive as being too demanding? How can the Church determine if reform is necessary, and if the reforms suggested are consistent with Catholic belief?

## Scripture Search

The passage states that God demands our faith and loyalty, but that secular leaders are also deserving of our trust and loyalty. Today that still means that we must observe laws, pay taxes, be involved in the processes of government (by voting, for example), and offer our support.

## SECTION 2

### Text Questions (Student text pages 245–253)

**Page 247**

(10) Answers will vary.

**Page 252**

(11) Answers will vary but may include Franciscans, Dominicans, Sisters of Saint Joseph, or Marist Brothers.

(12) Answers will vary and might include St. Patrick's Cathedral in New York City or Lourdes in France.

**Page 253**

(13) Faith is not based on reason, which is linked to logic. Faith is connected with belief. The deeper our faith, the deeper our ability to understand.

(14) People are often judged by their looks and those judgments are often wrong. There is no connection between a person's appearance and his or her intelligence.

## SECTION 2 Checkpoint! (page 254)

### Review

(1) The Crusades were organized as an attempt to win back the holy places from the Muslims. Militarily they were a failure, but they did unify Christianity.

(2) The Benedictines lived in solitude and the new orders lived in society instead of retreating from it, and they preached and taught.

(3) The orders have produced teachers, preachers, scholars, and confessors.

(4) Gothic cathedrals were used for meetings, and as inns, schools, and meeting places.

(5) Pilgrimages were taken to obtain special favors, atone for sins, fulfill a vow, or express faith.

(6) The aim of scholasticism was to take all knowledge by faith and reason and arrange it systematically.

(7) Words to Know: *crusade* (a religious-military expedition to the Middle East which attempted to free the Holy Places from Muslim control); *mendicant* (a beggar or one who lives on charity); *Franciscans* (order of friars founded by Saint Francis of Assisi and dedicated to "Lady Poverty") *Dominicans* (order of preachers founded by Dominic and dedicated to scholarship and preaching); *pilgrimage* (a trip to the Holy Land or other holy place as an expression of faith or to atone for sin); *scholasticism* (a scholarly movement of the twelfth and thirteenth centuries which attempted an intellectual synthesis of Catholicism); *mystic* (a pious person whose life is dedicated to prayer and the experience of God's presence).

## In Your World

1. Help students locate reference materials on any of the famous Gothic cathedrals. Emphasize the way the building itself becomes a form of religious expression.

2. Try to get students to capture the details of their trip just as medieval pilgrims would have. Prepare students in advance by telling them about the place they are to visit. Try to arrange a tour or talk just for your class, if possible.

3. Use the Encyclopedia of Religion or a text on medieval Christianity for information. Emphasize the special and unique contribution of women to the development of the mendicant orders.

## Scripture Search

These passages present conflicting images of the poor. The passage from Psalms stresses that the poor are blessed and protected, while the sections from Proverbs imply that poverty is the result of ignorance. Other passages from Proverbs say that one must be kind to the poor, and state that it is better to be poor and have integrity than to be rich and have no integrity. Matthew encourages the faithful to give all their possessions to the poor and 2 Corinthians shows that Jesus made himself poor for our sakes. All these passages show a confusion or ambivalence about the condition of poverty. It is true that some people are poor because they do not use their God-given gifts. It is also true that none of us is in a position to judge those who have less than we do. Mendicants use the poverty of Jesus as a model for their own lifestyle. Finally, all people, no matter what their social or economic status, are open to God's blessing and protection.

## SECTION 3
## Text Questions (Student text pages 255–262)

### Page 256

(15) If the Holy Father were to move there would probably be confusion, and possibly bad feelings, perhaps of betrayal by those left behind in the Vatican.

(16) Answers will vary.

(17) The Church remained holy even during this period even though many of its earthly representatives did not remain faithful.

### Page 258

(18) People will often do strange things during a time of crisis or in order to keep from contracting a disease, even if those things are known not to be of any help.

### Page 260

(19) Excessive asceticism can lead to physical injury or even starving to death. It can also become the end instead of the means. People can begin to focus too much on the ascetic activity itself and not the results it is supposed to bring.

(20) Answers will vary and may include expelling people from the Church, compromising, or holding meetings or councils.

### Page 262

(21) The artistic contributions to the Church were expressions of faith and piety. They were a gift.

(22) Many people may not even have known about the scandals in Church leadership because communication was so difficult (no newspapers or TV!). Or possibly, some people may not have been surprised to hear about this behavior on the part of leaders but did not allow that information to threaten their faith.

9

# SECTION 3 Checkpoint! (page 263)

## Review

(1) The Avignon Captivity was the period when seven Holy Fathers lived at Avignon instead of in Rome.

(2) The Western Schism ended when Gregory XII legalized the Council of Constantine and it elected Martin V as pope.

(3) The Black Death killed one-third to one-half of the population of Europe. Economies were paralyzed, people despaired, and all of western Europe was in disarray.

(4) The Waldensians were disobedient to Church leadership and rejected the clergy. The Cathari practiced excessive penance and asceticism.

(5) The Inquisition was created to root out heresy from within the Church.

(6) The artwork and literature of the Renaissance illustrated and reflected the faith of the people. Religion inspired artists and writers.

(7) Words to Know: *Avignon Captivity* (period when seven Holy Fathers resided in Avignon and not in Rome); *Great Western Schism* (period when two or three rival claimants to the papacy confused the Church); *Black Death* (fatal epidemic that swept Europe leaving chaos and economic paralysis); *Waldensians* (heretical group that rejected the clergy).

## In Your World

(1) Students might want to read about the Plague in a historical text or encyclopedia before beginning this activity. Focus on the sights and sounds of everyday life during this epidemic. How does this imaginary figure cope with his or her own fear and the fear of others?

(2) Use the Sistine Chapel artwork, for example, and stress its biblical sources.

## Scripture Search

Jesus instructed us to heal the sick or to treat them with compassion as he did (example of Good Samaritan). The medieval mendicants used his example as a source of strength. Those today who work with the sick (sufferers with AIDS, for example) draw the same strength from the model Jesus provided.

# CHAPTER 9 Review (pages 264–265)

## Study

(1) Strengthened Church laws concerning worship, tithing, and reception of the sacraments. Charlemagne introduced the filioque controversy and made bishops civil servants.

(2) Lay investiture removed the appointment of bishops from the pope. Bishops became responsible to civil governments, not the Church.

(3) Monks from Cluny owed allegiance only to the pope, not to any secular leader, and therefore they had an integrity others lacked.

(4) Answers might include language, the inclusion of the filioque, the primacy of Rome, the use of icons, or celibacy for all priests.

(5) Gregory VII initiated free episcopal elections and celibacy, and he removed simony and lay investiture from the Church.

(6) The popes' weapons included excommunication, papal bulls, and canon law. The emperor could use exile, anti-popes, and confiscation of Church property.

(7) Pope Boniface was slapped by an ally of Philip IV after being captured.

(8) The Crusades were to win back the Holy Land from Islam. They became a means for gaining personal wealth by some rulers.

(9) The mendicants were beggars who lived on alms in the world, and who formed communities dedicated to teaching, healing, and preaching. They carried the message of God to the world.

(10) The cathedral served as town hall, library, concert hall, Bible, and school, as well as a place of worship.

(11) People went on pilgrimages to obtain special favors, atone for moral failing, fulfill a sacramental penance or private vow, gain a special indulgence, or express their faith.

(12) Thomas Aquinas was a student and scholar who tried to demonstrate that true faith and true science are one and are not contradictory.

(13) The Great Western Schism was a dispute over who could elect the pope and who was head of the Church, but it did not result in a real split in the Church.

(14) The Black Death was a fatal plague which struck Europe in 1348. One-third to one-half of the population died within two years. Religious

houses were deserted, priests were poorly educated, the economy became paralyzed, and people despaired.

(15) Some cultural contributions include artwork, literature, poems, and music. They reflected people's experience of God's presence in the world.

## Action

(1) Be sure to present the primary issues clearly: the *filioque*, the primacy of Rome, and celibacy are three important points of debate. Ask students to volunteer opinion on how the two sides can be reconciled.

(2) Allow the students to choose the events they feel are important and to balance both good and bad.

## Prayer

Do this exercise in class and encourage the class to take it seriously. Physical preparation for prayer can be as important as spiritual preparation. Have the class repeat the prayer silently and then aloud as a group.

**9**

185

# Building Christendom: A.D. 800–1500

**OVERVIEW:** The aim of this chapter is to cover some of the main developments which happened between 800–1500. They include the split between East and West, and the struggle between Church and state. Positive change is traced through the rise of the mendicant orders, intellectual growth, and the contributions of the Renaissance, all despite the devastation to Europe caused by the Black Death.

**OBJECTIVES: The students will:**

- Confront some of the negative developments in the Church in the early Middle Ages;

- Discuss the meaning of the crusades, the birth of new religious orders, the purpose of pilgrimage, and the contributions of scholasticism;

- Debate the arguments that split the Church in the fourteenth century and learn about the bright light of the artistic and cultural contributions of the Renaissance.

**TIME FRAME: One to one-and-a-half hours.**

**MATERIALS: Map, time line.**

**PROCEDURE:**

*Into:* Prayer—Begin class with Saint Francis's Prayer for Peace.

*Through:*

Activity One:

1. Ask if any students have ever heard of Charlemagne. Place him on the time line and describe the changes in the Church during his reign.

2. Ask students what the word "reform" means and why reforms are often hard to introduce. Use a contemporary example such as women getting the right to vote. Describe the Cluniac Reform.

3. Ask students to describe the differences between the Eastern Orthodox and Roman Catholic Churches. Develop the list and explain the events that led up to the split.

Activity Two:

1. Ask for a definition of "holy war." Use question 10 on page 247. Describe the Crusades. Discuss the successes and failures of the Crusades.

2. Make a list of as many religious orders as students can name. Talk about Saint Francis and his goals.

3. Ask if any students have been on a pilgrimage or know what they are. Show a photo of a Gothic cathedral and discuss its uses.

Activity Three:

1. Present the "Great Western Schism" and have each student say how they would have resolved it.

2. Ask for a definition of a plague. Use polio or AIDS as a modern example. Discuss the effects of the Black Death.

3. Mention Michelangelo, Chaucer, and Thomas More. See if students can identify them. Discuss artistic expression as a part of faith.

***Beyond:*** Suggest that students read "A People at Prayer," page 256 and complete activity 2 from Section 3, "In Your World," page 263.

***Prayer:*** Close class with the Jesus prayer from "Prayer," page 265.

**9**

Name: _____     Score: _____

**CHAPTER 9 QUIZ**
# The Building of Christendom: A.D. 800–1500

Place the letter of the best answer on the line.

___ 1. Charlemagne was too (a) much, (b) little a Christian ruler.

___ 2. The question of whose authority was supreme, pope or emperor, (a) was clearly spelled out, (b) was confused and uncertain.

___ 3. Most of the problems that plagued the medieval Church (a) stemmed from feudalism, (b) were not related to feudalism.

___ 4. The greatest struggle between Church and state was over (a) lay investiture, (b) the temporal power of the pope.

___ 5. Church reforms (a) began with the monasteries, (b) ignored the monasteries.

___ 6. The break between East and West in 1054 (a) came as a surprise, (b) was a culmination of long standing differences.

___ 7. The basic difference between Eastern and Western Christianity is in their (a) relationship to the pope, (b) liturgical language and cultural differences.

___ 8. The crusades were an attempt to (a) convert the Muslims, (b) regain and defend the Holy Land.

___ 9. Cultural and economic results of the crusades were (a) negligible, (b) far-reaching.

___ 10. The mendicants helped combat (a) Church worldliness, (b) monastic strictness.

___ 11. Francis' and Dominic's influence was spread by (a) the crusades, (b) their Second and Third Orders.

___ 12. Medieval cathedrals were primarily (a) corporate enterprises of hundreds of unnamed artisans and Christians, (b) the achievement of well-known architects and artists.

___ 13. Pilgrimages were (a) a medieval development, (b) part of the Church's early tradition.

___ 14. Scholasticism attempted to reconcile faith and (a) reason, (b) religious experience.

___ 15. During the Avignon "Captivity" the Holy Father lived in Avignon by (a) choice (b) force.

___ 16. The Great Western Schism was a time when (a) large numbers broke away from the Church, (b) multiple papal claims confused the Church.

___ 17. The Hundred Years' War and the Black Death left the Church (a) stronger than ever, (b) weakened and full of contradictions.

___ 18. Heresies came primarily from attempts to (a) understand its doctrines, (b) reform its lifestyle.

___ 19. Renaissance popes were (a) patrons of the arts, (b) opposed to stressing temporal affairs.

___ 20. The scandals and abuses of the fourteenth- and fifteenth-century Church were the result of (a) ignorance of the need for reform, (b) inability to carry out reforms.

# CHAPTER 9 QUIZ
Answer Key

**1.** a

**2.** b

**3.** a

**4.** a

**5.** a

**6.** b

**7.** a

**8.** b

**9.** b

**10.** a

**11.** b

**12.** a

**13.** b

**14.** a

**15.** a

**16.** b

**17.** b

**18.** b

**19.** a

**20.** b

## Praying with Thomas

Directions: (Can be used with Section 2, Schools and Scholars) Divide class into three groups. Assign each group a stanza of "Pange Lingua" to read aloud—side I, side II, and side III. Ask for a prayer leader to do the readings of leader. Ask another student to read words of Saint Thomas.

Song: "Pange Lingua" (Written by Saint Thomas Aquinas for Corpus Christi Vespers)

Side I: Praise we Christ's immortal body, and his precious blood we praise:

Side II: Born of royal Virgin Mother, he shall reign for endless days!

Side III: Dying once to save all nations, evermore he wins our praise.

Side I: Coming forth from spotless Virgin, he for us was born a man.

Side II: Sowing seeds of truth among us, he fulfilled the Father's plan;

Side III: Then his final night upon him, wondrously that night began!

Reader: "O Banquet most holy, in which Christ is food for man, O wondrous Sign, O great mystery of his passion, death, and resurrection! Here the soul is filled with life, here the darkness yields to Light, and the hope of the glory to come."

*All:* Silent meditation on Thomas' antiphon, written for Corpus Christi.

*Leader:* Thomas, your words on the Eucharist are very deep. Help us to appreciate this great gift of Christ which meant so much to you. For all your knowledge and intelligence, you were basically a simple person. To you, the Eucharist was Christ, the all-consuming goal and purpose of your life. Help us to find Christ in this Sign as you did. And if Christ should ask us, as he did you, what we would like above all else, help us to say, as you did, "Only yourself, Lord."

Song: "Pange Lingua" (continued)

Side I: On the eve of that Last Supper, breaking bread with chosen friend

Side II: He obeys the Law's direction, even as the Old Law ends.

Side III: Now he hands the Twelve a new Bread: his own flesh with their flesh blends!

Side I: By a word, the Word embodied, changes common bread and wine:

Side II: Bread becomes his holy Body, wine is made his Blood divine!

Side III: Though this truth evades the senses, faith unveils the sacred sign!

*Leader:* Please respond: Give us only Yourself, O Lord.

Lord Jesus, as we seek you in the service of our brothers and sisters,

As we work to make this world a better place,

Rather than wealth, honor, success, power, or pleasure,

When we meet with opposition and persecution in preaching your Word,

When things go well for us and we are happy and grateful,

As we try to forget ourselves and help each other,

In every celebration of the Eucharist,

In every moment of our lives and for all eternity,

*All:* O Jesus, we adore you in our midst—in the beauty of creation, in one another, in the sacrament of your Body and Blood. We believe your word, "I am with you all days." Send your Holy Spirit to make us instruments of your peace and justice on earth. And at the moment of death, let us see your face in glory, since here on earth we have believed without seeing you.

Song: "Without Seeing You"

## The Imitation of Christ
"On friendship with Jesus"

"What can the world offer you without Jesus? To be without Jesus is hell most grievous; to be with Jesus is to know the sweetness of heaven. If Jesus is with you, no enemy can harm you. Whoever finds Jesus finds a rich treasure, and a good above every good. He who loses Jesus loses much indeed, and more than the whole world. Poorest of all men is he who lives without Jesus, and richest of all is he who stands in favour with Jesus."

What word might today's world substitute for "Jesus"?

"On death"

"Of what use to us is a long life, if we amend so little? Alas, a long life often adds to our sins rather than to our virtue! Would to God that we might spend a single day really well! Many recount the years since their conversion, but their lives show little sign of improvement. If it is dreadful to die, it is perhaps more dangerous to live long. Blessed is the man who keeps the hour of his death always in mind, and daily prepares himself to die."

Is it a healthy sign to be mindful of death?

"On the true lovers of Jesus"

"Jesus has many who love his kingdom in heaven, but few who bear his cross. He has many who desire comfort, but few who desire suffering. He finds many to share his feast, but few his fasting. All desire to rejoice with him, but few are willing to suffer for his sake. Many follow Jesus to the breaking of bread, but few to the drinking of the cup of his passion. Many admire his miracles, but few follow him to the humiliation of his cross. Many love Jesus as long as no hardship touches them.... They who love Jesus for his own sake, and not for the sake of comfort for themselves,

bless him in every trial and anguish of heart, no less than in the greatest joy. And were he never willing to bestow comfort on them, they would still always praise him and give him thanks."

What is this passage really saying about suffering?

"A Prayer"

"Grant me, Lord, to know all that I should know, to love what I should love, to esteem what most pleases you, and to reject all that is evil in your sight. Let me not judge superficially by what I see, nor be influenced by what I hear from ignorant men, but with true judgment to discern between things spiritual and material, and to seek your will and good pleasure at all times and above all else."
                                    —Thomas à Kempis

Quoted in *Eerdman's Handbook to the History of Christianity* (Grand Rapids, MI: Wm. B. Eerdman's Publishing Company, 1977), p. 356.

## Warnings
"Ah Constantine! to how much ill gave birth, not thy conversion, but that dower which the first rich Father took from thee!" (Dante, *Inferno*, XIX, 115–117).

"The Church of Rome, by confounding two powers in herself, falls into the mire, and fouls herself together with her burden" (Dante, *Purgatorio*, XVI, 127–9).

"Come, infamous Church, listen to the words of your Lord: 'I have given you splendid robes, but you have made them cover idols; I have given you precious vessels, but you have used them to exalt your false pride. Your simony has profaned my sacraments; lechery has made of you a pockmarked harlot. And you no longer even blush for your sins! Whore that you are!' You sit on Solomon's throne, and beckon to all who pass you by. Those who have money you bid a welcome to, and have your pleasure of them; but the man of goodwill is cast outside your doors!' " (Girolamo Savonarola).

"Helmets and swords are fashioned here from chalices. The blood of Jesus Christ is sold dirt cheap" (Michelangelo, speaking of Rome).

## Panel Discussion Questions
1. How did the Pope become a temporal ruler and what did this mean for the Church?

2. What were the important elements in the Christianization of Europe?

9

**3.** How are monks, mendicants, and crusaders different and yet alike?

**4.** What were the glories of medieval Christendom? The scandals?

**5.** Why was the Renaissance both a triumph and a disaster?

**6.** Why is reform so difficult?

## Bernard's Prayers

**1.** *Prayer to Mary:* "In dangers, in doubts, in difficulties, think of Mary, call upon Mary. Let not her name depart from your lips, never suffer it to leave your heart. And that you may more surely obtain the assistance of her prayers, neglect not to walk in her footsteps. With her for guide, you shall never go astray, while invoking her, you shall never lose heart. So long as she is in your mind, you are safe from deception. While she holds your hand, you cannot fall. Under her protection, you have nothing to fear. If she walks before you, you shall not grow weary. If she shows you favor, you shall reach the goal."

**2.** *Hymn to Jesus*
"Jesus, the very thought of thee, With sweetness fills the breast, But sweeter far thy face to see, And in thy presence rest" (Bernard of Clairvaux).

## Additional Reading

Comby, Jean and Diarmaid MacCulloch. *How to Read Church History. Vol. 2: From the Reformation to the Present Day.* New York: Crossroad, 1989.

Knowles, David. *Medieval Theology: The Evolution of Medieval Thought.* New York: Vintage Books, 1962.

Meyendorff, John. *Byzantine Theology: Historical Trends and Doctrinal Themes.* New York: Fordham University Press, 1979.

**9**

CHAPTER 10

# FAMILY RIFTS: A.D. 1500–1600
### (Text pages 266–297)

## FOCUS
**Doctrinal:** The rejection of Roman Catholicism by nearly half of Christendom was the most devastating phenomenon in the Church's experience.

**Personal:** How can I better understand the splintering of Christendom so as to work for the reunion of all Christians?

## OBJECTIVES
**Cognitive:** (a) to understand the forces and motives that created the Lutheran, Calvinist, and Anglican Churches; (b) to realize the extent of the abuses in which the Church was immersed and the way in which reform occurred; (c) to understand the splintering process of Protestantism and the areas of Catholic-Protestant shared belief and practice.

**Affective:** (a) to feel the scandal and tragedy of disunity among Christians; (b) to respect the faith, truth, and goodness found within the Protestant churches.

## Chapter 10 Outline

### SECTION 1
**The Launching of the Reformation**

Luther's Concerns

The Special Conditions

Scandal Continues

*On This Rock* (margin feature)

A Tormented Soul

The Challenge

*A Changing Europe—The New Map* (text feature)

The Papal Bull

A Final Departure

### SECTION 2
**A New Era**

The Lines Are Drawn

Calvin—A Prophet with a Mission

The Geneva Community

The "Reformed Churches"

*Doctor of the Church, Saint, Mystic* (text feature)

Henry VIII—England's First Lay Pope

Henry's Problem

*Communion of Saints* (margin feature)

The Church of England

## SECTION 3
### Losses and Gains

**⑩**

# TEACHER'S RESOURCE 10A

## Historical Notes

### The Reformation

Ironically, the movement known as the Reformation was not a reform, but an explosion—a series of new religious systems based on revolutionary theological theories that altered the entire course of history. Protestantism was no simple separation from Rome as the Greek Schism of 1054 had been, but a condemnation of the very structure of the Church—dogma, hierarchy, priesthood, liturgy. It even went so far as to designate the Roman Church as the Church of the anti-Christ.

Clamors for reform from within the Church were heard long before Luther's protest. Dante had painted cardinals in hell. Erasmus had depicted Saint Peter as driving some popes from the gates of heaven. In England, John Colet had pleaded with the clergy of Canterbury: "The Church, the spouse of Christ, is become foul and deformed. I have come here today, fathers, to admonish you with all your minds to deliberate, in this your council, concerning the reformation of the Church." Egidio da Viterlo, head of the Augustinian Order to which Luther belonged, told the assembled Fifth Lateran Council in 1512: "Unless we force our greedy desire for human things … to yield to the love of divine things, it is all over with Christendom." In nations which heeded the call to reform—such as Italy, Ireland, and Poland—the Protestant Reformation failed to take root. When Luther appeared on the scene, the popes already had more problems than they could handle. France and Spain were dueling for control of Italy.

The Turkish Armies threatened to conquer all of Europe. Epidemics of plagues ravaged Rome. How was one to reform the Church when Rome itself (1527) was being sacked by troops of the Catholic Emperor, Charles V. Only the heroism of the Swiss guards, who gave their lives, down to the last man, allowed Clement VII (1523–1534) to escape with his life. When Paul III (1534–1549) directed a papal commission to draw up a list of the abuses in need of correction, the Church took the first decisive step toward its own reformation.

### Martin Luther

To a large extent, recent studies on Luther have enabled us to see the genius as well as the weaknesses of the man more objectively. Luther began by attempting to correct one Church evil. His Ninety-five Theses were not Protestant—they criticized excesses and set limits to the dogma of papal infallibility, still imperfectly defined. The controversy grew out of an overwhelming, almost pathological sense of sin which led him to unusual insights into the role of faith and the sacraments. In September, 1983, the U.S. Lutheran and Roman Catholic Dialogue came to an agreement on the role of faith in justification.

Ultimately, however, for Luther the controversy led to a rejection of the authority of the Church, which he saw as placing the pope's power above God's word. By hindsight, poor communication and perhaps some bad will on both sides led to the tragic break. Luther's first reaction to his excommunication in 1520 bears testimony to this: "I am in grievous pain, like a child abandoned by its mother." Already at the Diet of Worms Luther declared, "I believe in neither pope, nor councils, which have often been mistaken." His final rupture with the Church came in 1524 when he discarded his Augustinian habit.

Luther was a tenderhearted, brutal, sentimental, violent, muddleheaded, dogmatic, arrogant, hardworking, poetic, and obscure man. Doing the work of five men, he supplied the needs of his people for a vernacular Bible, catechism, liturgy, and hymnbook. "I endeavored to make Moses so German," Luther boasted, "that no one would suspect he was a Jew." More than a thousand German printing houses were at hand to disseminate his works.

With the onslaught of the Peasants' Revolt, Luther's first concept of the Church as a spiritual reality gave way to a Church in which secular princes replaced the authority of the pope. Within ten years, Church lands—nearly one-third of German soil—were confiscated and secularized, leaving Germany in religious chaos.

Luther supplied no real remedies to the evils from which the sixteenth-century Church suffered. His response to papal and clerical abuses was to abolish both papacy and clerics. His remedy for excesses in pious devotions was to discard them altogether—indulgences, the rosary,

devotion to the saints, pilgrimages, holy water, fasting, and confession. Luther died as he had lived: tormented and engaged in spiritual conflict, perhaps even feeling that his ideals were betrayed by the church that would bear his name.

## The Emperor Charles V

A significant factor in winning Germany from Catholicism to Lutheranism was the frequent absence of Catholic Emperor Charles V. His early leniency toward Luther, offering him safe conduct to the Diet of Worms, and his lack of vigorous enforcement of the ban against heretics, left the German princes free to embrace Luther's doctrines. Only at the Peace of Augsburg (1555) after decades of strife, when the principle "*cuius regio, huius religio*" ("whoever has the kingdom controls the religion") became the new basis of Germanic law, did Charles seem aware of what he had allowed to happen. By then it was too late. Germany was already permanently divided into a Protestant north and a Catholic south. The Emperor divested himself of his lands and retired to a monastery in Spain where he spent the last three years of his life in prayer and penance. Charles ordered his body to be buried under the monastery altar table in such a way that when the priest celebrated Mass he would stand on the Emperor's breast and head, in token of his eternal humiliation. But there were other factors in society that supported a break from the Roman Church. The spirit and writings of the Renaissance had been critical, advocating a return to the Scriptures and the pure faith of the primitive Church. Anti-clericalism created a readiness among many people to accept the Bible as the only religious authority. A decline in Scholasticism left theological studies uncertain and confused. In addition, there was the anti-Roman spirit of German nationalism, and the efforts of the newly formed national states to concentrate power in the hands of national monarchs.

## John Calvin

Calvin left the Catholic Church at age twenty-four, not over a crisis of conscience, like Luther, but through the religious upheaval that followed in Luther's wake. Although Calvin appeared a generation later than Luther, it was Calvin's *Institutes* that gave Protestantism its much-needed systemization. While Lutheranism remained basically a German phenomenon, Calvinism became international and free of the patronage of princes. Its discipline, rather than its doctrine, drew followers. Lay people ran Calvin's churches, and the Academy of Geneva produced learned and capable clergymen. There, the theological concept of predestination, humanity's total dependence on God, produced disciples of indomitable wills. The signs of "election" were specific: acceptance of the gospel, reception of the Lord's Supper, and moral living. For Calvin the road to heaven was straight and narrow. He, more than anyone else, gave Protestantism its hardworking, no-nonsense ethic.

Whereas Lutheranism had unintentionally undermined the basis of morality, Calvin reestablished it on unshakable foundations, making Geneva the European capital of the Reformation. The strictness of the Geneva community can be seen in the fact that, during the first five years of Calvin's rule, there were fifty-eight death sentences, seventy-six banishments, and over a thousand excommunications. In France, Calvin's followers faced Catholic persecution. Cardinal Baudrillart testified that with unwavering constancy Calvinists endured "horrible punishments no less terrible than those which the last pagans inflicted on the early Christians." The blood of Calvinist martyrs encouraged other people to become Calvinist.

## The Church in England

In 1530, four years prior to Henry VIII's Act of Supremacy, the Church of England was already in bad shape. Only four of its 30 bishops resided in their own dioceses. The abbots of its 800 religious houses were nominated by the king, a fact that made Henry's dissolution of the monasteries relatively easy. Cardinal Wolsey had the prerogative of a papal legate, and from 1518–1529 was the sole intermediary between the English clergy and Rome. His ambition, lack of scruples, and immoral lifestyle, matched the king's. Henry, both the "Bluebeard" of the Reformation and the "Defender of the Faith," was a strange mixture of contradictions. On hearing that Bishop John Fisher of Rochester—the only member of the English hierarchy who had refused to acknowledge Royal Supremacy, had been named a cardinal—the king vowed: "He will have no head for his cardinal's hat." Yet at the news of Thomas More's execution, Henry blamed Anne Boleyn, shouting, "You are responsible!" A year later to the very day, Anne mounted the scaffold steps.

Henry's policies of death to Catholics who refused to take the Oath of Supremacy, and death to Protestants who dissented from Catholic dogma, caused one foreign visitor to exclaim, "Merciful God! What a way these people live! They hang papists on one side of the street and burn anti-papists on the other."

Confiscation of monastic properties helped solve the king's financial problems. The distribution of these properties as gifts to the English nobility tied these nobles to the king. At Henry's death in 1547, the English Church was a hybrid—neither papist nor Protestant. Under Edward VI, a sickly child of nine, Archbishop Cranmer guided the kingdom toward Protestantism. Mary Tudor's biggest mistake was to make Protestant martyrs of men of repute and integrity. Cranmer was deposed, sent to the tower, and later burnt as a heretic. With nearly 300 deaths to her credit "Bloody Mary" succeeded in equating church tyranny with Rome.

Considered illegitimate by the Roman Church, Elizabeth I had no choice but to be Protestant, though no one knows what her real religious convictions may have been. She ensured the final break with Rome, passing such fearful anti-Catholic legislation that all but the most heroic complied. *The Book of Common Prayer* and the 39 Articles, incorporating many of the heretical ideas of both Luther and Calvin, were completed under Elizabeth.

## The Council of Trent

The Council of Trent (1545–1563) had a hard time getting off the ground. When the bull summoning a council was issued, Germany and France were at war and forbade their bishops to attend. At the first session, only 31 bishops appeared. The majority were Italian and none came from really Protestant territories. Opposition to the council sprang from every quarter—from bishops who feared conciliarism, from Catholic rulers and prelates content with the *status quo*, from mutual suspicion between Catholic and Protestant forces, and from a fear of interference by Emperor Charles V. The first session of eight meetings, 1545–1547, set the tone for the doctrinal conservatism of the entire council.

Prior negotiations between Catholics and Lutherans had all collapsed and the council itself made no attempts at reunion.

The second session of the Council, 1551–1552 had only 59 Church members and a few Protestants. Their presence was due to the fact that Charles V forbade the German bishops to attend until Protestants were invited. Their views only serviced to bring out the theological chasms which had developed between Catholicism and Lutheranism since 1517. This session defined transubstantiation and reaffirmed the sacramentality of Extreme Unction and Penance, which had been rejected by the reformers. The bishops, fearing that they would be captured by the French, recessed for ten years.

The third and most productive council session, 1562–1563, had more than 250 bishops present, about 80 percent of them Italians. Even though Clement VII (1523–1534) had been willing to concede communion under two species and marriage of the clergy as a prerequisite for a Lutheran return to the fold, the council debates over clerical celibacy, the use of the vernacular, and offering the chalice to the laity were heated. When the actual documents of Trent called for the vernacular, communion of both sacramental bread and wine, and active lay participation in the Mass, the clergy ignored these rulings as "too Protestant."

Trent reviewed traditional Catholic teaching that had been distorted or rejected by Protestant critics and reaffirmed its authenticity. Abuses in clerical life and the preaching of indulgences were corrected. The Church emerged from Trent highly structured, with the papacy elevated to a role of absolutism and isolationism that lasted until John XXIII. It stressed the need of all churches to conform to Rome in matters of liturgy, government, and discipline rather than to incorporate local customs and traditions. A defensive attitude toward Protestantism halted biblical studies and downplayed the reading of the Bible. Trent's closing off of doctrinal speculation in the Church caused a shift of interest to the area of morality, increased the use of confession, and developed the sin-conscious and scrupulous mentality characteristic of many Catholics prior to Vatican II.

Along with Trent's legislation, the Church experienced a burst of holiness seldom equaled before or since. Amid a flood of mystics and missionaries, new orders were created and older ones reformed. The Society of Jesus was the most powerful instrument of Catholic revival and resurgence in the post-Conciliar years. Fifteen years after its founding, it already numbered over 1000 members. The Jesuits' fourth vow of obedience to the Holy Father gave him a spiritual militia which was powerful and mobile.

## Eastern Christians

There are five million Eastern Christians in North America, four million of them belonging to the Orthodox Church. The Greek Orthodox have nine dioceses in the United States: one in Canada, one in South America; they are all headed by the Archbishop of New York and number 1.9 million members. The Orthodox came to Florida in 1764, the Greek Catholics of New Orleans in 1864. The Greek communities reside mainly east of the Mississippi and above the Ohio River. One million Russian Orthodox became independent of the Russian Church in 1970 against the will of Patriarch Athenagoras I.

## Pedagogical Notes

To pique student interest in this topic, refer to the Ecumenical Handbook in this text (page 408) in conjunction with this chapter.

## TEACHER'S RESOURCE 10B

## Theological Notes

There are many complex and interrelated factors that led up to the Reformation of the Church launched by Martin Luther in 1517. In this chapter, students become better acquainted with many of the reasons for this tragedy of separation. But besides learning what the Reformation was, why it occurred, and who was responsible for it, students of Reformation history should also have an opportunity to think about what we might learn from the Reformation. In a sense, the Reformation had a similar impact on the Church that the death of a loved one has on a family. It was a devastating event. It was final and irreversible and it left us wondering about how we could cope with the future.

The best that we can do in the face of a traumatic situation like this is to try to "integrate" our loss—to face it with all the courage and hope we can muster. Then, over a period of time as our faith promotes a measure of healing, we can step back and consider what this moment of suffering might reveal to us about our lives and our futures.

There are several lessons about our lives as disciples of Christ that we can learn from the "death experience" of the Reformation.

1. The unity that Jesus prayed for and the "oneness" that we claim to be a mark of the Church is *both a gift* of God's Spirit *and a task* for God's people. Unity is given to us in the person of God's word (Jesus), yet we must also work to achieve and preserve that unity. Before the Reformation, Catholics tended to assume that the Church would always maintain its mark of unity because of the strength of its institution, its magisterium, and its papacy. Today we realize the need to foster unity by making concrete signs of healing in our broken world. It's not enough to say we are one. We have to *create* unity too.

2. The second lesson flows from the first. The Church of Jesus Christ must keep a healthy distance between itself and the political structures of society. It cannot become so institutionally involved in social governance that its freedom to critique society and preach the Gospel is compromised. During the sixteenth century, the Church was seen as a political entity that competed with other national states for the allegiance of its citizens. As a result, what Martin Luther intended to be a debate that would lead to genuine reforms within the Church quickly escalated into a political battle between Rome and the Germanic states. In the end, everyone in the Body of Christ lost because the distinction between the Church's secular interests in Europe and its religious mission was insufficient.

3. There's a third lesson to be learned from the experience of the Reformation, and that's the lesson of humility before the Word of God. Church officials demonstrated little interest in discussing Luther's theological concerns. Their response was simply to condemn him and demand that he be silent. In their enthusiasm to preserve the legitimate teaching authority

of magisterium, Church leaders conveyed the impression that the Church was beyond reproach. As the Council of Trent (1545–1563) and Vatican II (1962–1965) clearly indicated, however, the Church was indeed in dire need of reform. Trent made important and necessary changes regarding the conduct of priestly life and the preparation for priesthood. Many years later, Vatican II took up several of the questions Luther had originally proposed for discussion in 1517. Had Catholics been more humble before God's word in 1517, we might wonder, would the separation prompted by the Reformation ever have occurred?

History is a great teacher. We cannot change the past, but by remembering our past, we can gain important insights to help us deal with the present and plan for the future. The Reformation is now part of our history. Its lessons may not be entirely pleasant for us to learn, but that does not make them any less important.

**10**

199

# Time Line A.D. 1500–1600

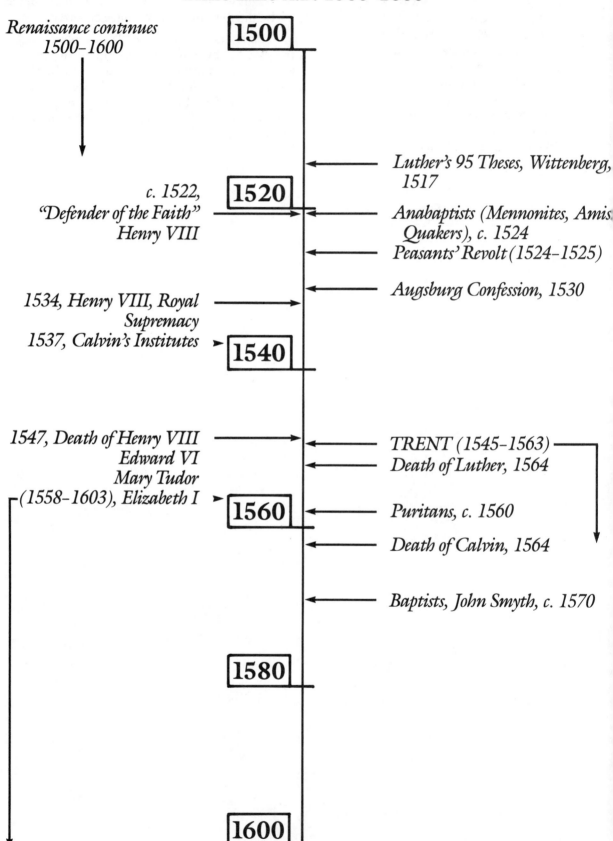

*Renaissance continues*
*1500–1600*

**1500**

Luther's 95 Theses, Wittenberg, 1517

*c. 1522,*
*"Defender of the Faith"*
*Henry VIII*

**1520**

*Anabaptists (Mennonites, Amish, Quakers), c. 1524*
*Peasants' Revolt (1524–1525)*

*Augsburg Confession, 1530*

*1534, Henry VIII, Royal*
*Supremacy*
*1537, Calvin's Institutes*

**1540**

⑩

*1547, Death of Henry VIII*
*Edward VI*
*Mary Tudor*
*(1558–1603), Elizabeth I*

*TRENT (1545–1563)*
*Death of Luther, 1564*

**1560**

*Puritans, c. 1560*

*Death of Calvin, 1564*

*Baptists, John Smyth, c. 1570*

**1580**

**1600**

# CHAPTER 10  Test

## Family Rifts: A.D. 1500–1600

I.  **Matching:** Place the letter of the correct term on the line. There are extra terms.

a. Anne Boleyn     d. Bishop John Fisher     g. Martin Luther
b. Bloody Mary     e. Henry VIII     h. Philipp Melanchthon
c. John Calvin     f. Ignatius of Loyola     i. John Wycliffe

___ **1.** Author of the *Spiritual Exercises*

___ **2.** Restored Catholicism in England

___ **3.** Controversy over indulgences

___ **4.** Martyred in England under Henry VIII

___ **5.** Established a religious dictatorship in Geneva

___ **6.** First declared Royal Supremacy in England

___ **7.** Wrote the *Augsburg Confession*

II.  **Incorrectly classified:** Write the letter of the item that **does not belong** on the line.

___ **1.** Associated with Luther: (a) Wittenberg, (b) Augsburg Confession, (c) Peasants' Revolt, (d) Edward VI.

___ **2.** Associated with Calvin: (a) Institutes, (b) John Tetzel, (c) Geneva, (d) predestination.

___ **3.** Associated with Anglicanism: (a) Royal Supremacy, (b) Elizabeth I, (c) Charles V, (d) Book of Common Prayer.

___ **4.** Denied or abolished by Protestantism: (a) clerical celibacy, (b) papal authority, (c) Scripture, (d) Seven Sacraments.

___ **5.** Reforms of Luther: (a) use of the vernacular, (b) justification by faith alone, (c) abolition of monasticism, (d) rejection of the Bible.

___ **6.** Associated with Trent: (a) Puritans, (b) tightening of Church discipline, (c) Paul III, (d) Diocesan seminaries.

___ **7.** Lost to the Church through the Reformation: (a) England, (b) Spain, (c) most of Germany, (d) Switzerland and the Low Countries.

___ **8.** Associated with the Counter-Reformation: (a) Jesuits, (b) Index, (c) numerous saints, (d) Ninety-five Theses.

III.  **Chronology:** Write the letter of the term which occurred first in the story of the Reformation.

___ **1.** (a) Anglicanism, (b) Calvinism, (c) Lutheranism

___ **2.** (a) Anne Boleyn, (b) Catherine of Aragon, (c) Elizabeth I

___ **3.** (a) Royal Supremacy, (b) deaths of Fisher and More, (c) Bloody Mary

Name: _____  Score: _____

___ **4.** (a) persecution of Catholics in England, (b) excommunication of Luther, (c) Council of Trent

___ **5.** (a) Death of Thomas More, (b) Ninety-five Theses, (c) abuses in the preaching of indulgences

**IV. Short answers:** Define the following terms. Use the reverse side of this paper.

**1.** Reformation

**2.** Augsburg Confession

**3.** predestination

**4.** Royal Supremacy

**5.** Counter-Reformation

**V. Essay: C**hoose two.

**1.** What did the three major Protestant groups have in common?

**2.** Would the Church have renewed and reformed itself without the Reformation?

**3.** What do you consider the saddest aspect of the Protestant Reformation? Why?

**10**

# CHAPTER 10 Test
## Family Rifts: A.D. 1500–1600
**Answer Key**

**I.**

1. f
2. b
3. g
4. d
5. c
6. e
7. h

**II.**

1. d
2. b
3. c
4. c
5. d
6. a
7. b
8. d

**III.**

1. c
2. b
3. a
4. b
5. c

**IV.**

Answers will vary.

**V.**

Answers will vary.

# CHAPTER 10

## SECTION 1
### Text Questions (Student text pages 267–275)

**Page 269**

(1) Answers will vary but may include the fall of the Berlin Wall and the war in the Persian Gulf.

(2) People may leave the Church over a problem dealing with a specific issue, or because they are disillusioned by its human failings and weaknesses.

**Page 274**

(3) Luther hoped to initiate reforms in the Roman Church and to make it more aware of its excesses and corruption.

(4) Luther's sense of sin made him feel that salvation is a free gift of God and that faith is the only proper response to that gift. He felt that we cannot do anything to initiate the process of salvation because of our sins.

## SECTION 1 Checkpoint! (page 276)
### Review

(1) Some historical factors leading to the Reformation were increased levels of education and questioning of faith, the availability of books, the rise of nationalism, and the increased interest in independence.

(2) The excesses of the clergy, stress on ritual, and internal rivalries scandalized the people.

(3) Luther was almost killed during a storm, and he vowed to become a monk after living through it. He was pessimistic, often depressed, and a despairing person. These feelings can be seen in his stress on human unworthiness and justification by faith alone.

(4) Luther burned a papal bull and a copy of canon law ordering him to retract his views and destroy his writings.

(5) Luther advocated a priesthood of the laity, justification by faith, doing away with celibacy and monasticism, and he rejected the primacy of Rome. He used the primacy of Scripture as his proof.

(6) Words to Know: *Reformation* (the movement that established Protestantism); *Wittenberg* (city in Germany where Luther posted his Ninety-five Theses); *Ninety-five Theses* (Luther's criticisms of the way Johann Tetzel preached and of the practice of indulgences); *indulgence* (remission of temporal punishment still due for a sin after penance gained through prayer, good works, or an offering); *1517* (the year Luther posted the Ninety-five Theses in Wittenberg); *papal bull* (a special document from the pope).

## In Your World

**(1)** Discuss some of the similarities and differences before attending the Lutheran service. Be sure students are looking and listening for them. Try to arrange a tour around the church before or after the service.

**(2)** Use any text on the Reformation and the Encyclopedia of Religion.

**(3)** Again, encourage students to do a little bit of research before writing their articles. Try to get them to speculate on the reaction, both positive and negative.

## Scripture Search

Paul is saying that faith makes righteousness and cuts across cultural boundaries (like the ones between ancient Jews and Greeks). Paul clearly states that observance of Jewish law is not required as a basis for faith. Be sure students see the need for looking at these passages in their proper contexts. Luther did not mean that works are unimportant or unnecessary. He stressed a balance between one's inner disposition in faith and its outer expression in good works.

## SECTION 2

## Text Questions (Student text pages 277–285)

**Page 279**

**(5)** Luther introduced the vernacular Bible, hymn books, a readable psalter, and catechism.

**(6)** The use of the vernacular in worship has been introduced, the use of hymns, and more involvement of lay people in service and structure.

**Page 281**

**(7)** Answers will vary.

**(8)** Calvin's contributions included a stress on discipline and morals, and on lay government.

**Page 285**

**(9)** The marriage might have been annulled or Henry might have been given more power over the running of the Catholic Church in England. Henry might also have gone along with the wishes of the pope and have remained married.

**(10)** Answers will vary.

## SECTION 2 Checkpoint! (page 286)

### Review

**(1)** The Peasants' Revolt estranged Luther from the masses and tied his movement to the Germanic princes and the secular state.

**(2)** Luther produced a Bible in German which could be read by all literate people, put together a hymnal that used music, and wrote a psalter and catechism that were easily understandable.

**(3)** Predestination says that God has already determined the fate of all people for either reward or punishment.

**(4)** Calvin believed in strict discipline. He said that personal virtue reflected God's election and laws to regulate behavior made those elected by God more visible.

**(5)** Calvin added discipline, order, structure, and the witness of martyrs.

**(6)** Henry VIII wanted to divorce Catherine of Aragon and marry Anne Boleyn. Rome refused to annul the marriage or allow a divorce so Henry declared himself the head of the Church of England.

**(7)** Words to Know: *Peasants' Revolt* (uprising of German peasants against the nobility and the Church; Luther rejected the movement); *Augsburg Confession* (formal statement of Lutheran beliefs drawn up by Melanchthon); *predestination* (Calvinist belief that God has already determined the final fate of every individual); *Institutes* (Calvin's statement of his own religious beliefs); *Royal Supremacy* (Henry VIII's claim to be supreme head on earth of the Church of England).

### In Your World

**(1)** Reforms could include items about dress, conduct, or seating arrangements. Make sure you keep the reforms as a package and debate them together. What kinds of reforms, changes, and compromises are made before the package is accepted? How do you decide as a class—by a vote or by letting one student (or the teacher) make the final decision?

**(2)** Try to read through some of the works beforehand and pick out a section that will be clear and not too difficult. A passage that deals with the papacy or with monasticism might be helpful since those disputes have been covered in this chapter.

## Scripture Search

These passages contain moral codes for deacons and guides for behavior for slaves, children, and parents. The harshness of the rules may guarantee some degree of compliance. If they represent ideal behavior, they can be used as goals or models for our behavior. The people mentioned in the letters give us good ideas about what kinds of people made up the earliest Christian communities and about the high standards required of leaders.

## SECTION 3

### Text Questions (Student text pages 287–294)

**Page 288**

(11) Some might think that loyalty to Rome takes precedence over loyalty to a secular leader.

**Page 289**

(12) Answers will vary.

(13) Answers will vary. The holiness of the Church as institution is unaffected by the weaknesses and sins of its human representatives. Lay Catholics may be disillusioned by corruption and sin, or they may want to try to correct the problems.

**Page 292**

(14) The Council of Trent emphasized reorganization in order to try to root out corruption by rearranging and introducing new structures that countered the Protestant's changes.

**Page 294**

(15) Answers will vary, but may include Presbyterians, Methodists, and Baptists.

## SECTION 3 Checkpoint! (page 295)

### Review

(1) Elizabeth used fines, confiscation of property, imprisonment, and laws against attending Mass. Rome used excommunication.

(2) Bernard meant laziness, not tithing, and immorality of all kinds.

(3) Adrian VI barely granted any privileges and tried to get Germany to act against Lutheranism.

(4) The Oratory of Divine Love was a clerical support group of common prayer and simple living.

(5) The changes made at Trent include reorganization of the Curia and Inquisition, provisions for seminaries, removal of abuses and tightening of discipline, and formation of new orders.

(6) Words to Know: *Council of Trent* (meetings held to renew and reform the Catholic Church in response to Protestantism); *1545* (the date of the beginning of the Council of Trent); *Jesuits* (teaching order founded by Ignatius of Loyola); *Counter-Reformation* (reform movement following the Reformation which renewed the Church through the Jesuits and other religious orders).

### In Your World

(1) Try to include legislation that might have to do with indulgences, the use of the vernacular in prayer, and the compilation of new and revised prayer books or hymnals.

(2) Use any encyclopedia such as *The Encyclopedia of Religion*, or a book of saints, and also encourage students to use maps.

### Scripture Search

This passage from John gives us Christ's own repeated prayer "that all may be one," and his own motive for unity, "that the world may believe that you sent me." These make our striving for unity a matter of Christian conscience.

## CHAPTER 10 Review (pages 296–297)

### Study

(1) Luther originally intended to change how indulgences were gained.

(2) Indulgences are blessings which remove any temporal punishments caused by sin. They were being sold to pay Church debts.

(3) The Renaissance had awakened an interest in the common people. There were questions about the authority of the Church. Technology increased the availability of books and nationalism was on the rise.

(4) Johann Tetzel was a Dominican friar who preached indulgences and who notified Rome of Luther's criticisms.

(5) Luther advocated a priesthood of the laity, justification by faith, abandoning celibacy and monasticism, and rejected the primacy of Rome.

(6) Peasants in Germany followed Luther's calls to seek social justice and looted castles and Catholic cloisters. Later, Luther repudiated the peasants, and Protestantism became connected to the princes and secular leaders.

(7) John Calvin was a very severe and disciplined person, rigid and reserved. He was a brilliant scholar who saw God as a strict judge. This vision led him to inject the idea of predestination into his reforms and to encourage passing laws to regulate behavior.

(8) Henry VIII wished to have his marriage to Catherine annulled. The pope would not agree to the annullment.

(9) Henry VIII refused to pay Church taxes, then declared himself head of the Church in England.

(10) In the Church of England, English was used for worship, the communion supper replaced Mass, clerical marriage was allowed, and a new prayer book was written.

(11) Under Elizabeth I, Catholics were persecuted, fined, imprisoned, and lost their property.

(12) Before Trent, the Fifth Lateran Council tried to impose some reforms.

(13) The Council of Trent reaffirmed the basic truths of Catholic belief (renewal) and reorganized Church structure such as the Curia (reform).

(14) New religious congregations and orders provided teachers, missionaries, advisors, and spiritual leaders for the Church.

(15) The Church has introduced the vernacular into worship and developed new roles for the laity.

## Action

(1) Use both the *Ecumenical Handbook* (408) and any encyclopedia to obtain information. Be sure to include historical information as well as details about beliefs and practices.

(2) Again, be sure students consult some outside sources and encourage them to choose an individual who interests them.

## Prayer

Use this prayer in class daily while reading through this chapter. Discuss how easy it is to become discouraged and how a prayer like that of Ignatius of Loyola can re-center one's thoughts and intentions.

**10**

# Family Rifts: A.D. 1500–1600

**OVERVIEW:** This chapter covers the period of painful division for the Church. It outlines Martin Luther's criticisms, the social and political conditions in Europe, and the ultimate split between the Protestants and Rome. Reflection on the need for reform and the most effective ways of bringing it about should be the focus.

**OBJECTIVES: The students will:**

- Talk about what they know about Martin Luther, Protestants, and the idea of historical context.

- Identify some positive accomplishments of Luther and tie Henry VIII to the birth of the Anglican Church.

- Ask students what reforms they would like to see in the Church and discuss the Council of Trent as an example of Church-initiated reform.

**TIME FRAME: One to one-and-a-half hours.**

**MATERIALS: Map, copy of the Augsberg Confession and the Institutes.**

**PROCEDURE:**

*Into:* Prayer—Begin class with the prayer from the Spiritual Exercises given in the "Prayer" section, page 297.

*Through:*

Activity One:

1. Ask students how Protestants are different from Catholics. Make a list on the board.

2. Discuss briefly Luther's early life. Did students know he was a monk? Talk about his feelings of inadequacy. Can students relate to this? Tie Luther's feelings to the idea of justification by faith.

3. Define the term "context." Ask students why it is important to know about the social, political, economic, religious, and cultural conditions at the time of a certain event or change. There were excesses and abuses in the Church and there was political change. These factors are important. Use modern Eastern Europe as an analogy.

Activity Two:

1. Explain the term "vernacular" and ask what positive changes are made by translating the Bible and conducting worship in the vernacular. Use questions 5–6 on page 279 as a guide.

2. Ask students to identify Henry VIII. What do they know about him? Discuss his dilemma. How would students solve it?

3. Describe the results of Henry's dispute with Rome. The king or queen of England is still head of the church there.

Activity Three:

1. Describe briefly the antagonism between Catholics and Protestants, especially in Britain, that led to the permanent split between them. Use question 11 on page 288 as a guide.

2. List reforms that students think the Church should have made then and now. Use question 13 on page 289 to guide discussion.

   3. Discuss the Council of Trent and list some of its reforms and
      results. Ask how internal change can lead to renewal.

**Beyond:** Suggest that students read "A Changing Europe—The New Map,"
on page 272 and "Catholic Missionaries—A New Breed," on page 291.
Encourage them to complete activity 2 from "Action," page 297.

**Prayer:** Close class by reading silently the opening statement from Vatican
II in "A People at Prayer," page 292.

Name: _____     Score: _____

## CHAPTER 10 QUIZ
# Family Rifts: A.D. 1500–1600

Mark true (+) or false (o).

___ 1. Luther's criticism came at a time when the Church was in great need of reformation.

___ 2. Luther, Calvin, and Henry VIII had a great deal in common.

___ 3. The main ideas of the Reformation were not new.

___ 4. Church scandals, politics, technology, nationalism, and religious superstition all helped the Reformation to succeed.

___ 5. Luther was ideally suited for monastic life.

___ 6. Luther's ninety-five theses were a modest criticism of existing abuses.

___ 7. Politics and personal jealousies played a part in Luther's condemnation.

___ 8. Once excommunicated, Luther found peace.

___ 9. Luther's doctrine of justification by faith alone has no basis in Scripture.

___ 10. The Peasants' Revolt and the Augsburg Confession determined the future course of Lutheranism.

___ 11. Calvin built his new religion on predestination.

___ 12. Calvinism included many of Luther's teachings but was more radical and international.

___ 13. Unlike Luther, Calvin kept all the sacraments.

___ 14. Religion under Calvin was entirely separated from the state.

___ 15. Religious wars deepened the zeal of Calvinists.

___ 16. England's move to Protestantism was completed under Henry VIII.

___ 17. Royal Supremacy in England was imposed without opposition.

___ 18. Mary Tudor temporarily restored Catholicism.

___ 19. Catholics in England were savagely persecuted under Elizabeth.

___ 20. The sixteenth-century Church seemed unaware of its need for reform.

___ 21. The Council of Trent and the Counter-Reformation were identical.

___ 22. Trent worked at both renewal and reform.

___ 23. Many of Trent's regulations put Roman Catholicism on the defensive.

___ 24. Much of Trent's success was due to the leadership of the new religious orders.

___ 25. Luther's reforms were condemned by both Trent and Vatican II.

**10**

# CHAPTER 10 QUIZ
Answer Key

1. +
2. o
3. +
4. +
5. o
6. +
7. +
8. o
9. o
10. +
11. +
12. +
13. o
14. o
15. +
16. o
17. o
18. +
19. +
20. o
21. o
22. +
23. +
24. +
25. o

## PRETEST

    Classification: If the statement applies to Catholics only, write **C**. If Protestants only, write **P**. If it applies to both, write **B**.

____ 1. Scripture contains all that is necessary to salvation.

____ 2. Believe in Christ's death, resurrection, divinity, and Second Coming.

____ 3. A Christian can grow in grace and holiness by works of love and prayer.

____ 4. Believe in the Bible as God's word.

____ 5. Emphasize Scripture and preaching.

____ 6. Since all believers share in Christ's priesthood, there is no need for an ordained priest.

____ 7. The Church is a fellowship of believers.

____ 8. Each Christian is free to interpret Scripture.

____ 9. Christ is really present in the Eucharist; once the bread and wine are consecrated they are no longer bread and wine.

____ 10. Believe in heaven and hell.

____ 11. Believe in the Trinity.

____ 12. Christ is our only mediator with God.

____ 13. Obedience to the pope is a visible sign of our unity with Christ's Church.

____ 14. The saints can help us both as models and as intercessors.

____ 15. Mary deserves no special honor.

## PRETEST
Answer Key

1. P
2. B
3. C
4. B
5. P
6. P
7. B
8. P
9. C
10. B
11. B
12. P
13. C
14. C
15. P

## Discussion Starters

• What was Martin Luther attempting to do in 1517?

• Are good works necessary for salvation?

• What is an "invisible" church?

• Should top political and religious authority be held by the same person?

• How does a Church Council bring about reform?

• Will the pursuit of ecumenism water down Catholic faith and practice?

## Wycliffe's Bible

"These thingis Jesus spak; and whanne he hadde cast up hise eyen into hevene, he seide: 'Fadir, the our cometh; clarifie thi sone, that thi sone clarifie thee; as thou hasy yovun to hym power on ech fleische, that al thing that thou has yovun to hym, he yyve to hem, everlastynge liif. And this is everlastynge liif, that thei knowe thee very God aloone, and whom thou hast sent, Jesu Christ. Y have clarified thee on the erthe; Y have endid the werk that thou hast yovun to me to do. And now, Fadir, clarifie thou me as thisilf, with the clereness that Y hadde at thee bifore the world was maad. Y have schewid thi name to the men whiche thou hast yovun to me of the world; thei weren thine, and thou has yovun hem to me, and thei han kept thi word' " *(John 17:1–6).*

[From the second version of Wycliffe's Bible, 1388, as quoted in *Eerdman's Handbook to the History of Christianity* (Grand Rapids, MI: Wm. B. Eerdman's Publishing Company), p. 339].

## Additional Reading

Chadwick, Owen. *The Reformation.* Pelican History of the Church, vol. 3. New York: Penguin Books, 1972.

Luther, Martin. *Selections From His Writings.* Edited by John Dillenberger. New York: Doubleday, 1961.

Penaskovic, Richard. "Roman Catholic Recognition of the Augsburg Confession." *Theological Studies,* 41:2 (1980); 307–14.

**10**

**CHAPTER 11**

# FROM TRENT TO VATICAN II:
## A.D. 1600 TO THE PRESENT

(Text pages 298–327)

## FOCUS

**Doctrinal:** Whatever its need for reform, the Church has been constantly guided in its growth and renewal by the power and presence of the Holy Spirit.

**Personal:** Am I proud of my heritage and role as a member of the post-Second Vatican Council Catholic Church in America?

## OBJECTIVES

**Cognitive:** (a) to understand how the Church, in the centuries following Trent, moved to a defensive and conservative position; (b) to see Vatican II as a turnabout in the Church's attitude toward itself and its relation to other Christians and the world; (c) to learn how the Church in America grew from a handful of despised papists to the nation's largest religious denomination.

**Affective:** (a) to love the outward-moving Church created by Vatican II; (b) to appreciate the unique contributions of American Catholicism to the world-Church.

# Chapter 11 Outline

### SECTION 1
**An Era of Change**

After Trent
New Worlds for Christ
From Faith to Skepticism
*Athens and Jerusalem* (text feature)
Twilight
*On This Rock* (margin feature)
Revolution in France
Crown and Altar Tumble

### SECTION 2
**The Wonderful Century**

Catholicism on the Defensive
Simple People and Popes
*Bernadette and the Miracle of Lourdes* (text feature)
A Papal Renaissance
*Communion of Saints* (margin feature)
Hope, Despair, and Dreams
Conceived in Liberty
The Infant American Church

**11**

⑪

# TEACHER'S RESOURCE 11A

## Historical Notes

In reaction to the shock of division that occurred in the Protestant Reformation, the Church emerged from Trent a highly authoritarian and centralized structure that was a throwback to medieval times. As a result, Church-state relations remained obscure and ill-defined. Despite these drawbacks, a new spirituality, accompanied by the work of the new religious orders was injected into the Church. The skepticism that accompanied the Enlightenment led to the downfall of both the French monarchy and the French Church. The Revolution took an anti-clerical turn and Church buildings and images were destroyed.

Vatican I (1870) saw power centralized in Rome and the doctrine of infallibility reach its final definition. By this time, Catholicism in the United States was already fighting religious prejudice and developing parish communities and a strong educational system. John XXIII's leadership at Vatican II and the social encyclicals of John, Paul VI, and John Paul II brought the Church head on into the twentieth century where it has confronted many of the major issues facing the Church and its members worldwide.

## Church Development

Like all social institutions, the Church's development was gradual. Trent's official papers, made available from the Vatican archives at the end of the nineteenth century, show that the Council had not developed a clear concept of the Church as a whole, but limited itself to individual acts of reform or doctrinal explanation. The Church itself had to wait until the twentieth century. What emerged in the wake of the Protestant Reformation was a highly authoritarian, centralized structure that was basically a throwback to medieval times—a monolithic Church. In opposition to the modernizing innovations of the Reformation, there was a single universal language—Latin; one theological system—neo-Scholasticism; one universal expression of Catholic worship—the Tridentine Mass; and one system of government—the Code of Canon Law. For 400 years Catholics assumed that all this was unalterable.

Perhaps the greatest omission of the Council of Trent was to leave the area of Church-state relationships insufficiently defined. Because of this, governments appointed bishops and interfered with papal elections until our own century. Tridentine spirituality, based on the sacraments, self-discipline, and good works, characterized the new religious orders and strongly influenced Catholic life until Vatican II.

## Counter-Reformation

The Church's Counter-Reformation, begun before Trent and continuing along after it, created so strong a religious revival that it gave birth to the Baroque—a new art form. Baroque's heavy ornamentation, sweeping curves, vast proportions, and sharp contrasts of light and shadow, combined the humanist tradition of the Renaissance with the beauty of medieval Catholicism. The art, literature, music, and architecture of such men as El Greco, Rubens, Velásquez, Bernini, Cervantes, and Palestrina, had little in common with the sober piety of the Protestant north and did much to stimulate the popular devotions rejected by the Reformers.

Among the many new religious orders that emerged after Trent to sustain the Counter-Reformation, the Jesuits were unique. They dispensed with communal life and choir recitation of the Divine Office. Their large numbers, their special vow of obedience to the Holy Father, and their spiritual and intellectual acumen, made them a powerful force.

Counteracting the exuberance of the age was the heresy of Jansenism, which introduced a rigidity into Catholicism similar to that of Puritanism. Influenced by Calvin's insistence on human unworthiness before the Divine Majesty, Jansenism practiced the late reception of first Communion. Because of Jansenism, many of the laity stopped receiving the sacraments.

## Treaty of Westphalia

The Treaty of Westphalia (1648) not only marked the end of a united Christendom, but also set up a series of essentially anti-religious principles. The first was that the people were to follow the religion of the prince. The second was a denial of the Church's authority as a moral guide in public affairs. With nothing left to restrain their self-interest and passion, Catholic princes, using

the "divine right of kings," tended to enslave the Church, making it an organ of the state. This situation, as disastrous as Protestantism, led inevitably to totalitarianism and the French Revolution.

## Revolution in France

Following Westphalia, Protestantism moved into a state of Deism. It was a Christianity which rejected dogmatic beliefs entirely, making religion an affair of "good will to men." Born of the Enlightenment, it rejected the supernatural and saw Catholicism as an enemy. By May 5, 1789, the Enlightenment had long since sown the seeds of skepticism and disbelief that were to destroy both the French monarchy and the French Church.

In July of 1790, the Estates-General had passed the Civil Constitution of the Clergy. It dissolved monasteries, abolished religious orders, directed the wholesale confiscation of Church properties, and changed dioceses and Church structures so that Bishops and priests were to be elected by the people in the same way as other municipal officers. The Constitution was as drastic as the reformation of the Church of England under Henry VIII; it was perhaps the Assembly's greatest political mistake. Church and nation were divided into those who accepted it and those who would not. Of the 160 French bishops, only six agreed to take the oath. More than 40,000 priests and religious chose exile. Rome waited until the following spring to condemn the Constitution as schismatic and heretical, and decreed excommunication for all who would not retract their oaths to it.

By 1792, the Revolution had become anti-clerical. It attempted to sweep away the entire structure of organized Christian institutions and persecuted even the clergy who had taken the oath. In many respects the French Revolution was worse than the Protestant Reformation, where, at least, loyalty to the Gospel and the Christian faith had been asserted. The Revolution had begun by attempting to combine the new faith with the old religion through a Constitutional Church separated from Rome and closely bound up with the new state. The compromise was abandoned under Robespierre and the Jacobins.

During the Revolution, famous abbey churches and cathedrals throughout France were

leveled. By 1796 a completely new religion, with hymns to nature and readings from philosophers, had been invented. Toynbee points out the supreme paradox of the French Revolution. By disposing of the traditional Christian establishment, it opened the way for a return to the pre-Christian religions—the worship of collective human power which had been practiced in Rome.

In many ways what happened in France in 1789 parallels what happened in Russia in 1917. Both revolutions began in a blood bath. Both had their purges, fell short of freedom, and ended with a dictator. Both provided a new ideology that was almost a religion. In the name of freedom and equality, existing political and religious authority were destroyed.

## Napoleon and the Pope

Although Napoleon's armies swept over Europe, in his battle with the Church he would have done well to remember his own words: "There are only two powers on earth, the sword and the spirit.... In the long run the sword is always beaten by the spirit." First Pius VI was imprisoned and suffered the indignity of having the fisherman's ring torn from his finger by a French officer. Then Pius VII spent five years (1809–1814) in captivity at Napoleon's orders. When the Emperor annexed the Papal States in 1809, Pius excommunicated him. In the end, it was the "cardboard pontiff," as Pius VII styled himself, who won. During Napoleon's fatal retreat from Moscow, his uncle, Cardinal Fesch, said: "My nephew is lost, but the Church is saved." Ironically it was Pius VII who offered Napoleon's family refuge in Rome when the Emperor's downfall exiled them. When the Congress of Vienna (1815) restored the Papal States to the Church, England stood ready to assume world leadership.

## Vatican Council I

Vatican Council I (1870) came as a climax to the centralization of power in Rome and reflected Rome's anti-liberalism. The Council, the largest until that time, included 774 bishops, 46 of them from the United States. After only seven months, it was suspended because of the outbreak of the Franco-Prussian War and never officially reassembled. In many respects, Vatican II completed its unfinished work.

The Council's pronouncement on papal infallibility was not a new idea. The primacy of the pope had already been so clearly defined by the Council of Florence (1439) that Vatican I simply took over the formula. As the topic was debated, strong pros and cons were voiced. Dissenters to its proclamation were not so much against the doctrine itself as against its timing. Cardinal Newman, for example, thought it premature and unnecessary. Because 60 dissenting bishops left Rome early, the vote was 535 to 2 in favor. American Bishop Fitzgerald of Little Rock, Arkansas, cast one of the two "nay" votes.

By the doctrine of papal infallibility, the Church holds that when the Roman Pontiff "speaks *ex cathedra*, that is, when exercising the office of pastor and teacher of all Christians, he defines with his supreme apostolic authority a doctrine concerning faith or morals to be held by the universal Church, through the divine assistance promised to him in Saint Peter, is possessed of that infallibility with which the divine Redeemer willed his Church to be endowed in defining doctrine concerning faith and morals: and therefore such definitions of the Roman Pontiff are irreformable of themselves and not from the consent of the Church." This doctrine was the death blow to conciliarism.

Papal infallibility was no sooner defined than it spawned the Dutch schism. Prompted by the writings of German Church historian, J. J. Dollenger, the Church of Utrecht, sometimes called the Old Catholics, separated from Rome. They remain independent to this day. Among the other long range results of Vatican I were: theological schools, other than that of Thomas Aquinas, were looked upon with suspicion; the Curia grew in power as no new theological experimentations were permitted; Catholic political parties were seen as potential separatists; and because of Italy's annexation of the Papal States, Italian Catholics were forbidden to take part in political life. Linked to his isolation from the world, a kind of mystique grew up around the Holy Father, an aura of being the last citadel of truth, yet hostile to democracy, freedom, and social reforms. Vatican I's failure to read the signs of the times gave Roman support to old kingships and treated liberals as less than loyal.

## Leo XIII

Pope Leo XIII is regarded as the greatest papal ruler since Trent. Expected to die soon after his election, his 25 years in office (1878-1903) came as a surprise. Sixty-nine when elected, Leo was an informed political genius who had the wisdom to choose able collaborators. He modernized Church government, advanced biblical studies, and worked to represent Catholicism as a guarantee of true liberty.

Leo is best known for his social encyclicals. The word "encyclical" comes from the Greek (*en* = in, *kyklos* = circle) and means a letter meant to go in a circle—to make the rounds of all the dioceses of the Church. Papal encyclicals apply Gospel values to concrete historical problems. They are written in Latin and take their title from the first two or three words of the text. The following three encyclicals are among Leo's most significant. *Aeterni Patris* (August 4, 1879) restored Aquinas to first place in Catholic philosophy and theology. *Immortali Dei* (November 1, 1885) gave the Catholic teaching on the state and became the Magna Charta of democracy. *Rerum Novarum* (May 15, 1891) was an answer to Karl Marx's *Das Kapital.* It upheld both the capitalist's right to profit and the workingman's right to form associations, to receive just wages, and to have a day of rest.

## Spanish Expansion

When the national power of Spain became joined to the religious cause of the Counter-Reformation, it gave the Spanish monarchy an ecclesiastical prestige and power unequalled in Europe. Spaniards came to the New World with the idea that the Faith was to be propagated. Centuries of conflict with the Muslims had primed the Spanish character for its policies of forced conversions as well as exploitation of the American Indians.

From the time Christopher Columbus claimed the lands of the New World for their "most Catholic Majesties" Ferdinand and Isabella, missionary activities were supported by the crown. Spain colonized Central America, South America, and the entire Southwest and Pacific coast of the United States. Saint Augustine, Florida (1545), and Santa Fe, New Mexico (1609), were America's first two cities. Junipero Serra (1713–1784) who established 26 missions along the coast of California, was only one of the many Franciscan friars who spent their lives working among the Indians.

## John Carroll, First American Bishop

John Carroll, singularly blessed by both nature and grace, was a fitting spiritual father and founder of the Catholic Church in the United States. He was born in Upper Marlborough, Maryland, on January 8, 1735. While he was still a young Jesuit, the Society of Jesus was suppressed and he opted to serve as a secular priest in Rock Creek, Maryland. As Father John Carroll, he accompanied Benjamin Franklin to Canada seeking aid for the American cause against England. Carroll was not quite 50 years old when he was made Prefect Apostolic, head of the mission territory of the United States. Five years later, March 25, 1789, the Assembly of American clergy elected Carroll as their first bishop. His official appointment by Pius VI followed. After 26 years spent in directing the energies of the American Church, Carroll found a final resting place in the Cathedral of the Assumption in Baltimore, Maryland. This Mother Church of United States Catholicism, begun by Carroll, was completed after his death.

## A Victim of Prejudice

From its very beginnings, the Church in the United States was a victim of prejudice. This was almost to be expected, since Protestant groups looked to America as a place for Christianity to be free of "Catholic corruptions and infidelities." Only Catholic and Quaker settlements seemed to recognize the principle of religious freedom. The oldest Catholic Church in the original 13 colonies was the Jesuit Church of Saint Ignatius in Maryland, dating from 1637. But when Catholics lost political control of Maryland, they faced persecution even there. Many foreigners who aided the colonists during the Revolutionary War were Catholics—Count Pulaski and General Kosciusko among them. Daniel and Charles Carroll, cousins of Father John Carroll, both played important roles in the colonial struggle for independence and nationhood.

Organized bigotry against American Catholics surfaced in the 1830s and 1840s. *The Protestant*, a religious weekly, kept the fires of anti-Catholicism burning. Nativist propaganda included such books as *Six Months in a Convent*

and *The Awful Disclosures of Maria Monk.* Anti-Catholic riots in Philadelphia brought loss of life and Church burnings. The Know-Nothing political party succeeded in having a New York law passed forbidding clergymen to hold property. The Ursuline Convent in Charlestown was also burned at Know-Nothing instigation. As the nation continued to move west of the Mississippi, St. Louis Cathedral, built in honor of King Saint Louis IX of France, became the Mother Church of the West. The Belgian-born Jesuit, Peter de Smet, famous as "the Blackrobe," proved himself worth more than a whole army in keeping peace between the United States and the Indians. Senator Benton called him "the best friend the Indians ever had."

The Ku Klux Klan, a Southern secret society aimed at keeping freed Blacks poor and powerless, directed their prejudice against Catholics as well. In 1928, Al Smith, the Catholic governor of New York, was defeated in the presidential race partially because America still wasn't ready to trust a papist.

## John XXIII

With the papacy of John XXIII (1958–1963), papal autocracy and the negative effects of the Council of Trent came to an end. Like Bishop John Carroll, Pope John was "the right person, in the right place, at the right time." He supplied the communication between hearts that Christianity needed, and worked to lead humanity toward becoming "one family." To visiting rabbis at Vatican II his simple welcome was, "I am Joseph, your brother."

Pope John took off the Italian glasses the papacy had worn for so long. He sought for peaceful coexistence with all peoples. The Church was to be Christ to the world, to show itself "the loving Mother of all." In incidentals there was to be diversity; in essentials, unity; in all things, charity.

With unassuming goodness, John XXIII's social encyclicals confronted the world. *Ad Petri Cathedram* (May 29, 1959) spoke of the need for peace and union among nations through justice. *Princeps Pastorum* (November 28, 1959) covered mission needs: respect for native cultures, the conversion of the learned, and social welfare work. *Mater et Magistra* (May 15, 1961) dealt with Christianity and social progress, the proper distribution of wealth, the rights and duties of

218

labor, subsidiarity and the dignity of the person. *Pacem in Terris* (April 10, 1963) presented the basis of right order among human beings, the rights and duties of individuals and states, the divine origin of authority, the duty of taking part in public life, and interreligious cooperation. As head of a worldwide Church, he called for aid to the oppressed, a realization of the nature of Christian baptism, the need for collegiality of the episcopate, ecumenism, and acculturation of the Church in the Third World.

## Pedagogical Notes

1. This chapter covers a very long period of time and many different developments in politics, economics, philosophy, and culture. Encourage students to enhance their classroom study with other materials, maps, and even primary sources.

2. The effects of Vatican II need to be clarified, especially with reference to many of the changes that were made in practice and worship. The end of this chapter lends itself well to a discussion of the role the Church can play in the daily life of all Catholics.

## TEACHER'S RESOURCE 11B

## Theological Notes

The Church's official response to the Reformation was the Council of Trent which began in 1545 and ended in 1563. Exactly 400 years after the conclusion of that General Council, another ecumenical gathering of Catholic bishops, Vatican II (1962–1965), published its first document: *"The Constitution on the Sacred Liturgy"* (December 4, 1963).

While it is true that these two councils were convened for different purposes and under different circumstances, a comparison between their respective approaches to worship (to mention but one example) speaks volumes about the kind of developments that occurred between Trent and Vatican II. We can, of course, see the expected continuity in Church teaching in the liturgical documents from both periods. Yet there are also important differences in tone, manner of presentation and emphasis which suggest the dramatic changes in the Church's self-understanding that took place between the middle of the sixteenth century and the middle of the twentieth century.

Two textual examples can help illustrate this point.

1. From the Council of Trent ("Decree on the Sacraments," No. 1605) comes the following statement: "If anyone says that [the] sacraments are instituted only for the sake of nourishing faith, *anathema* sit." The affirmation of the statement, of course, is that the sacraments do more than simply nourish faith. But notice the tone of the teaching; it's combative. The manner of presentation is harsh, even accusatory. The emphasis of the teaching seems to be punitive in that after stating what the Church declares to be a false belief, it spells out the consequences in no uncertain terms: *anathema sit* (literally, "let him be damned").

2. From Vatican II ("The Constitution on the Sacred Liturgy," Par. 59) comes the statement: "It is ... of the greatest importance that the faithful should easily understand the sacramental signs, and should eagerly frequent those sacraments which were instructed to nourish the Christian life." This Vatican II teaching does not contradict the teaching of Trent cited above, but it affirms (rather than challenges) belief in the sacraments as "nourishment" for Catholics. What is more, the tone of the declaration is affirmative. Its manner of presentation is loving. Its emphasis is pastoral. Quite a difference!

This simple example of development in the Church's proclamation of faith regarding the sacraments during the 400-year period from Trent to Vatican II suggests four important lessons about changes that have occurred in practically any era of Church history we choose to study.

**(1)** Development is part of the Church's nature. It is almost a fifth "mark" of the Church.

**(2)** Development in doctrinal understanding or self-understanding does not threaten the survival and growth of the Church. Just the opposite seems to be the case.

**(3)** While the guidance of legitimate Church authority and doctrine help the Body of Christ stay on course toward the kingdom of God, the primary teacher in the Church—the Holy Spirit—

has a habit of surprising us with new insights, attitudes, and pastoral concerns. Pope John XXIII, who convened Vatican II, was one of God's delightful surprises for us. His efforts at Church renewal could not have been predicted.

(4) The "Golden Age" of the Church should not be identified with some past historical period.

Building upon a rich past, we still look forward to the Golden Age of the future—the final fulfillment of God's kingdom in Christ Jesus. This allows the Church to be hopeful and confident in the face of new situations, experiences and historical developments. It helps us keep our eyes, not simply on ourselves, but on Jesus Christ.

# Time Line—Trent to Vatican II: A.D. 1600 to the Present

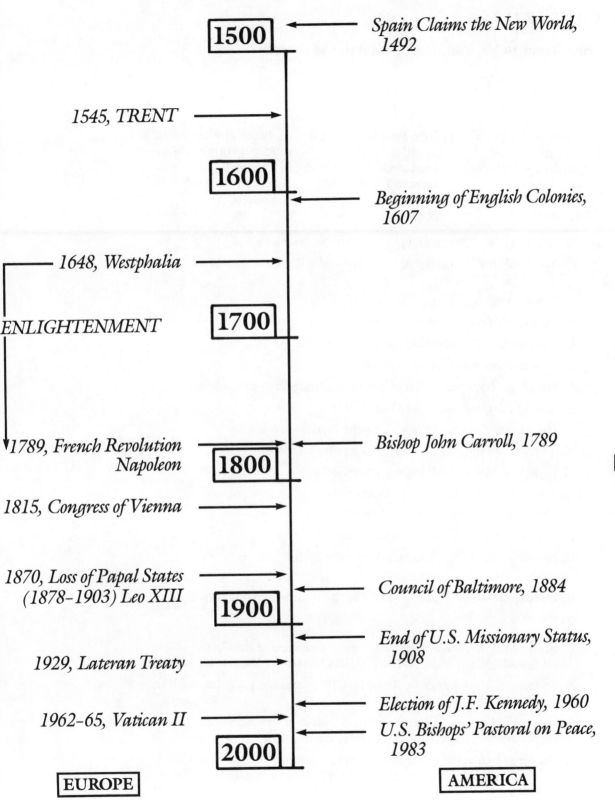

**1500** ← *Spain Claims the New World, 1492*

*1545, TRENT* →

**1600**

← *Beginning of English Colonies, 1607*

*1648, Westphalia* →

*ENLIGHTENMENT*  **1700**

*1789, French Revolution Napoleon* → ← *Bishop John Carroll, 1789*

**1800**

*1815, Congress of Vienna* →

*1870, Loss of Papal States (1878–1903) Leo XIII* → ← *Council of Baltimore, 1884*

**1900**

← *End of U.S. Missionary Status, 1908*

*1929, Lateran Treaty* →

← *Election of J.F. Kennedy, 1960*

*1962–65, Vatican II* → ← *U.S. Bishops' Pastoral on Peace, 1983*

**2000**

**EUROPE**    **AMERICA**

221

Name: _____ Score: _____

# CHAPTER 11 Test

## From Trent to Vatican II: A.D. 1600 to the Present

I.  **Matching:** Place the letter of the best answer on the line. There are extra answers.

a. Congress of Vienna
b. Council of Trent
c. Enlightenment
d. Isaac Jogues
e. Jansenism
f. John XXIII

g. John Paul II
h. Karl Marx
i. Las Casas
j. Lateran Treaty, 1929
k. Leo XIII
l. Napoleon

m. Peace of Westphalia, 1648
n. Propagation of the Faith
o. Vatican II
p. Vincent de Paul
q. Voltaire

___ 1.  Reformed the Church and placed it on the defensive

___ 2.  Tried to bring all missionary activity under Roman control and direction

___ 3.  Noted for his social encyclicals

___ 4.  Architect of modern-day communism

___ 5.  Led the French religious revival

___ 6.  French missionary and martyr

___ 7.  Fought for legal protection of the American Indians under Spain

___ 8.  Settled the question of the Papal States

___ 9.  His writings prepared the way for the French Revolution

___ 10. Tried to use the French Church as a political tool

___ 11. Ended a century of religious wars in Europe

___ 12. Strong opponent of present-day communism

___ 13. Heresy which resembled Calvinism

___ 14. Was inspired to call for a Church Council

___ 15. Redefined the Church and its role in the world

II. **Incorrectly classified.** Place the letter of the term which *does not belong* on the line.

___ 1.  Showed the weakness and conservative character of the Church: (a) Peace of Westphalia, (b) Leo XIII, (c) Congress of Vienna, (d) Pius IX.

___ 2.  Enemies of the Church: (a) Karl Marx, (b) Napoleon, (c) Voltaire, (d) Las Casas.

___ 3.  The early American Church suffered from (a) poor leadership, (b) prejudice, (c) small numbers, (d) lay trusteeism.

___ 4.  Blessings that came to the American Church included (a) John Carroll, (b) emphasis on education, (c) large numbers of immigrants, (d) Know-Nothings.

11

___ 5. Significant milestones in the American Church story: (a) 1789,
(b) 1884, (c) 1917, (d) 1960.

___ 6. Famous American Catholics include (a) Elizabeth Seton, (b) Franklin
D. Roosevelt, (c) James Gibbons, (d) Isaac Hecker.

___ 7. Characteristics of Vatican II: (a) autocratic spirit, (b) worldwide
representation, (c) liturgical reform, (d) use of modern technology.

___ 8. Characteristics of the American Church: (a) outreach to the
immigrants, (b) emphasis on education, (c) largely urban, (d) few
vocations.

___ 9. The only non-Italian to sit on the throne of Peter since 1523 was
(a) John XXIII, (b) John Paul II, (c) Paul VI, (d) John Paul I.

___ 10. Some characteristics of present-day American Catholicism are
(a) unity in diversity, (b) one-sixth of the nation's population,
(c) uninvolved in social justice, (d) active in support of the foreign
missions.

**III. Essay:** Choose two.

1. Why was the Church of John XXIII in need of Vatican II?

2. What aspects of the Catholic Church in America, past and present, make
you proud to be a member?

3. What was unique about Vatican II? How did it change the Church?

⑪

## CHAPTER 11 Test

### From Trent to Vatican II: A.D. 1600 to the Present

Answer Key

**I.**

1. b
2. n
3. k
4. h
5. p
6. d
7. i
8. j
9. q
10. l
11. m
12. g
13. e
14. f
15. o

**II.**

1. b
2. d
3. a
4. d
5. c
6. b
7. a
8. d
9. b
10. c

**III.**

Answers will vary.

# CHAPTER 11

## SECTION 1

### Text Questions (Student text pages 299–305)

**Page 300**

(1) Answers will vary but will probably include the reunification of Germany and the Persian Gulf Crisis.

(2) Some answers might include Mother Teresa, John Paul II, or the priests who serve in Latin America.

**Page 301**

(3) Customs and culture form a part of a people's identity and links to the past. Some practices which might have to be changed could include polygamy or idol worship.

**Page 303**

(4) Both Rousseau and the Church teach that human nature is good, but the Church teaches that its goodness comes from God who created it that way. Rousseau removed God from the picture.

(5) Answers will vary. People who rely on reason only are always looking for proof which is not necessary for faith.

**Page 304**

(6) People often fear change. Galileo was suggesting that the earth was not the center of the universe and that was threatening. It might have implied that Church teaching was in error.

(7) The people who were angry at their government for its abuses also remembered the Church and its past and took revenge for both at the same time.

### SECTION 1 Checkpoint! (page 306)

### Review

(1) The Peace of Westphalia ended the Thirty Years' War and resulted in Europe being divided into northern Protestant and southern Catholic regions.

(2) In France new religious orders were established. They were not cloistered, they cared for the sick, worked for the reform of the clergy, and preached missions to the laity.

(3) The Office of the Propagation of the Faith was set up to regulate missionary activity under Roman control.

(4) Deism says that God exists and that God created the world, but has no further role in it. It reflects the reliance of the Enlightenment on the use of human reason and the belief in the independence of human beings.

(5) During the French Revolution the Church was wealthy and was seen as a center of abuses by the poor.

(6) Words to Know: *Vincent de Paul* (leading figure in the French religious revival who worked for the sick and poor); *Propagation of the Faith* (papal society created to bring about a uniform policy in the Church's missionary activity); *Descartes* (French philosopher who denied anything not able to be evaluated by scientific reason); *Enlightenment* (age in which skepticism and philosophies that stressed reason over faith flourished); *Galileo* (astronomer who discovered that the earth revolves around the sun and who was condemned by the Church); *French Revolution* (revolt of the French people against the injustices of their society, 1789).

## In Your World

(1) Locate the place where the missionary served on a map. Put the experience into its political, economic, and cultural context so that students see the whole picture.

(2) Use a historical time line or book that traces developments. Encourage students to find as many changes in as many different areas as they can.

(3) Supply a world map or have students trace one from an atlas. Or have students work in groups and break up the globe into sections.

## Scripture Search

In this passage, the people demand that God give them a king. They wanted a monarchy instead of judges to rule over them. Samuel, one of the leaders, feels rejected. God understands the motivation of the people and has Samuel warn them of the consequences of a monarchy. They refuse to listen and God grants their request. The Israelites were not thinking of their best interest. They acted selfishly.

## SECTION 2
## Text Questions (Student text pages 307–317)

### Page 310

(8) Answers will vary.

(9) Answers might include renewal of interest in spiritual power or concentration on social issues instead of political ones.

(10) Leo XIII stressed care for the poor, orphans, and the oppressed in imitation of Jesus, just as the earliest Christians did.

### Page 312

(11) The Churches in Eastern Europe have become legitimate again and are encouraging people to return to worship, have begun training priests again, and are returning to and rebuilding churches.

### Page 314

(12) With separation of Church and state, the Church can make its own decisions about its leaders and policies.

(13) The people who founded the United States came here to escape religious persecution, so they wanted to be sure that everyone here would be free to worship as they wished.

(14) Today there are the Ku Klux Klan, the John Birch Society, and the various groups of White Supremicists.

### Page 317

(15) Answers will vary.

(16) The Catholic school system gave the immigrant populations a sense of community and familiarity in a new place. The people knew what kind of education their children would be getting and what values and traditions would be taught.

## SECTION 2 Checkpoint! (page 318)
## Review

(1) There were many new discoveries, inventions, and exploration in the 1800s. There were also new systems of thought that threatened the Church, such as atheism and materialism.

(2) Pius IX had to flee Rome and was seen as being out of touch with the times. The Papal State lost its independence and temporal power during his pontificate. Leo XIII expressed concern for social

issues like the labor movement, established Catholic universities, and was a champion of Catholic social action.

**(3)** John Carroll was the first bishop of Baltimore, encouraged the opening of the first Jesuit college, started a seminary, and was instrumental in the founding of new religious orders in America.

**(4)** Some answers might include Elizabeth Seton (founded the Sisters of Charity and Catholic school system); Mother Katherine Drexel (missionary to the Indians); or Cardinal Gibbons (organized Catholic labor).

**(5)** The Lateran Treaty set aside 100 acres in Rome as the Vatican. It became fully independent as a Papal State, and therefore released the Church from political obligation to anyone.

**(6)** Before Vatican II, the Church had been developing from all its missionary activity. Catholics became integrated into all levels of society. Political developments like the election of John F. Kennedy, and rapid social changes throughout the world, led to the calling of the Council.

**(7)** Words to Know: *Lateran Treaty* (1929 document giving full sovereignty to Vatican City); *Know-Nothings* (an American political party opposed to all foreigners and Catholics); *Lay trusteeism* (lay members' control of parish government).

### In Your World

**(1)** Use any of the reference materials mentioned throughout these chapters (*Encyclopedia of Religion*). Focus on the accomplishments of the person chosen and the hardships he or she may have had to face.

**(2)** Some of the countries which might provide a good focus are Russia, Romania, or Poland. Have a librarian show students how to find journal articles. Focus on the role of various religions in the independence movements of these countries.

### Scripture Search

The Council dealt with the questions of how converts from a different cultural and religious background should be admitted to the new faith. This made Christians realize the true nature of following Jesus. Groups of Catholics from different cultures have to learn to be tolerant of other Catholics whose customs may be different. This chapter follows the development of an American Catholic Church which has its own character and also fits into the universal Church.

## SECTION 3
### Text Questions (Student text pages 319–324)

**Page 320**

**(17)** Advances of this century made it easier for all the bishops to communicate at the Council and for the Council to be understood by the rest of the world, Catholic and non-Catholic.

**Page 322**

**(18)** Other changes included: religious women were freed from the traditional habit, lay people were given a greater role in worship and government (eucharistic ministers), and women took on greater participation in the liturgy.

**Page 324**

**(19)** Answers will vary, but some students may have heard criticisms that giving up the habit or not using Latin is being too liberal and breaking with tradition.

**(20)** Many people find tradition a stabilizing factor and are reluctant to change because it means they will have to modify their own behavior or attitudes.

**(21)** Answers will vary but will probably include the shortage of priests, materialism, poverty, and the abortion debate.

## SECTION 3 Checkpoint! (page 325)
### Review

**(1)** Vatican II dealt with the Church's role in the modern world, and was worldwide in its representation. It also used modern technology.

**(2)** Scripture provided the key to understanding how the original Church saw itself, and how we can continue that image. New ways of interpreting Scripture were important for defining and understanding that self-image.

**(3)** Since Vatican II there have been meetings, papal encyclicals, and World Synods of Bishops.

**(4)** Some Catholics are alienated by the increased role for women, the new emphasis on Scripture, and the vocation crisis.

**(5)** Optimists see increased lay involvement in ministry, shared responsibility, a service-oriented authority, and a renewal of ecumenism. Pessimists see a decline in Catholic schools, a decline in Church attendance, and a drop in the number of vocations.

**(6)** Words to Know: *John XXIII* (pope who ushered in a new age of the Church by summoning the Second Vatican Council to update the Church); *Vatican II* (Council held to create a Church open to change, and committed to religious freedom, ecumenism, and a new role for the laity); *John Paul II* (the first non-Italian pope since 1523).

## In Your World

**(1)** Be sure the person invited has a balanced opinion about the changes. Have students ask questions about very practical and visible aspects of the differences.

**(2)** Choosing the issue is important. It might be the ordination of women, celibacy in the priesthood, or an issue that is related to education. Be sure that both sides are represented.

**(3)** Bring a copy (or copies) of the documents from Vatican II. Choose a short portion dealing with prayer, ecumenism, or another issue in which students express an interest.

## Scripture Search

Luke presents the activity of the Spirit in relation to Jesus. At Jesus' baptism the Spirit descends upon Jesus, enabling him to initiate his mission. At the end of his earthly mission, Jesus tells his disciples that they should not worry about what they will say in their own defense because the Spirit will teach them what to say. As John explains, the Spirit bears witness to Jesus and still does today. The role of the Spirit today is to guide us to truth.

## CHAPTER 11 Review (pages 326–327)
## Study

**(1)** Three-fourths of the peasant population of Germany perished during the Thirty Years' War.

**(2)** The Sisters of Charity did not remain confined to their convents. They cared for the sick and poor, and were active in society.

**(3)** Missionary journeys were voyages to explore and open up new worlds for the Church, and to evangelize. French efforts in the United States did not lead to any permanent gains for the Church,

and in some areas, missionaries were not sensitive to the local customs and cultures.

**(4)** Descartes believed that everything must be able to be proved by scientific reason, including faith. Rousseau regarded all human nature as naturally good without God's playing a part in this. They challenged the roles of faith and mystery in human life.

**(5)** Galileo discovered that the earth revolves around the sun and not vice versa. His discovery challenged Church teaching of the centrality of the earth.

**(6)** The French Revolution was caused by unjust taxation, extremes of wealth and poverty, and a general economic crisis. The Church was seen as a bastion of wealth and privilege. As a result, the Church was forced to rid itself of wealth and to identify more with the poor people.

**(7)** During the 1800s, many countries in the "New World" became independent. Some European countries were unified, and new systems of thought were introduced. The Church defended itself against atheism and charges that it was linked to outdated political systems. It was seen as being resistant to change.

**(8)** Some leading Catholic figures include John Henry Newman, Thérèse of Lisieux, Leo XIII, and Mother Cabrini.

**(9)** Leo XIII supported the rights of workers, opened the Vatican archives to scholars, founded several Catholic universities, and championed Catholic social action.

**(10)** The two world wars resulted in the establishment of Vatican City, and in efforts by the Vatican to prevent war. After World War II, many communist governments began to persecute the Church and other religious organizations in many countries.

**(11)** Carroll loved both the Church and America. Under Carroll's direction the Church grew and prospered in America.

**(12)** The influx of immigrants increased the Church's numbers in the United States. The Church provided education, Americanization, orphanages, etc.

**(13)** Vatican Council II was called to address the Church's role in the modern world.

**(14)** Vatican II returned the Church to its early roots. It emphasized tradition and Scripture.

**⓫**

Vatican II worked to make Catholicism a credible voice to the world. Vatican II also introduced liturgical changes and addressed the issues of human freedom and dignity.

## Action

(1) Use the time line from the previous chapter as a guide. Encourage students to include as many different kinds of events as they can.

(2) This activity will mean that students will have to become familiar with the events and activities sponsored in their parishes.

(3) The speaker could be a teacher, missionary, nurse, or other professional. Be sure students make the connection between religious vocation and the daily life of the person.

## Prayer

Discuss the effect music has on all of us. Does it distract or enhance the prayer experience? What about music in the dentist's office, or the shopping mall? How can music be used as an expression of spirituality? Try using music in class. Experiment with different types.

**11**

# From Trent to Vatican II: A.D. 1600 to the Present

**OVERVIEW:** The goal of this chapter is to trace the positive and negative political and religious changes over the past 400 years, culminating in the rise of American Catholicism and the accomplishments of Vatican II.

**OBJECTIVES:** The students will:

- Discuss the rapid developments, both positive and negative in the world and the Church from 1600–1800.

- Learn about the origins of the American Catholic community and the rise of new ways of thinking and governing that threatened the Church.

- List and discuss the reforms made, and those still needed in the Church, and the challenges the Church faces in the future.

**TIME FRAME: One to one-and-a-half hours.**

**MATERIALS: Time line, documents from Vatican II, map.**

**PROCEDURE:**

*Into:* Prayer—Begin class with this prayer spoken from the Apollo 8 Moon mission: "Give us, O God, the vision which can see Your love in the world in spite of human failure. Give us the faith, the trust, the goodness in spite of our ignorance and weakness. Give us the knowledge that we may continue to pray with understanding hearts and show us what each one of us can do to set forth the coming of the day of universal peace."

*Through:*

Activity One:

1. Ask students to name some explorers of the seventeenth and eighteenth centuries. Where did they go? How were native peoples treated? Describe early conversion attempts which tried to force people to adopt European customs, and their failure. Use question 3 on page 301 to encourage discussion.

2. Ask students to discuss the differences between reason and faith. Do they conflict with each other? Describe the challenges and changes in society that accompanied scientific discoveries (like Galileo's) and the emergence of new philosophies. Use question 5 on page 303 as a guide for discussion.

3. Introduce the French Revolution. Did students know that the French used the American Revolution as a model? The Church was identified with the old order and therefore blamed for many problems facing society. Show how closely the Church was related to social, economic, and political matters. Is this good or bad?

Activity Two:

1. Ask for definitions of atheism, materialism, nationalism, and secularism. How could the Church defend itself against these new movements? Are all "isms" necessarily a threat? Of resisting change, assimilation, or adaptation, which is the best way to treat such a threat (or is there a best way)?

**⑪**

2. Do students know when Catholics began to arrive in America? What contributions can immigrants of all kinds make to a country (even today)? And what problems may arise? Why are people often intolerant of immigrants? Show how the Church evolved as a structure that could care for and build up the immigrant populations into an American Catholic Church.

3. Have students name as many changes as they can that have occurred so far in the twentieth century (airplanes, automobiles, moon landing, VCR, nuclear weapons). Give the dates of both world wars and discuss the establishment of the Vatican in the time between them. Introduce the Holocaust and make sure students understand the horrors of genocide. Discuss racial and religious hatred with the students.

Activity Three:

1. Can students identify John XXIII? Discuss Vatican II as the Council that brought the Church into the twentieth century and the modern world in a number of ways. Bring in the Council documents.

2. Have students discuss the kinds of objections and disputes that are being raised in the Church today. What feelings are at the source of these divisions?

3. Take a poll. Is the Church's future optimistic or pessimistic and why? List the specific changes students think the Church, and their parish(es) will face in the next 50 years. What role will today's students and tomorrow's adults play in the development of the Church?

**Beyond:** Suggest that students read "John XIII—The Interim Pope," on page 321, and focus on questions 19–21 on page 324. Encourage them to complete activity 3 from Section 3, "In Your World," page 325.

**Prayer:** Close class with the prayer found in "A People at Prayer," page 320.

**⑪**

**CHAPTER 11 QUIZ**
# From Trent to Vatican II: 1600 to the Present

**I.** Place the letter of the *best* answer on the line.

___ **1.** The century following Trent was marked by (a) peace and prosperity, (b) religious wars, (c) natural disasters.

___ **2.** Leading figure in the French religious revival: (a) Ignatius, (b) Voltaire, (c) Vincent de Paul.

___ **3.** Carried the faith to the New World: (a) Spain and Italy, (b) France and England, (c) Spain and France.

___ **4.** The Age of Enlightenment (a) strengthened the Church, (b) undermined the Church, (c) had no connection with the Church.

___ **5.** The French Revolution (a) split and weakened, (b) did not affect, (c) helped the Church.

___ **6.** Napoleon attempted to (a) use the Church, (b) ignore the Church, (c) destroy the Church.

___ **7.** Liberalism put the Church on the (a) alert, (b) offensive, (c) defensive.

___ **8.** The nineteenth century was the century of (a) great pontiffs, (b) little saints, (c) totalitarianism.

___ **9.** His efforts put the Church in touch with the world: (a) Pius IX, (b) Leo XIII, (c) Pius X.

___ **10.** Greatest threat to the twentieth-century Church: (a) communism, (b) Third World, (c) Holocaust.


**II.** Mark true (+) or false (o).

___ **1.** The English planted the Church in America.

___ **2.** The American ideal has come to be identified as white, Anglo-Saxon, and Protestant (WASP).

___ **3.** Colonial America had little use for Catholics.

___ **4.** The U.S. Constitution helped Catholics by forbidding an established Church.

___ **5.** John Carroll's diocese, established in 1789, was small in both Catholic population and area.

___ **6.** Carroll's policies set the Church and the nation at odds with one another.

___ **7.** Immigration has been the primary cause of the growth of the American Church.

___ **8.** The Civil War strengthened the image of the Catholic Church in America.

___ **9.** Most of the Church's energies in the post-Civil War decades were devoted to evangelizing blacks.

___ **10.** Cardinal Gibbons identified the American Church with the working class.

___ **11.** Until the twentieth century, the American Church occupied a missionary status.

___ **12.** The American Church was never divided by schism.

___ **13.** Catholic ghettos lasted until World War II.

___ **14.** The election of John F. Kennedy was a turning point in America's acceptance of Catholicism.

___ **15.** American Catholics have always presented a united front.

Name: _____ Score: _____

**III.** Mark true (+) or false (o).

Vatican II...

___ **1.** was enthusiastically welcomed by Church leaders.

___ **2.** developed from an inspiration of John XXIII.

___ **3.** was aimed at renewal of the Church and the unity of all Christians.

___ **4.** tried to resist change.

___ **5.** saw the Church as apart from the world.

___ **6.** emphasized law, obedience, and uniformity.

___ **7.** made use of modern technology.

___ **8.** changed attitudes as well as practices.

___ **9.** was wholeheartedly accepted by all Catholics.

___ **10.** helped centralize Church authority in Rome.

⑪

# CHAPTER 11 PRE-TEST

Mark true (+) or false (o).

In the period from 1600 to the present ...

___ **1.** Christendom fell apart and was replaced by rival national states.

___ **2.** Europe expanded its horizons and territorial possessions.

___ **3.** the Church crossed the Atlantic and penetrated into Asia.

___ **4.** democratic ideas battled against absolute kings.

___ **5.** science opened new worlds and technology changed the way people lived and worked.

___ **6.** the Church defined the doctrine of papal infallibility .

___ **7.** the Papal States were reduced to one-sixth of a square mile within the city of Rome.

___ **8.** saints, martyrs, and religious communities multiplied.

___ **9.** two world wars brought disillusionment with progress and plunged the world toward atheism.

___ **10.** Vatican II turned the Church in new directions.

## Chapter 11 Quiz
## Answer Key

**I.**

1. b

2. c

3. c

4. b

5. a

6. a

7. c

8. b

9. b

10. a

**II.**

1. o

2. +

3. +

4. +

5. o

6. o

7. +

8. +

9. o

10. +

11. +

12. o

13. +

14. +

15. o

**III.**

1. o

2. +

3. +

4. o

5. o

6. o

7. +

8. +

9. o

10. o

# CHAPTER 11 PRE-TEST
Answer Key

1. +

2. +

3. +

4. +

5. +

6. +

7. +

8. +

9. +

10. +

## Panel Questions

1. Why did the Protestant Revolt put the Church on the defensive?

2. Why did the French Revolution make the Church suspicious of democracy?

3. Was the Church's loss of the Papal States a blessing in disguise?

4. What makes the American Church unique?

5. How was Vatican II different from any other Church Council?

## Simulation: The Nineteenth-Century Church

Divide students into four groups: (1) European Bishops, (2) European Common People, (3) American Bishops, and (4) American Catholics.

Give each group its corresponding task sheet from below.

**1. EUROPEAN BISHOPS:**

*Read:* Michael Pennock. *Your Church and You* (Notre Dame, IN: Ave Maria Press, 1983), pp. 205-7.

*Background:* The Church has survived because it is the establishment, linked to wealth and power. The liberal revolutionaries intend to overthrow the Church when they overthrow the kings of Europe. You are "establishment" yourselves, from old families in old dioceses, and very comfortable.

*Your Task:* (1) to decide the relationship between Church and state, (2) to tell what the Church (you) will do for the common people, and (3) to formulate two statements; one for Rome and one for the people of your dioceses.

**2.** EUROPEAN COMMON PEOPLE:

*Read:* Wm. H. McNeill, *Ecumene: Story of Humanity* (New York: Harper & Row, 1973), pp. 583-4, 589-90.

*Background:* You are working too many hours for too little pay. The quality of your homes, workplaces, and cities are getting richer while you are getting poorer. The existing governments are ignoring your requests for help and you are beginning to listen to people like Karl Marx who offers hope for the workers.

*Your task:* (1) to decide what the Church should do for the common people, and (2) to formulate a statement to your bishops stating your position.

**3.** AMERICAN BISHOPS:

*Read:* Linden, *et al., History of Our American Republic* (Laidlaw, 1981) pp. 342-6.

*Background:* Most of you were born in Europe and came to America as missionaries to the immigrants from your homeland. You have built big ethnic parishes. You remember what it was like back home, when you were part of the "established Church," but now you are in a religious and ethnic minority, holding together poor and uneducated immigrants who are feared and distrusted by many American citizens, and some influential government leaders and lawmakers.

*Your tasks:* (1) to decide the relationship between Church and state, (2) to tell what the Church (you) will do for the common people, and (3) to formulate two statements: one for Rome and one for the people of your dioceses.

**4.** AMERICAN CATHOLICS:

*Read:* Morison, *et al. Concise History of the American Republic* (Oxford University Press, 1977), pp. 386-8.

*Background:* Nearly all of you are immigrants and laborers in the factories or on the railroads. Your parish is the center of your daily life: Sunday Mass (with the sermon in your native language, *not* English), a school where your children learn American ways, social organizations, a newspaper, a credit union, and financial assistance when needed.

*Your tasks:* (1) to decide what the Church should do for the common people, and (2) to formulate a statement of your position to your bishops.

Allow 20–30 minutes for groups to make their assessments and decisions. If the suggested readings are not readily available, others of a similar nature can be substituted. When groups are ready, have the American bishops meet the American Catholics, while all the Europeans observe. The people present their case and the bishops respond. Reverse the procedure with the Americans as observers. Next have all the bishops meet and laity observe.

The simulation is intended to show students how the Church in Europe began to separate itself from the "establishment" connections and was able to help its people, even though, in some ways, it may have upset Rome.

## Additional Reading

Church, F. Forrester and Terrence J. Mulry, eds. *The Macmillan Book of Earliest Christian Prayers.* New York: Macmillan, 1988.

McDonnell, Kilian. "Infallibility Again?" *Worship* 53:1 (1979): 56–66.

Rahner, Karl. "Towards a Fundamental Theological Interpretation of Vatican II." *Theological Studies* 40:4 (1979): 716–27.

Sherry, Gerard E. "Church Authority: Not All Roads Lead to Rome." *U.S. Catholic* 48:9 (1983): 45-51.

Wojtyla, Karol. *Prayers of Pope John Paul II.* Edited by John F. McDonald. New York: Crossroad, 1982.

⑪

## CHAPTER 12

# Christ Gathering His People Today

(Text pages 328–353)

## FOCUS

**Doctrinal:** Christ's mission of establishing God's reign is carried out in the Church by proclamation of the word, sanctification of the faithful, and witness of loving service to the world. Proclamation of the word is achieved mainly through evangelization and catechesis.

**Personal:** How can evangelization become a part of my daily life?

## OBJECTIVES

**Cognitive:** (a) to understand Christ's mission and how it is continued in the Church today; (b) to learn the process of evangelization and the role of catechesis in the church.

**Affective:** (a) to appreciate the ongoing need for catechesis and existing opportunities for it; (b) to grow in love for my faith and to want to share it with others.

## Chapter 12 Outline

### SECTION 1
**God's Mission for the Church**

> The Mission of Jesus
> The Mission of the Church in Our World
> *Prophet, Priest, and King—Israel's Leaders* (text feature)
> *On This Rock* (margin feature)
> Gathering the People—Evangelization

### SECTION 2
**An Evangelizing People**

> How to Be a Successful Evangelizer
> Who Needs Evangelization
> Active Catholics
> *Communion of Saints* (margin feature)
> Inactive Catholics
> Those Outside the Church
> The RCIA: Evangelization in Action
> Catechesis
> Content and Methods
> *Rebellion and Renewal—Thomas Merton* (text feature)
> New Emphasis in Catechesis

TEACHER'S
PREVIEW

## SECTION 3
### The Many Missions of the Church

Twenty Years in India

New Direction

Evangelization and Progress

*A People at Prayer* (margin feature)

*Missions and a Nobel Peace Prize* (text feature)

The Sleeping Giant of Evangelization

⑫

# TEACHER'S RESOURCE 12A

## Historical Notes

In only 200 years, the American Catholic Church has grown tremendously. The Catholic population of the United States has grown from 1 percent in 1776 to 26 percent in 1990. Still, today an average of one-third of every Catholic's relatives and friends are inactive in the Church. Forty percent of all Americans have no Church affiliation. It has been shown that 81 percent of all converts are made through personal contact with active Church members.

## Pedagogical Notes

1. As you introduce the last three chapters of the text, you might want to return to the "image" motif presented in the first five chapters. You can now contrast the external and internal images of the Church traced throughout its history. These last three chapters reflect the way the Church and its members are the image of Christ's encounter with the world.

2. There are many good reference works available that deal with world religious traditions and with the statistics about world populations. One that you might want to consult is the *World Christian Encyclopedia,* compiled by David B. Barrett (New York: Oxford University Press).

3. This chapter is a good opportunity to discuss the purpose and methods of evangelization. Respect for the beliefs and traditions of others is important. Evangelization will not be successful if it is approached with a feeling of superiority or dominance. Sincerity and faith are needed.

# TEACHER'S RESOURCE 12B

## Theological Notes

Christ continues to gather his people today. We are now, as we have always been, a ministering community; a community called Church. The Greek word for Church describes in detail what it means to be a ministering community. "*Ekklesia*" (Church) in the language of the New Testament comes from two Greek words: "*EK*" and "*kalein*" which means "to call out." The Church is the "called-out" people. We are called out of the narrowness of our own self-

concern and gathered together by the Spirit to go forth on a mission that Jesus gave us.

Being Church, therefore, implies being a missionary people. We may not travel to distant lands as Saint Paul and other great missionaries of the past and present have done, but the obligation to proclaim the Gospel to all the nations rests upon us just the same. **How** we feel called to follow Christ as his disciples and ministers is a personal question, answered by the unique personal signs of our commitment. **That** we respond to the call, however, is absolutely necessary if we claim to belong in and to the ministering Church.

There are many images that might be used to help students understand the missionary imperative of Christianity, but the one that seems to bring the message home to many Catholics these days is the image of hospitality. The Church—especially as experienced at the level of parish—should be a place and a people of hospitality.

Everyone knows what good hosts and hostesses do. There's nothing difficult about the concept. First, hospitable people place a high value on making others feel welcome. While they treasure their privacy, they also recognize that setting the table for guests and attending to their needs are tangible, human gestures of the love of God that Jesus asks us to profess. Table fellowship, as we recall from Scripture, is a sign of the kingdom of God. When we share our food and ourselves with others, therefore, we proclaim the kingdom of God.

What is more, when we make signs of hospitality, we are attempting to love as God loves—with no strings attached. The gracious host, for example, doesn't invite people to join the family for dinner with the provision that the guests promise to return the favor! It's a poor hostess indeed who adds to her invitation: "There will be a modest charge of $12.95 for my dinner party. Cash, check or Visa accepted." People of welcome and hospitality don't keep track of who owes them invitations or favors in return.

Finally, hospitable people go out of their way to identify those who need special attention: The man who recalled that his friend's wife was deployed in the Middle East during the Iraqi War and invited his friend out to a movie or dinner was being a Christian host. The mother who takes time from her busy day to bring a card and gift to someone in the hospital displays the hospitality of Jesus. Teens can be hosts and hostesses too by paying attention to friends who seem to be angry or discouraged for no apparent reason.

It doesn't really matter how simple the gesture of self-giving is. Whenever we respond to the needs of others by making of ourselves signs of welcome, concern and healing, we are ministers of hospitality in the kingdom of God. We are missionaries in the sense that we accept Christ's call out of ourselves, and because we do, we are his Church in the world.

**12**

# The Father's Plan Unfolding: Hebrew History

## *Hebrew History*

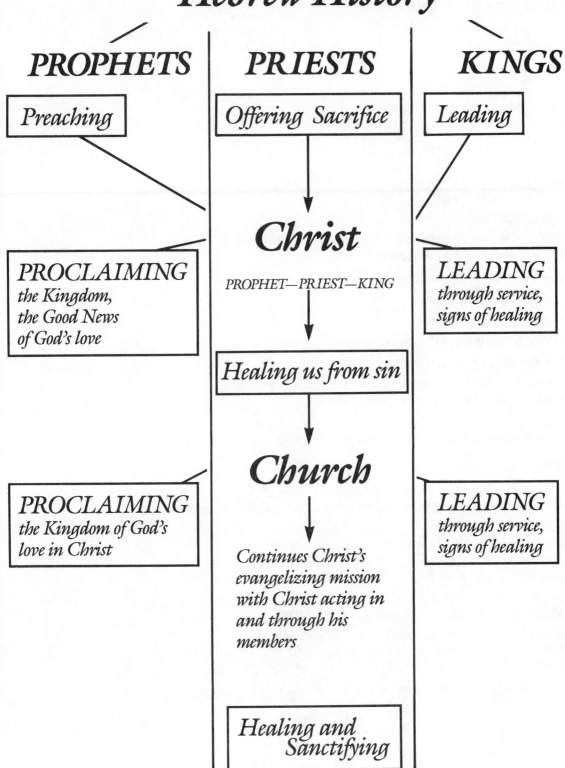

### PROPHETS

Preaching

PROCLAIMING
the Kingdom,
the Good News
of God's love

PROCLAIMING
the Kingdom of God's
love in Christ

### PRIESTS

Offering Sacrifice

## *Christ*

PROPHET—PRIEST—KING

Healing us from sin

## *Church*

Continues Christ's
evangelizing mission
with Christ acting in
and through his
members

Healing and
Sanctifying

### KINGS

Leading

LEADING
through service,
signs of healing

LEADING
through service,
signs of healing

**12**

239

Name: _____  Score: _____

## CHAPTER 12  Test

## Christ Gathering His People Together

I.  **Matching.** Place the letter of the *best* answer on the line. There are extra items.

a. CCD                  f. catechumens          k. missions
b. PSR                  g. converson            l. priest
c. RCIA                 h. evangelization       m. prophet
d. Age of the Church    i. kingdom              n. utopia
e. catechesis           j. mission

___ 1. An image for the state of creation in which all things are in order according to God's will

___ 2. A turning to Christ

___ 3. The activity by which the Church proclaims the Gospel so that faith may be aroused, unfold, and grow

___ 4. Efforts to plant the Church in lands where Christ has not been preached

___ 5. One who announces salvation

___ 6. A program for catechumens

___ 7. Interval between Christ's first and second coming

___ 8. Persons turning to Christ for the first time

___ 9. Any activity that helps people to hear, understand, interiorize, and respond to God's will in service and celebration

II.  **Incorrectly classified.** Place the letter of the item that *does not belong* on the line.

___ 1. Jesus told his Apostles (a) to spread the Good News, (b) to share his mission, (c) to complete the kingdom, (d) that he would remain with them.

___ 2. Evangelization (a) means sharing Christ's mission, (b) requires becoming a "born-again" Christian, (c) originated with Jesus, (d) is a mind-set.

___ 3. Evangelization is carried out primarily through (a) catechizing, (b) healing and miracles, (c) missionary work, (d) preaching.

___ 4. Successful evangelizers need to be (a) argument winners, (b) enthusiastic, (c) sensitive to the Holy Spirit, (d) witnesses to Christ in their own life.

___ 5. All people need evangelization except (a) Catholics, (b) Protestants, (c) unbelievers, (d) none of the above.

___ 6. The RCIA (a) is found in every parish, (b) has several stages, (c) is a powerful agent of evangelization, (d) involves the whole Christian community.

___ 7. Catechesis (a) answers the questions that arise after we accept Jesus, (b) is a lifelong process, (c) should be centered in God's Word, (d) should avoid contemporary problems.

___ 8. Evangelization in the missions (a) involves medical service, (b) embraces education in secular subjects, (c) employs all that is valuable in a given culture, (d) avoids social reform.

___ 9. Jesus came to save us by fulfilling the Old Testament roles of (a) evangelist, (b) king, (c) priest, (d) prophet.

**III. Essay.** Choose two.

1. How could you be an evangelizer in your home? neighborhood? school? parish?

2. Why is the Church committed to a program of evangelization?

3. What was the mission of Jesus and how is it carried out in the world today?

⑫

## CHAPTER 12  Test
## Christ Gathering His People Together
Answer Key

**I.**

**1.** i

**2.** g

**3.** h

**4.** k

**5.** m

**6.** c

**7.** d

**8.** f

**9.** e

**II.**

**1.** c

**2.** b

**3.** b

**4.** a

**5.** d

**6.** a

**7.** d

**8.** d

**9.** a

**III.**

Answers will vary.

# CHAPTER 12

## SECTION 1

### Text Questions (Student text pages 329–335)

**Page 330**

**(1)** Being sent on a mission means being given a purpose to take a journey or act as a representative. It is a responsibility.

**(2)** It means that the reign of God has started in Jesus' words and deeds, and mostly by his resurrection, but that it will not be complete until the Second Coming.

**(3)** Examples of kingdom living might include being active in a charitable activity like a soup kitchen or shelter, being politically active in social causes, volunteering for work in your faith community or as a missionary, or donating time as a doctor, dentist, or lawyer to help those who cannot afford your services.

**Page 332**

**(4)** Signs of global unity are the unification of East and West Germany, the changes in South African society and the freeing of Nelson Mandela, efforts to improve our environment, and to wipe out disease and human rights abuses. The common people help by putting pressure on political leaders, boycotts, volunteering, etc.

**(5)** Oppression exists today in bigotry against African-Americans, Asians, Hispanics, the poor, and Jews. Oppression slows progress, lessens human dignity, and makes everyone suffer.

**(6)** Answers will vary.

**Page 335**

**(7)** Answers will vary and may include peer pressure, temptations from the media, economic worries, or political obstacles.

**(8)** Jesus evangelized by preaching and by his own example. He ate with the disenfranchised and preached the Sermon on the Mount.

## SECTION 1 Checkpoint! (page 336)

### Review
**(1)** Before Jesus, the will of God was revealed through Israel's prophets, priests, and kings.

**(2)** Jesus carried out his mission by announcing that the Father was offering salvation through him, by gathering followers and being an example of service, and by giving his life in a sacrifice of worship.

**(3)** This saying means that the reign of God is initiated or started in Jesus' life and death, but that it is not complete until the Second Coming.

**(4)** Evangelization is carried out through preaching, catechizing, missionary work, and witness of life.

**(5)** The six elements are Christian witness, proclaiming the Gospel, inner acceptance, entry into Church community, participation in the sacraments, and initiating evangelization.

(6) Words to Know: *mission* (being sent on an official task which may be religious, political, scientific, or military); *kingdom* (an image for the state of creation in which all things are in accord with God's will); *evangelization* (proclaiming the Gospel so that faith may be aroused, unfold, and grow); *conversion* (to turn completely away from present beliefs or behavior).

## In Your World

(1) Stress the dedication and commitment needed, and the difficulty faced when talking to people about the faith.

(2) Be sure your description of kingdom living includes as many aspects of personal and professional life as students can come up with.

## Scripture Search

In Mark, Jesus is preaching the Gospel message of God; In John, Jesus is represented as the Son of God, and the embodiment of God and as an emissary of God sent to do God's will. In Luke, Jesus proclaims God's will and acts as an example.

## SECTION 2

## Text Questions (Student text pages 337–345)

### Page 338

(9) People do not respond well to threats or fear tactics. When evangelizers appear superior, the personal touch is lost.

(10) The media can reach those who are homebound, can relay information to large numbers of people effectively, and can also relay visual images of daily lived discipleship.

### Page 340

(11) It shows that the work is not yet complete and that we all have a lot to learn and room to grow.

(12) Just as Jesus led by example, we can also live the Gospel message and show people how our faith is expressed daily in our actions.

### Page 342

(13) Formation in the catechumenate echoes the ancient process of conversion adopted by all followers of Jesus, especially Gentiles who had a three-year period of learning precede their baptism and full inclusion in the Christian community.

(14) Answers will vary.

### Page 345

(15) Answers will vary.

(16) Catechesis reminds us that we are the body of Christ and that our whole being is dedicated to carrying out the Gospel message.

(17) Today the Church should be addressing such issues as homelessness, war and peace, and oppression.

## SECTION 2  Checkpoint! (page 346)

### Review

(1) A good evangelizer should be enthusiastic and willing to share. She or he should also be individual oriented, interested in others, and able to live the Gospel as well as teach it.

(2) The five groups are: (a) active Catholics; (b) inactive Catholics; (c) those outside the Catholic Church (Protestants); (d) religious non-Christians; and (e) those without religious affiliation.

(3) The RCIA is a version of the baptismal rite for adults revised in 1974 which restored the period of the catechumenate to the conversion process.

(4) Catechesis aims to deepen our understanding of the mystery of Christ and to help others to do the same. It can include teaching, preaching, or other missionary work.

(5) Catechesis should enhance our personal lives and our understanding of ourselves as Catholics. History is a part of our identity, but not the sum total of it. Catechesis should touch every aspect of our Catholic identity.

(6) Words to Know: *enthusiastic* (means "in God" or being inspired by the Spirit); *RCIA* (Rite of Christian Initiation of Adults—revised baptismal rite that restored the catechumenate); *catechesis* (stage in the evangelization/conversion process which aims at developing an understanding of the mystery of Christ).

## In Your World

(1) Supply copies of *The Rites* and allow students to read through the information and the rituals themselves.

(2) Focus on your own classroom first and then on a way to bring evangelization outside it to the rest of the school or parish. This might include a special Bible study for your class, a trip, or special prayer time. Then arrange for students to visit

**12**

other classes to share their experiences, or perhaps make a presentation during adult education at a local parish. Emphasize the sharing aspect of evangelization.

## Scripture Search

(1) These passages present Paul eager to preach the Gospel message as a servant of God. He describes his ministry as one of preaching. This desire to preach gave him the strength to withstand torture, shipwreck, hunger, and ultimately death. He also expresses great humility in his understanding of his mission.

(2) The Prodigal Son shows that, like the father in the parable, God's love is unconditional and always offered. Anyone who enters (or returns) to the Church with sincere faith will be welcomed no matter what he or she has done.

## SECTION 3

## Text Questions (Student text pages 347–350)

**Page 350**

(18) Answers will vary.

(19) Young people often go through a rebellious phase of rejecting much of their upbringing or what is identified with their parents. As they become more independent they may realize their need for the Church, especially when they marry and have children.

## SECTION 3 Checkpoint! (page 351)

## Review

(1) Missionaries may provide medical services, education, and vocational training, as well as act as spiritual guides.

(2) The Church can provide services needed by the communities and be a witness to Christ by starting new communities, supporting missions, and meeting the needs of all people.

(3) Missionaries imitate Christ by caring for the poor and oppressed, and showing people how to recognize their self-worth.

(4) Evangelization is the responsibility of every Catholic adult and child.

(5) Words to Know: *secularism* (refers to ideas and values that are worldly).

## In Your World

(1) Stress the mutual respect and shared goals of all the people involved in the activity despite specific differences in practice or belief. Discuss the experience both before and after. What expectations did students have and what were their impressions afterwards?

(2) A short-term experience could be in a soup kitchen or shelter. Any student interested in a more in-depth experience should consult her or his parents and pastor.

## Scripture Search

1 John speaks of witness to Christ; the mission of the Church, directing evangelization at the pilgrim Church itself (which is always in need of reform); expectation of anger and rejection during evangelization, the need for missionaries to discern and use what is of value in the native culture; the focus of evangelization and catechesis on works of mercy and social justice; and the reliance of evangelizers on God's grace to accomplish their mission.

## CHAPTER 12  Review (pages 352–353)

## Study

(1) Jesus announced the gift of salvation, he gathered together a community of disciples, he led by example, and he gave his life.

(2) Kingdom living is living according to God's will as taught by Jesus and his mission gave us this concept by his teaching and personal example.

(3) The kingdom now is the inauguration of the kingdom of God and its slow coming to completion, when evil will be finally destroyed in the fullness of life.

(4) There is tension now between the place Jesus takes in the heart of each believer, and the visible kingdom on earth, which still includes suffering and oppression.

(5) We are commissioned by Jesus to be his agents. It is our responsibility to proclaim the kingdom; and he gives us the strength to do so.

(6) Evangelization requires ongoing renewal and growth,  while  witnessing to Jesus daily in our lives.

(7) Catholics can evangelize every day, by living committed to the Gospel and by proclaiming the Good News to others.

(8) Active Catholics need to renew their faith and increase their understanding of the mystery of God.

(9) The RCIA stresses the period of the catechumenate as a time of formation, of conversion, and of coming to a mature faith.

(10) Catechesis leads to genuine conversion.

(11) Catechesis must touch a person individually. Therefore it must adapt to the age, development, and readiness of the learner.

(12) Missionaries witness to Christ in all they do, just by their life in his service and in sacrificing home and family for the kingdom.

(13) The Church cares for the handicapped, teaches people to help themselves, breaks down barriers between people, and fights for all human rights in society.

(14) Today many local customs are retained, such as traditional furniture, music, and dance. Local workers and more lay people are involved in missionary activities, and there is more ecumenical cooperation.

(15) Decreased Catholic Church membership can be traced to more intermarriage, dissatisfaction with leadership or changes, secularism, and increased mobility.

(16) At the beginning of the century, the United States was a missionary territory. Now it supports 40 percent of all the world's missionaries.

## Action

(1) This activity can be done individually or in groups. Circulate letters around the classroom and try to contact missionaries in a variety of places, including some in the United States.

(2) Use photos or drawing or a combination. Be sure to capture as many different aspects of kingdom living as possible including RCIA, local outreach, Bible study, education, and ecumenism.

### Prayer

Obtain recordings of African or Asian music from a library and use them in class. The goal here is to demonstrate how hard it is for us to feel at home in the culture of another people. Think how hard it is for people of another culture to be forced to immerse themselves in Western music for worship.

# Christ Gathering His People Today

**OVERVIEW:** This chapter focuses on the mission of the Church to establish the reign of God in all people through evangelization and catechesis.

**OBJECTIVES:** The students will:

- Define the term "mission" and relate it to the life of the People of God in evangelization.
- List the names of those groups to be evangelized and catechized, and the best way to approach each.
- List the function of missionaries and discuss the need for witnesses in foreign lands as well as at home.

**TIME FRAME: One to one-and-a-half hours.**

**MATERIALS:** *RCIA manual.*

**PROCEDURE:**

*Into:* Prayer—Begin class with the prayer in "A People at Prayer," page 348.

*Through:*

Activity One:

1. Ask students to define the word "mission" and to give secular examples from science or politics.

2. What was Jesus' mission? Discuss what it means to carry out God's will. Give some concrete examples. Use questions 4–6 on page 332 as a guide for discussion.

3. Define evangelization as sharing Christ's universal mission. To whom does this apply? Why does it apply to everybody? What can each student do to share in the mission?

Activity Two:

1. Ask students to describe a good evangelist. List the characteristics of both a good evangelist and an unsuccessful one.

2. Who needs evangelization? Add the list made previously by the students and explain why even all active Catholics need evangelization.

3. What is catechesis and who is it for? Is it just dull history and dates? Explain the use of the RCIA, and even focus on the catechumens in a local parish if possible.

Activity Three:

1. Name a missionary, his or her job, and how that reflects in service to God.

2. How can evangelization and missionaries help liberate people here and in other countries? Discuss the concept of liberation. What kinds of liberation are there besides political (from oppression, poverty, physical handicaps, reliance on others).

⑫

3. Ask why people move away from the Church, especially between the ages of 18 and 22. Make a list of reasons on the board. How could this loss be turned around? What conditions or events do students think cause young people to return to the Church? How can the Church respond to people who move away?

**Beyond:** Suggest that students read "Rebellion and Renewal—Thomas Merton," on page 343 and focus on question 14 on page 342. Encourage them to complete activity 2 from Section 1 "In Your World," page 336.

**Prayer:** Close class with the prayer that began it on page 348.

12

Name: _____ Score: _____

## CHAPTER 12 QUIZ
# Christ Gathering His People Today

Mark true (+) or false (o).

___ **1.** Jesus' mission was to launch the kingdom and to empower us to continue his work.

___ **2.** Jesus' mission involved teaching, leading, and sanctifying God's people.

___ **3.** The Church exists to carry out Christ's mission.

___ **4.** We are all involved in Christ's mission.

___ **5.** The life of a real Christian is peaceful and free of tension.

___ **6.** Evangelization began with Vatican II.

___ **7.** Evangelization is primarily concerned with work in the foreign missions.

___ **8.** Evangelization is meant to lead to an acceptance of Jesus and a commitment to his Church.

___ **9.** Most Catholics are active convert-makers.

___ **10.** The best evangelizers have all the answers and know how to argue in favor of the Church.

___ **11.** Personal witness can be a powerful force in evangelization.

___ **12.** All people have need of evangelization.

___ **13.** The RCIA restored some of the ancient traditions of the Church surrounding Baptism.

___ **14.** Catechesis is directed toward teaching children the faith.

___ **15.** Catechesis is concerned primarily with knowing the faith.

___ **16.** A new emphasis in missionary catechesis is respect for the culture and customs of the people being evangelized.

___ **17.** Evangelization and human progress should work together.

___ **18.** The Church uses nearly one-fifth of its resources in outreach to the unchurched, inactive Catholics, and non-Catholics.

**⑫**

___ **19.** Really committed Christians feel the need to share their faith with others.

# CHAPTER 12 QUIZ
Answer Key

1. +
2. +
3. +
4. +
5. o
6. o
7. o
8. +
9. o
10. o
11. +
12. +
13. +
14. o
15. o
16. +
17. +
18. o
19. +

## Twenty Ways to Evangelize
(Can be used with Section 2, How To Be a Successful Evangelizer)

1. Lead a profoundly Christian life.

2. Establish or join a Parish Council Committee on Evangelization and Growth.

3. Hold a Visitors' Sunday regularly or write people who might be interested.

4. Help compile a mailing list of every household in the parish.

5. Many people stop going to church when they move into a new neighborhood. Hold a Newcomers' Gathering to meet and welcome them.

6. Exhibit posters and other signs of welcome in the church hall or vestibule.

7. Send flowers or cards to hospitalized Catholics and those with no religious affiliation. Include the pastor's phone number and a note from him saying that he is available if the sick person wishes spiritual help.

8. Have musical groups perform on street corners and issue invitations to parish activities.

9. Join usher teams responsible for extending hospitality at services.

10. Include those in need of evangelization in the Prayers of the Faithful.

11. Participate in a study or prayer group.

12. Help publish a parish newsletter.

13. Help publish a brochure presenting the parish, its people, its organizations, its buildings, and its programs. Leave it in the pews and/or mail it to everyone in the neighborhood.

14. Begin a monthly prayer vigil or Holy Hour to pray for inactive Catholics. Invite parishioners to come and pray for someone in particular.

15. Visit inactive Catholics before Christmas and Easter. Invite them to church.

16. Help serve a banquet to introduce interested people to the parish. Send invitations to everyone in the geographic territory of your parish.

17. Use the bumper sticker, "We care to share. The friendly family of American Catholics," available from the Paulist Catholic Evangelization Center, 3031 Fourth Street, NE., Washington, D.C. 20017.

18. Hold an open house to introduce people to the Church. Distribute brochures as in #13. Give tours and demonstrations.

19. Lend Catholic books and literature to friends.

20. Direct interested people to information that the Knights of Columbus supply: Knights of Columbus, Home Study Service, 4422 Lindell Boulevard, St. Louis, MO 63108.

ADDITIONAL
RESOURCES

# A Vatican II Concept of the Parish Mission in Action

(Can be used with Section 1, The Mission of the Church in our World)

## A VATICAN II CONCEPT OF THE PARISH MISSION IN ACTION

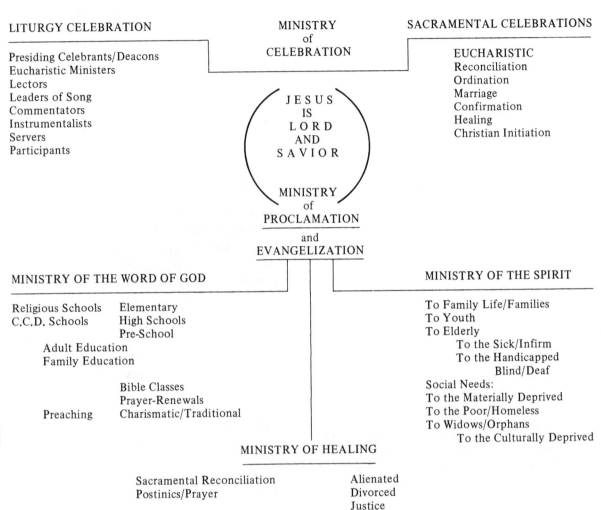

LITURGY CELEBRATION

Presiding Celebrants/Deacons
Eucharistic Ministers
Lectors
Leaders of Song
Commentators
Instrumentalists
Servers
Participants

MINISTRY
of
CELEBRATION

JESUS
IS
LORD
AND
SAVIOR

MINISTRY
of
PROCLAMATION
and
EVANGELIZATION

SACRAMENTAL CELEBRATIONS

EUCHARISTIC
Reconciliation
Ordination
Marriage
Confirmation
Healing
Christian Initiation

MINISTRY OF THE WORD OF GOD

Religious Schools    Elementary
C.C.D. Schools    High Schools
     Pre-School
   Adult Education
   Family Education

     Bible Classes
     Prayer-Renewals
Preaching    Charismatic/Traditional

MINISTRY OF THE SPIRIT

To Family Life/Families
To Youth
To Elderly
   To the Sick/Infirm
   To the Handicapped
     Blind/Deaf
Social Needs:
To the Materially Deprived
To the Poor/Homeless
To Widows/Orphans
   To the Culturally Deprived

MINISTRY OF HEALING

Sacramental Reconciliation      Alienated
Postinics/Prayer      Divorced
     Justice

## Worth Quoting

"The Church invites or repels others by everything it says or does." (Anonymous)

"Evangelization means bringing the Good News into all the strata of humanity, and through its influence transforming humanity from within and making it new." (Pope Paul VI)

"Here on earth God's work must truly be our own." (John F. Kennedy)

"Our response to Vatican II's demand that the Church become actively involved in society may well decide the future of American Catholicism." (Barbara Beckwith)

"Evangelization is more than an attack on religious illiteracy; it is an attempt to dig the only foundation that can support religious commitment in today's world." (James J. DiGiacomo, S.J.)

"The first service that one owes to others ... consists in listening to them. Just as love of God begins with listening to his word, so the beginning of love for the brethren is learning to listen to them." (Dietrich Bonhoffer)

250

12

## Brief History of the Society for the Propagation of the Faith

Pauline Jaricot was a wealthy nineteen-year-old girl living in France. One day, inspired to action on behalf of missionaries, she appealed to friends, relatives, and the miners in her town, asking them to donate a penny and a prayer. Then she had each person promise to contact ten others and ask the same of them. Pauline's plan for pennies and prayers evolved into the Society for the Propagation of the Faith. Today this official mission organ of the Church continues to support world missions financially and spiritually.

# The Faithful of Yesterday, Today, and Tomorrow

**THE FAITHFUL OF YESTERDAY, TODAY, AND TOMORROW**
**(Adherents in millions and as a percentage of world population)**

| Religion | 1900 | % | 1980 | % | 2000 | % |
|---|---|---|---|---|---|---|
| Christian | 558 | 34.4 | 1,443 | 32.8 | 2,020 | 32.3 |
|    Roman Catholic | 272 | 16.8 | 809 | 18.5 | 1,169 | 18.7 |
|    Protestant & Anglican | 153 | 9.4 | 345 | 7.9 | 440 | 7.0 |
|    Eastern Orthodox | 121 | 7.5 | 124 | 2.8 | 153 | 2.4 |
|    Other | 12 | 0.7 | 155 | 3.6 | 258 | 4.1 |
| Non-religious & atheist | 3 | 0.2 | 911 | 20.8 | 1,334 | 21.3 |
| Muslim | 200 | 12.4 | 723 | 16.5 | 1,201 | 19.2 |
| Hindu | 203 | 12.5 | 583 | 13.3 | 859 | 13.7 |
| Buddhist | 127 | 7.8 | 274 | 6.3 | 359 | 5.7 |
| Chinese Folk Religion | 380 | 23.5 | 198 | 4.5 | 158 | 2.5 |
| Tribal & Shamanist | 118 | 7.3 | 103 | 2.4 | 110 | 1.8 |
| "New Religions" | 6 | 0.4 | 96 | 2.2 | 138 | 2.2 |
| Jewish | 12 | 0.8 | 17 | 0.4 | 20 | 0.3 |
| Other* | 13 | 0.8 | 36 | 0.8 | 61 | 1.0 |
| World population | 1,620 | | 4,384 | | 6,260 | |

*including Sikh, Confucian, Shinto, Baha'i, Jain, Spiritist, Parsi
Due to rounding off, percents do not equal 100.
SOURCE: *World Christian Encyclopedia* as quoted in "Counting Every Soul on Earth," *Time* 119:18 (May 3, 1982), p. 66

## The Church in a Changing World

Vatican II pointed out that it is necessary for the Church to listen to the world. Our own age is one of tremendous dynamism because it is an age of tremendous change. As you draw from the class the causes and results of the many changes in the modern world, ask them to think of ways in which (a) these changes have affected Christians; (b) the Church has already changed to accommodate the cultural shifts; (c) they personally can respond to the mission of the Church today; (d) they can be more willing to accept and expect change; and (e) they can become ministers to alleviate anxiety in others.

1. *Causes of Change:*
   - technological progress
   - scientific progress
   - scholarship
   - educational explosion
   - communications explosion
   - publicity explosion

2. *Results of Changes:*
   - a greater complexity of all issues
   - a more eager search for order
   - questioning of values and authorities
   - less mystery and awe surrounding persons in authority

- a tendency to independence
- challenge to tradition
- a demand for efficiency
- more personalism
- fewer ghettoes of ignorance
- greater affluence and pleasure
- desire for total experience of the person
- family no longer the center
- faith not "needed," solutions from science
- profound mysteries turned up by science
- faster and more complete/confusing communication
- higher mobility
- greater understanding of the Bible and early history of the **Church**

The Church has continually evolved. Each epoch has had its own influence and its own problems. The Church today is still very much alive—growing, developing, evolving. Some theological shifts effected by the global situations are reflected in the views of various contemporary theologians:

"The Church is too complex to be viewed under one theological category." (Avery Dulles)

"The Church must have a theology of politics and, being part of the world, must be subject to criticism." (Johannes Metz)

"Dialogue with the world is not to be seen merely as a missionary tactic but as an imperative because of the universality of God's saving presence. The secular world has already taught us religious liberty, pluralism and critical interpretation of our religious texts." (Gregory Baum)

"To be sacrament to the world the Church must be human in the world—with our brothers and sisters everywhere. We must embody and communicate the spiritual in the material. Our job is to give credible witness and more." (Edward Schillebeeckx)

"The Church can no longer be only European. A diaspora Church is not only permitted by God, but willed by him. The Age of Christendom is over. Christians today must be so not by accident of birth, but by mature choice. God's grace operates everywhere and in every age. We need different creedal formulas and updating of language and moral vision." (Karl Rahner)

"The human dignity of every person endows him or her with natural rights which the state's primary commitment is to protect, and duties which it must facilitate. The powers of government are limited by a higher order of human and civil rights. The Council's Declaration of Religious Freedom declares that in virtue of human dignity, everyone should be immune from coercion in matter of faith profession and that no one should be compelled to accept the Christian faith." (John Courtney Murray)

"It is through union with the community that the Christian is united to Christ." (Henri de Lubac)

"The Church is subordinate to the kingdom, a Pilgrim People under changeable forms, already adapting in New Testament times. Yet the Church is the sign of the kingdom, and manifests Christ's body. This makes it all the more in need of on-going reform because it will be credible only in so far as it serves, admits its faults, and corrects itself. Only thus can there be a reunion of Christian Churches, dialog with non-Christian religions, and real influence for good in society. [Three reforms initiated by Kung were the establishment of episcopal conferences, abolition of the Index of Forbidden Books, and simplification of the liturgy.]" (Hans Kung)

"The Church exists in itself but not for itself. Its aim is not great numbers, but to be a small community of quality believers who prepare the way for salvation of all in the kingdom—"a minority in the service of the majority." (Yves Congar)

## Additional Resources

For information on the "Home Missions," including videos, contact Director of Parish Services, The Catholic Church Extension Society of the USA, 35 East Wacher Drive, Chicago, IL 60601, (312) 236-7240.

**CHAPTER 13**

# Christ Calling His People to Holiness

(Text pages 354–381)

## FOCUS

**Doctrinal:** Christ calls his people to holiness and gives them the means to attain it.

**Personal:** How am I responding to my personal call to holiness?

## OBJECTIVES

**Cognitive:** (a) to understand holiness as a sharing in the life and powers of Jesus; (b) to realize the importance of prayer and the role of Mary in the life of the Church.

**Affective:** (a) to appreciate the variety and beauty of Christian holiness and prayer; (b) to grow in devotion to Mary as Mother and model of holiness.

## Chapter 13 Outline

### SECTION 1
**All Are Called**

Equal Privilege of Faith

What is Holiness?

Jesus, Our Model

*Holiness—A Universal Ideal* (text feature)

*On This Rock* (margin feature)

The Challenge of Holiness

Reflections of God's Holiness

Helps to Holiness in the Church

### SECTION 2
**Sharing the Power of Jesus**

The Virtues

Faith

Hope

Charity

The Cardinal Moral Virtues

Special Gifts

*Communion of Saints* (margin feature)

Gifts in Action

Understanding and Wisdom

Fruits

*Outpourings of the Spirit* (text feature)

Charisms

Prayer, an Indispensable Means to Holiness

Participation in Prayer
Liturgy of the Hours
Individual Prayer

## SECTION 3
### Many Models of Holiness

Community, A Help to Holiness
*A People at Prayer* (margin feature)
Mary Most Holy
Mary's Call
God's Presence in Mary
*Women as Models—Strength, Wisdom, Faith* (text feature)
Mary in Prayer
Mary—Of Us and For Us

**⑬**

# TEACHER'S RESOURCE 13A

## Historical Notes

Mary is presented in Scripture as the first and best disciple of Jesus. She is a model for everyone who follows the Lord. She has been the center of the group awaiting the Holy Spirit in Jerusalem, and honored as the Mother of God. During the Middle Ages, she was pictured as the queen of heaven and earth, worthy to have shrines and cathedrals built in her honor. Mary is the model of religious women and men who dedicate their lives to caring for the spiritual children of the Church rather than their own children. She is the model of mothers whose greatest privilege is to form Christ in their children. Among her titles are New Eve, Daughter of Zion, Glory of Jerusalem, Woman of Faith, and Mother of the Church.

## Pedagogical Notes

1. This chapter attempts to explain holiness in terms to which teen-agers might easily relate. If your class is mature, you may wish to present holiness in strictly theological terms, beginning with God who is beyond us, through Jesus Christ who incorporates himself with us and reveals God.

2. The Council's teaching on the role of Mary places her clearly within the context of the Church. It is summarized in Chapter 8 of the *"Dogmatic Constitution on the Church."* Pope Paul VI referred to this chapter as "the greatest Marian Doctrine that ever came out of any Ecumenical Council, even including Ephesus, which proclaimed Mary the *Theotokos*, Mother of God."

# TEACHER'S RESOURCE 13B

## Theological Notes

Holiness seems almost unmentionable in some circles these days. It suggests to many people the image of someone who doesn't have both feet on the ground, or someone who wants to flee the world because dealing with the struggles of this life is simply too difficult.

There certainly may be Christians who confuse holiness with flight from reality, but that kind of behavior is far from holy in the Christian tradition. Jesus, our best example of holiness, showed us how important it was for us to seek a deeper relationship with God by living whole lives in the world. In fact, some Christian writers speak of genuine holiness as "wholeness."

We, like Jesus, become whole or complete people by balancing our involvement in the down-to-earth business of daily living with a life of prayer and self-discipline, which calls our attention to the "more" of human existence. The majority of the saints honored by the Church are remembered for their concrete contributions to learning, justice, evangelization, or some other earthly endeavor. Holy people, therefore, are not trying to escape the world. They have both feet planted firmly on planet earth, and they keep their eyes on the God who created the earth and all creatures.

Mary is a particularly good example of Christian holiness. Though she is honored as the mother of God by the Church, Mary was also the mother of the human Jesus. She lived her life like any other Jewish family woman and she achieved her holiness by embracing all the joys and pain every mother experiences. What made her saintly was her dedication both to her parental responsibilities and to the God whose purpose for her she did not completely understand.

Two qualities of Mary's life describe her holiness and illustrate how she may be a good model for us. First, Mary's life demonstrates generativity. The word "generative" means life-giving. Every mother and father is generative in the literal sense of the word. The love of parents brings forth new life. But all of us, whether married or single, male or female, young or old, are called to generate life. Taking our cue from the God and Father of Jesus Christ, we become whole and complete human beings when we share the life that is in us. This is what Genesis 1:27 tells us when it reveals that we are created in God's "image" and "likeness." We are most human when, like God, we are life-giving people.

Second, Mary was not only a generative woman. She was also generous. Because she was human, we have to assume that she took care of her own needs. That's normal and legitimate. But there was more to her life than self-concern. She left room in her heart for the concerns of God and God's Son, Jesus. In fact, she oriented her entire life toward these concerns.

**13**

When Jesus was threatened by Herod, she and Joseph took their infant child to safety in Egypt (*Matthew 2:13–18*). When Jesus implied that those he was preaching to were his "mother and brother" (*Mark 3:31–35*), Mary accepted this apparent rebuff. When the Apostles abandoned her son on Good Friday, Mary was there (*John 19:26*). Her generosity seemed to know no bounds.

In a world that tempts us to selfishness and the acquisition of goods and power, Mary's life can help us see that true happiness lies in following Jesus and in accepting his call to self-transcendence. In this, she is a model of genuine Christian holiness: life lived in the world, and at the same time, life oriented toward the love of God.

# Prayer Types and Methods

Experiment with prayer forms which most appeal to you. Check those you've tried.

___ **1.** *Traditional Prayers:* How many, like the "Our Father," do you know? Slow down and ponder to bring out the meaning.

___ **2.** *Centering Prayer:* Whether it is localized in head, heart, or stomach, the aim is to journey inward to an awareness of God in whom we live and move and have our being; essentially deep listening.

___ **3.** *Extrovert Meditation:* Finding God through creative activity like dance, sculpture, painting, and music.

___ **4.** *Eucharist:* The basic prayer of Christians which sums up their life; a way to the Father in Jesus and the Spirit.

___ **5.** *Hermitage Prayer:* Learning to do nothing in order to listen to God; a difficult form, the Baroness de Hueck called it "Poustinia."

___ **6.** *Icon-templation:* Using a visual center such as a cross, a painting, a mosaic, an icon, a statue, or the tabernacle to aid the imagination and support one's prayer to an invisible God.

___ **7.** *The Jesus Prayer:* Repetition of the single line, "Lord Jesus Christ, Son of God, have mercy on me a sinner," or just the word "Jesus," while surrendering one's heart to the Lord.

___ **8.** *Mantra:* Repetition or chanting of any sacred word or phrase to close down thoughts and open oneself to the Lord of the Universe.

___ **9.** *Scripture:* Meditation on biblical phrases, scenes, or stories; praying of the psalms; listening to the Word proclaimed aloud.

___ **10.** *Prayer of Suffering:* A simple turning to the Lord in the midst of pain, instead of flight or seeking alleviation.

___ **11.** *Feasting:* Worship through meals or special days with food, wine, story, and song.

___ **12.** *Prayer of Christians:* Sanctification of time by reciting, together with believers around the world, prayers centered in the Psalms at regular intervals during the day.

___ **13.** *Chanting:* The running together of syllables on simple tones to affect the deep levels of the spirit. The Psalms lend themselves well to this type of prayer.

___ **14.** *Novenas:* Any nine-part devotion held on consecutive days, hours, or on a particular day for nine weeks or months; often held in preparation for special events or to petition favors.

___ **15.** *Rosary:* Fingering of beads arranged in decades while reciting Hail Marys and meditating on the Christian mysteries; a source of strength when recited by a group.

**⓭**

___ **16.** *Pilgrimage:* Prayer of the feet; a walking journey to a shrine or another prayer area.

___ **17.** *Way of the Cross:* Meditative ritual walking to, and reflecting upon, fifteen stations of the passion, death, and resurrection of Christ.

___ **18.** *Shrine Praying:* Establishing a corner or altar in your room or home where you can concentrate and pray; an icon, incense, candles, or flowers set it apart.

- What is the purpose of all prayer?

- What usually triggers your prayer?

- What are some good times and places you have found for prayer?

# Dogmatic Constitution on the Church—Chapter VIII

*The Role of the Blessed Virgin Mary, Mother of God,
in the Mystery of Christ and the Church*

Numbers in parenthesis refer to sections of the document.

## I. *Introduction*

Why do we venerate Mary? (52)

What is Mary's relationship to the Trinity? (53) How is she our Mother? (53)

Why was this chapter included in the document on the Church? (54)

## II. *The Role of the Blessed Virgin in the Economy of Salvation*

What is Mary's role in the Old Testament? (55)

How did Mary cooperate in the work of human salvation through faith and obedience? (56)

## III. *The Blessed Virgin and the Church*

What is the basis of Mary's mediation? (60)

Who is the one mediator between God and humanity? (61–62)

How can Mary be called mediatrix? (61–62)

How is Mary a model of the Church? (63–65)

—In her maternity:

—In her virginity:

—In her virtue:

—In her fidelity to God's Will:

—In her apostolic work:

## IV. *Devotion to the Blessed Virgin in the Church*

Why does the Church honor Mary? (66)

Why does it endorse many forms of piety? (66)

How are the offices and privileges of Mary to be explained by theologians and preachers? (67)

In what does true devotion to Mary consist? (67)

## CHAPTER 13 Test

## Christ Calling His People to Holiness

I. **Matching.** Write the letter of the word that best corresponds to the description. There are extra terms.

a. Ascension
b. Assumption
c. charism
d. chairty
e. divine maternity
f. Eucharist

g. faith
h. fortitude
i. holiness
j. Immaculate Conception
k. Liturgy of the Hours
l. moral

m. private prayer
n. prudence
o. religious
p. saint
q. theological
r. virtue

___ 1. Wholeness, fullness, permeated by God's love

___ 2. A capacity that enables us to perform good acts

___ 3. Virtues that regulate our relationship to one another

___ 4. The foundation of our relationship with God that involves our intellectual assent

___ 5. Source and end of all the virtues

___ 6. The Church's official prayer of praise

___ 7. Moral virtue which provides strength to handle difficulties and to overcome fear

___ 8. Personal communion with God

___ 9. The heart of liturgical prayer

___ 10. Gift of the Spirit given for service to the community

___ 11. Inclines a person to choose the best means to serve God in a particular situation

___ 12. Source and greatest of Mary's privileges

___ 13. Mary's being taken body and soul into glory

___ 14. One who vows chastity, poverty, and obedience as a sign of commitment to God and the Church

___ 15. One who dies in God's grace

II. **Incorrectly classified.** Write the letter of the item that *does not belong* on the blank.

___ 1. Holiness is (a) offered to all, (b) modeled by Jesus, (c) achieved without our efforts, (d) deeply related to prayer.

___ 2. Saints are (a) models, (b) witnesses to the Church's holiness, (c) drawn from every walk of life, (d) perfectly balanced individuals.

___ 3. The theological virtues or powers that relate us to God are (a) hope, (b) prayer, (c) faith, (d) love.

___ 4. The cardinal virtues which regulate our relations with other individuals include (a) prudence, (b) justice, (c) temperance, (d) holiness.

Name: _____   Score: _____

___ 5.  Fruits or effects of the Spirit include (a) health, (b) peace, (c) joy, (d) chastity.

___ 6.  Charisms open to us include (a) healing, (b) preaching, (c) tongues, (d) perfect sinlessness.

___ 7.  Prayer (a) finds its highest form in meditation, (b) can be vocal or mental, (c) is indispensable to holiness, (d) was taught us by Jesus.

___ 8.  Helps to holiness include (a) Christian Community, (b) feelings, (c) devotion to Mary, (d) prayer and the sacraments.

___ 9.  Mary's special privileges include (a) perpetual virginity, (b) divine maternity, (c) her Magnificat, (d) Immaculate Conception.

___ 10. Mary is (a) an image of the Church, (b) our model in holiness, (c) holy because of her privileges, (d) one of us.

**III. Essay.** Choose two.

1. Why and how do we honor Mary?

2. How would you describe holiness so that it would appeal to modern audiences? Make your description as complete as possible.

3. Explain the need for prayer and describe five ways of praying.

⑬

# How to Pray the Rosary

In praying the rosary, try to imagine scenes (mysteries) in Jesus' or Mary's life and relate them to your own life. Pray the rosary slowly, allowing time for thought.

Begin the rosary with the Sign of the Cross.

The Apostles' Creed is prayed while reflecting on the crucifix.

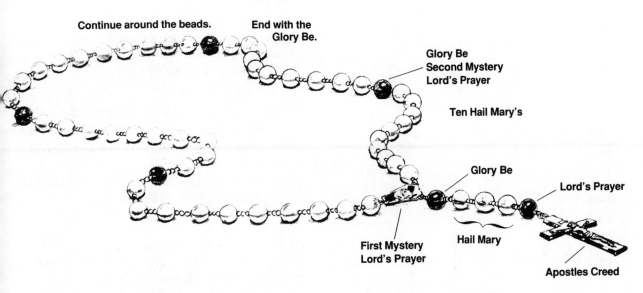

**Continue around the beads.**    **End with the Glory Be.**

Glory Be
Second Mystery
Lord's Prayer

Ten Hail Mary's

Glory Be

Lord's Prayer

First Mystery
Lord's Prayer

Hail Mary

Apostles Creed

Mysteries are chosen which fit the occasion, or the following arrangement might be used:

## Mondays and Thursdays — *The Joyful Mysteries*

(1) The Annunciation (Luke 1:26-38)

(2) The Visitation (Luke 1:39-56)

(3) The Nativity (Matthew 1:18-25)

(4) The Presentation (Luke 2:22-38)

(5) The Finding of the Child Jesus in the Temple (Luke 2:41-52)

## Tuesdays and Fridays — *The Sorrowful Mysteries*

(1) The Agony in the Garden (Matthew 26:36-46)

(2) The Scourging at the Pillar (John 19:1-3)

(3) The Crowning with Thorns (Mark 17:16-20)

(4) The Carrying of the Cross (Luke 23:26-32)

(5) The Crucifixion and Death of Our Lord (Matthew 27:33-56, Mark 15:22-41, Luke 23:33-49, John 19:23-42)

## Wednesdays, Saturdays, and Sundays — *The Glorious Mysteries*

(1) The Resurrection (Matthew 28:1-10, Mark 16:1-18, Luke 24:1-12, John 20:1-23)

(2) The Ascension (Acts 1:6-12, Luke 24:50-53, Mark 16:19)

(3) The Descent of the Holy Spirit upon the Apostles (Acts 2:1-13)

(4) The Assumption

(5) The Coronation of Mary as Queen of Heaven and Earth

Find the scripture passages for each mystery and use that passage as part of your reflection

**13**

## CHAPTER 13 Test
## Christ Calling His People to Holiness

**I.**

1. i
2. r
3. l
4. g
5. d
6. k
7. h
8. m
9. f
10. c
11. n
12. e
13. b
14. o
15. p

**II.**

1. c
2. d
3. b
4. d
5. a
6. d
7. a
8. b
9. c
10. c

**III.**

Answers will vary.

# CHAPTER 13

## SECTION 1
## Text Questions (Student text pages 354–361)

**Page 358**

(1) Answers will vary—pious, good, compassionate. People connect holiness with priests and saints, so it doesn't seem to be characteristics of everyday life.

(2) Answers will vary.

(3) Answers will vary but may include judging, merciful, stern, powerful, loving. God is perfect so all the adjectives show what God is but only in human and limited terms.

(4) We discover what God wants us to be through prayer, study, service, and education.

**Page 359**

(5) Jesus was tempted in the desert just after his baptism, and at his betrayal and death. In each case, he reaffirmed his faith in God.

(6) Answers will vary.

**Page 360**

(7) Answers may include drugs, alcohol, tobacco, sex, disrespect for others.

(8) Answers will vary.

**Page 361**

(9) Answers will vary.

## SECTION 1 Checkpoint! (page 362)
## Review

(1) Holiness is available to everyone and we are all called to it.

(2) Negative ways of describing God are sinless, not self-centered, not unfair, not unkind, or not mortal.

(3) God is totally complete—perfect, whole and without limit. God's holiness is part of God's being.

(4) The struggle for holiness is a challenge against our desires and temptations.

(5) Vowed religious free themselves from worldly obstacles to holiness and dedicate themselves in love to God's service.

(6) Sources of holiness include sacraments and liturgy (a share in the Spirit), confirmation (strength), and the People of God—community (support and example).

(7) Words to Know: *holy* (whole, complete); *secular* (worldly, not religious); *transcendent* (refers to realities beyond our selves); *chastity* (purity of character or conduct).

## In Your World

(1) Have students collect the results of their surveys. The definitions should consist of a couple of words. See how many examples appear repeatedly on the lists and discuss the results. Bring up again the issue of how we view people as holy.

(2) Allow students to become acquainted with the tensions and struggles that still exist in the life of a religious.

(3) Music could actually be played in class or the name or type of music can be discussed.

## Scripture Search

(1) According to Paul, sin is worshiping and serving the creature instead of the Creator. It can be caused by pride, and it leads to alienation from God, moral evil, and death. Specifically, idol worship and improper conduct are mentioned.

(2) The passage in Deuteronomy says that holiness is all around us and for everyone. It is up to each of us to choose holiness (life) instead of death. For the Israelites this meant accepting the responsibility of following the Law.

## SECTION 2

**Text Questions** (Student text pages 363–371)

### Page 365

(10) Answers will vary.

(11) People grow in holiness and never reach perfection. It is a goal that is always sought, and encourages us to work, pray, and study in imitation of Christ.

(12) Answers might include obedience, reverence, honesty, responsibility, loyalty, and respect.

### Page 369

(13) Answers will vary.

### Page 370

(14) Adoration might be offered at a major festival such as Easter. Thanksgiving would be offered after an illness has been cured. Contrition would be appropriate in repentance for an evil thought or act. And petition could be used to ask for strength during a difficult time or in making a difficult decision.

(15) The Eucharist allows us to share the life of Jesus and it forms a bond of unity between all Christians by our identity in it.

### Page 371

(16) Silence and solitude allow us to concentrate on God and to focus without distractions.

## SECTION 2 Checkpoint! (page 372)

### Review

(1) The theological virtues regulate our relationship with God.

(2) The three theological virtues are faith, hope, and charity.

(3) The moral virtues regulate our relations with one another and include prudence, justice, fortitude, and temperance.

(4) The Holy Spirit works in each person by endowing the individual with gifts which help him or her respond to the presence of the Holy Spirit in the world.

(5) Fruits and charisms are signs of the Holy Spirit active in a person's life.

(6) Meditative prayer leads to communion with the saints and insights from them; affective prayer is prayer from the heart and emotions; contemplative prayer transforms us into people of peace.

(7) Words to Know: *virtue* (capacity that enables a person to perform good acts in relation to God or to one another); *cardinal* (main or primary); *prudence* (moral virtue that enables a person to discern and choose the best means to serve God in a particular situation); *fortitude* (moral virtue of strength to handle difficulties, especially in overcoming fear of ridicule or pain); *temperance* (cardinal virtue that controls or moderates bodily tendencies in light of reason and God's plan); *charism* (gift or manifestation of the Spirit); *Liturgy of the Hours* (praise of God by hymns, psalms, readings, and prayers seven times daily).

**13**

## In Your World

**(1)** Use an edited version of the Liturgy if necessary. Stress the idea of shared prayer at a specific time. Discuss both its communal and personal aspects.

**(2)** The goal here is to make the theoretical virtues more concrete in applying them to everyday life. Try having students discuss situations when the virtues might be used first, and then encourage each student to adopt a virtue especially for themselves (it isn't necessary for them to divulge which they have chosen).

**(3)** Be sure that students do not choose a form of asceticism that is too extreme. Any student who wishes to fast even for one day must check with parents first. Solitude, donation of allowance to charity, or foregoing a usual activity (going out with friends) could also be forms of asceticism. Discuss the reasons for asceticism. It is not meant to serve as a punishment, but as a way to enhance the spiritual development of people by releasing them from the temptations of everyday life.

## Scripture Search

The gifts and charisms mentioned in these passages include prayer in heart and mind, prophecy, service, teaching, charity, mercy, wisdom, knowledge, healing, and administrative ability.

## SECTION 3

## Text Questions (Student text pages 373–378)

### Page 374

**(17)** Answers will vary.

**(18)** Answers will vary.

**(19)** Answers will vary and may include support in choosing a profession or in making friends.

### Page 377

**(20)** Answers will vary and may include mercy, love, and caring as female characteristics, and judging and powerful as male characteristics.

**(21)** Mary had to exercise her free will and her ability to respond to God's gift of grace. That is what makes us in God's image.

### Page 378

**(22)** Answers will vary.

**(23)** Mary understands the burden of motherhood, is a parent as a father is, can be a source of strength to teens as a mother or parent to whom one can turn, and is present as a model to all who need her care and love.

## SECTION 3 Checkpoint! (page 379)

## Review

**(1)** Charismatic groups were formed in order to revitalize Christian life by stressing the experience of the Spirit.

**(2)** A Christian community is a group of people with like goals and a like picture of their Christian life. It is a variety of people hoping to share their lives together as Christians.

**(3)** Mary exhibits nurturing, sensitivity, receptivity, and long-suffering.

**(4)** Eve was the mother of the human race, of all people, and Mary is the new mother of a saved and reborn humanity through Christ.

**(5)** Mary is a model of obedience, and of a lay woman filled with God's presence.

**(6)** The bishops warn us not to view Mary as a goddess or as a mediator between us and Christ. Mary is a human being.

**(7)** Words to Know: *synoptics* (taking a common view—refers to the gospels of Matthew, Mark, and Luke which present similar scenarios of Jesus' life and ministry); *Magnificat* (Mary's Song of Redemption which recalls the faithfulness of God in protection of the poor and weak); *Immaculate Conception* (belief that Mary was conceived free from original sin).

## In Your World

**(1)** Use, for example, Michelangelo's Pieta and several other paintings or sculptures. Note that Mary is often portrayed in her role as the mother of Christ either at his birth or death. She appears soft in some images and strong and protective in others.

**(2)** Some specific aspects of a Christian life could include ethics (how one approaches issues of war and peace or economics), or the study of Scripture and its application to daily life. Make the time spent in class discussing a shared Christian life distinct from other classroom activities by

rearranging chairs in a more informal fashion. Discuss how a Christian life can become part of everyone's life in the world.

## Scripture Search

Mary is shown in these accounts as loyal and a mother to all, and remaining with and ministering to Jesus until the end. The differences in the accounts show the different perspectives of the writers as discussed in Chapter 7.

## CHAPTER 13 Review (pages 380–381)

### Study

(1) In the Bible, God is represented as holy, perfect in all aspects, merciful, good, and in a living relationship with us.

(2) God's holiness is made present to us in God's attributes and in Jesus who embodies God.

(3) The forces that interfere with holiness are pride, greed, lust, anger, gluttony, envy, and laziness.

(4) Saints reflect God's holiness and there were people like us. Their lives on earth serve as models of holiness for us, and even today they intercede for us because of their holiness.

(5) Religious seek holiness by living the vows of poverty, chastity, and obedience.

(6) The sacraments link us to God and to holiness by connecting us to the Spirit.

(7) The cross has two beams. The vertical symbolizes the virtues that connect us to God and the horizontal represents our dealings with one another.

(8) Faith is the basis of our relationship with God. It is our knowledge of God grounded in love and our response to the offer of truth. It calls for surrender and acceptance.

(9) Hope and charity indicate our trust in God's love and our choice to do God's will.

(10) Prudence means making correct choices in serving God. An example would be what to do if you knew someone was involved in self-destructive behavior. Choosing the best way to help that person would be exercising prudence.

(11) Gifts of the Spirit include a good conscience, acts of mercy, counseling skills, teaching ability, good organizational skills, etc.

(12) The Holy Spirit is seen in the fruits of a person's labor.

(13) Charisms may seem like ordinary talents or skills like singing or teaching, and not charisms, or they may reflect destructive elements but seem like charisms.

(14) The four basic types of prayer are adoration (praise of God), thanksgiving (response to generosity), contrition (repentance); and petition (asking for God's presence).

(15) The Liturgy of the Hours sets regular prayer times for a community to offer praise to God (seven times during the day and night).

(16) Private prayer can become self-centered, but it can also help us cultivate a relationship with God, and a personal communion.

(17) Community means action, a lived commitment to Christ which is witnessed in the public arena.

(18) Mary's holiness is described as a special esteem. As Mother of God and the Church, she is obedient, faithful, and long-suffering.

(19) Mary is a model of patience, obedience, and service for us.

### Action

(1) Encourage students to represent as many attributes of Mary as they can. Discuss the variety of images used, and ask students which ones speak to them most.

(2) Use a theoretical situation to begin with in this activity. Discuss the feelings of each person involved. Why is it important for a person to understand the feeling of others? And why is it important for the individual to make changes or take action regardless of the reaction (or non-reaction) of the other involved?

### Prayer

Stress the meaning of the prayer, not just its repetitive nature. With each repetition, different aspects of Mary's holiness and character can come into sharper focus. Try to make this activity revitalize saying the Rosary for each student.

**13**

# Christ Calling His People to Holiness

**OVERVIEW:** This chapter focuses on the concept of holiness and its role in the personal and community life of each Christian. The virtues, use of prayer, and special love for Mary are used to illustrate the concept of holiness.

**OBJECTIVES: The students will:**

- Generate definitions of "holiness" and give examples from the secular and religious worlds.

- In small groups, define and provide a sample situation for the use of various virtues, gifts, and charisms.

- Discuss the many aspects of Mary's holiness and ways she acts as a model for us.

**TIME FRAME: One to one-and-a-half hours.**

**MATERIALS: Bibles, paper and pens, dictionaries, Rosaries.**

**PROCEDURE:**

*Into:* Prayer—Begin class with the prayer from the margin feature "A People at Prayer," page 374.

*Through:*

Activity One:

1.  Ask students to define the word "holy." Read the first paragraph of the chapter on page 355 and ask for reaction.

2.  Now ask students to give examples of living people who they think are holy. Encourage them to come with names from the secular as well as religious worlds.

3.  Discuss the source of our holiness in Jesus and his own personal struggles. Now list some of the things that we struggle with in our efforts to be holy and where we can get help.

Activity Two:

1.  As a class, define the term "virtue" and distinguish the theological from the moral virtues.

2.  Divide the class into small groups and assign a virtue or gift to each. Have each group define their concept and give an example of its use.

3.  List the reasons why and ways people pray. Cover individual and group prayer and the benefits of each type. Be sure the use of each type of prayer is clear.

Activity Three:

1.  Have the class describe Mary's role and list as many of her titles as it can.

2.  Ask students what they think makes Mary holy. Discuss the concepts presented in the text.

3.  Ask students to say what Mary represents to them personally as a mother.

*Beyond:* Suggest that students read "Holiness—A Universal Ideal," page 357 and focus on question 1 on page 358. Encourage them to complete activity 2 from Section 2, "In Your World," page 372.

*Prayer:* Close class with the Hail Mary found on page 377.

**CHAPTER 13 QUIZ**
# Christ Calling His People to Holiness

Mark true (+) or false (o).

___ 1. Striving for holiness is an essential part of the Christian vocation.

___ 2. Our ideas of holiness are rooted in the knowledge of God found in the Hebrew Scriptures.

___ 3. Human holiness is wholeness—being fully what God intended us to be.

___ 4. Holiness is easy to acquire.

___ 5. Saints lose their unique personality.

___ 6. Religious men and women are meant to witness to the Church's holiness.

___ 7. We have both natural and supernatural aids to holiness at our disposal.

___ 8. The sacraments and liturgy are indispensable sources of holiness.

___ 9. Our relationship to God is based on the gifts of faith, hope, and love.

___ 10. Moral virtues regulate our relations with others.

___ 11. The gifts of the Holy Spirit make it easier to respond to God's invitations.

___ 12. A charism is a fruit of the Holy Spirit.

___ 13. We need to be holy before we can pray.

___ 14. Liturgical and private prayer are not related.

___ 15. Fasting is an aid to prayer.

___ 16. Christian community is a way of living out one's commitment to Christ.

___ 17. Devotion to Mary is an option in the Church.

___ 18. The source and greatest of all Mary's privileges is her sinlessness.

___ 19. Mary did not need to be saved.

___ 20. Mary's holiness lies in her fidelity to God.

**13**

# CHAPTER 13 QUIZ
Answer Key

1. +
2. +
3. +
4. o
5. o
6. +
7. +
8. +
9. +
10. +
11. +
12. o
13. o
14. o
15. +
16. +
17. o
18. o
19. o
20. +

## Bible Service: Name of Mary
(Can be used with Section 3, Mary in Prayer)

**Directions:** Divide the class into two groups. Assign each group to read a part of this prayer, either Side I or Side II. Ask one person to serve as prayer leader, and three other people to serve as readers.

**All:** Song: "Immaculate Mary" or another Marian hymn.

**Leader:** The name of Mary means *Mistress.* In this reading, Queen Esther found favor with King Ahasuerus because of her exquisite beauty. She found favor with the King of Heaven because of her prayer and penance. At her request, the lives of the Jewish People were spared.

**1st Reader:** *New American Bible:* Esther 4:15–16, 5:1–3, 7:3–7

**Leader:** Esther saved her people. Mary gave us Christ through whom we were saved. Both Esther and Mary praised God for the marvels he did in them. Let us praise God in the words of Mary's canticle.

**Response:** *The Magnificat*

*Side I:* My being proclaims the greatness of the Lord, my spirit finds joy in God my savior.

*Side II:* For God has looked upon his servant in her lowliness, all ages to come shall call me blessed.

*Side I:* God who is mighty has done great things for me, holy is God's name.

*Side II:* God's mercy is from age to age on those who fear God.

*Side I:* God has shown a mighty arm; and has confused the proud in their inmost thoughts.

*Side II:* God has deposed the mighty from their thrones, and raised the lowly to high places.

*Side I:* The hungry have been given every good thing, while the rich have been sent empty away.

*Side II:* God has upheld Israel the servant, ever mindful of God's mercy, even as was promised our fathers, promised Abraham and his descendants forever.

**Leader:** The name of Mary also means *Spouse.* At the Annunciation, the Second Person of the Blessed Trinity became flesh through Mary by the overshadowing of the Holy Spirit. At the Annunciation, Mary became the Spouse of the Holy Spirit.

**2nd Reader:** Luke 1:26–38

**Response:** Psalm 45 (III)

*Side I:* Hear, O daughter, and see; turn your ear, forget your people and your father's house. So shall the king desire your beauty; for he is your lord, and you must worship him.

*Side II:* And the city of Tyre is here with gifts; the rich among the people seek your favor. All glorious is the king's daughter as she enters; her raiment is threaded with spun gold.

*Side I:* In embroidered apparel she is borne in to the king; behind her the virgins of her train are brought to you.

*Side II:* They are borne in with gladness and joy; they enter the palace of the king.

**All:** Song: "Sing of Mary" or another Marian hymn.

**Leader:** The name of Mary means *Mother.* Mary is not only mother of Jesus, but also of his body, the Church.

**3rd Reader:** John 19:25–27

**Response:** Prayer

Lord, when you gave your mother to Saint John, you gave her to each of us also. Thank you for this precious gift. Enable us to imitate Mary our Mother by seeking the food that remains to life eternal. Jesus, you made Mary the dwelling place of your presence and the abode of the Spirit. Make us, too, lasting temples of your Spirit.

**All:** Song: "Hail, Holy Queen, Enthroned Above" or another Marian hymn.

## Mary-Wise
(Can be used with Section 3, Mary Most Holy)

## Old Testament Prophecies

| | | |
|---|---|---|
| **(1)** Genesis 3:14 | Foreshadows Mary |
| **(2)** Isaiah 7:14 | Refers ultimately to Mary—Virgin, bearing a child |
| **(3)** Micah 5:1–3 | Includes Mary— "… she who is to give birth…" |

## Norms for Marian Devotion

**(1)** Rooted in the Bible, liturgy, and doctrine

**(2)** Based on solid faith

**(3)** Leading to Marian knowledge, love, and imitation

**(4)** Avoiding what might mislead others

## Exploring Holiness

Carefully study the following descriptions of holiness written by high school students. They are only excerpts of longer definitions. Say whether you agree or disagree with each statement **as it stands**. Be ready to tell why.

## Holiness is...

1. a state of mind.

2. doing extra things like reading the Bible even when it's not assigned.

3. saying the rosary.

4. having lots of friends and getting along well with others.

5. giving up all material wants and pleasures for a life devoted to the Spirit.

6. constantly trying to renew oneself in order to be the best person possible—this is the meaning of taking up the cross.

7. trying to be absolutely sincere in word and action.

8. loving others, even your enemies, in order to get to heaven to live with the Father.

9. imitating God and being happy and content with everything exactly as it happens.

10. trying your best to do everything that you know is right and that God wants of you.

11. being called and consecrated by the all-holy God as his own possession to share his life now as well as in the afterlife.

12. being happy with yourself and your neighbor because all can be forgiven and forgotten in Christ's forgiveness.

## Don't Be Shocked

When you get involved in your parish and really begin to work shoulder to shoulder with others, you may find one or more of the following situations:

- A pastor who drinks a bit too much.

- An associate pastor who seems more concerned about his clothes than about the sick and elderly.

- A Sister-principal who wants everything her own way.

- A council president whose main interest is his own glory.

- A musical director who is domineering.

- Jealousy among the women in the Altar Society.

- Stinginess in parishioner support of the Church.

- Lack of responsibility in the census or social committee.

- Apathy for the missions.

- Indifferent teen-agers.

Because Jesus came to make people holy, and the Church is supposed to carry out his mission, you may be tempted to throw up your hands in despair and give up. The parish is obviously a community with all the faults of human beings trying to share a common vision and a common goal.

- What good qualities do the faults of members of your family bring out in other family members?
- Name a good quality the faults of parish members might bring out in others.

## Saints are Human

The saints loved life and were very human. They used their talents. Don Bosco was an excellent juggler, Saint Hubert loved the hunt, and Teresa of Avila liked to dance to the click of the castanets. John of the Cross wrote poetry, Gertrude was a seamstress, and many saints played cards, chess, and ball games. Saint Edmund Campion, England's first Jesuit martyr, used his writing ability to bolster Catholic morale during the persecution of the sixteenth century. Blessed Marguerite, the Canadian-born founder of the Gray Nuns, successfully managed a store to pay off her husband's large debt and to educate her two sons.

The saints had the capacity to enter into deep and lasting relationships. Friendships among the saints resulted in mutual growth as well as good to the Church. With Francis de Sales as her spiritual director, Jane Frances Chantal founded the contemplative order of the Visitation. Saint Clare worked with Saint Francis of Assisi to inaugurate the Poor Clares, a monastery for contemplative nuns under Franciscan rule. Saint Margaret Mary Alacoque consulted the saintly Claude de la Columbiere through the joys and persecutions of her mission to spread devotion to the Sacred Heart of Jesus. Benedict and his sister Scholastica held prolonged spiritual conversations, taking their insights back to their separate monasteries. One of the best-known friendships was that between Saint Teresa of Avila and the Carmelite friar John of the Cross. Together they spread the reform of the Discalced Carmelites. Both were great mystics and have been honored as Doctors of the Church for their teachings on prayer.

Why would you expect saints to have hobbies and various talents as well as deep friendships?

Some saints were good-natured. Saint Thomas More, the personable Lord Chancellor of England who refused to acknowledge Henry VIII as head of the Church of England, had a healthy sense of humor which survived after two years in a foul dungeon. As he was led to the gallows for not signing the Oath of Supremacy, he quipped to his executioner, "Don't harm my beard. It did nothing to offend the King." When Pope John XXIII was asked how many people worked in the Vatican, he replied, "About half."

The saints' joy was not always rooted in personal good fortune. After her conversion, the beautiful Bostonian ex-socialite, Elizabeth Anne Bayley Seton, was rejected by friends and relatives alike. A penniless widow with five children and not enough to eat, she contracted many diseases. One of the most miserable was a rash of angry boils. Nevertheless, she could write in her journal, "Sometimes I can hardly contain my interior cheerfulness."

The saints loved animals as well as people. Saint Philip Neri played with his pet monkey in public to counteract exaggerated rumors about his holiness. Saint Julie Billiart of France lavished almost as much love on her cat as on one sinner to whom she wrote a thousand letters in the hope of winning her back to Christ. Saint Margaret of Cortona was converted when her lover's dog led her to his master, who had accidentally been killed during a hunt. Martin de Porres, rejected by his father for his mulatto color, loved animals so much that he would collect mice from the church drawers and feed them. The Poverello, Saint Francis of Assisi, is famous for his gift of knowing how to tame the animal kingdom. Having given away all his possessions to become poor like Christ, he gained all creation in exchange.

## Evil's Stranglehold

Without God we are capable of totally falling apart. Rod McGettrick, a successful stockbroker, turned to drugs to ease the pressures of his highly competitive job. He became addicted. Gradually all his savings were drained. He had to pawn his motorbike, his yacht, and two cars. Still he couldn't stop. When he piled up a debt of $10,000 in one month, his wife divorced him, taking custody of their son. When he lost his job, he finally sought professional help. Even after the sale of their house, it will take him years to pay off remaining debts. Looking back, Rod is stunned at the stranglehold evil had on him and at the swiftness of his ruin.

Without revealing names, recount a tragedy of someone you know.

## Prayer Preview

Have students respond to the following anonymously and tally the class response:

270

A = strongly agree; A = agree; D = disagree; SD = strongly disagree

. I know a lot about prayer.

. I pray frequently.

. I pray well.

. I would like to know how to make prayer more meaningful.

. I like to pray.

## How to Meditate on Scripture

*Procedure*

. Choose a favorite passage, such as the Agony in the Garden, and set a time. Begin realistically with five minutes or so.

2. Relax. Quiet yourself by slow, deep breathing. Recall God's presence and pray for help.

3. Use your imagination to reconstruct the time, place, persons, or images of the passage.

4. Read the passage slowly; reread it using only a small portion. Dwell on words or phrases that light up for you.

5. Make yourself part of the scene. Speak with the characters or directly to Jesus about your insights. Speak from your heart: praise, faith, gratitude, sorrow for sin.

6. Just before the conclusion, focus on the affection that most influenced you. Thank God for his graces.

7. Note any resolutions or thoughts in your journal.

## The Holy as Feminine

"Mary of course is not a 'goddess' in the sense that the Greek or Indian goddesses are, but devotion to Mary stripped of all the oddities which have grown up through the centuries, plays a role in Catholicism that is the functional equivalent of the role of the female deity in the best of the nature religions. In other words, there is something about the nature of man's relation to The Holy which seems to require that The Holy be perceived as containing both male and female elements. The Blessed Mother is the Catholic tradition's response to this valid human need" (Andrew M. Greeley, *The Life of the Spirit*).

## Mary in the New Testament

Infancy narratives: *Matthew 1:18–2:23*: Fulfillment of the Old Testament prophecies.
*Luke 1–2*: Part of the faithful remnant.

Other:

*Mark 3:31–35, 6:3–4*: Model of all Christians following the Word

*John 2:1–4*: The Church, Wine, "Woman"

*John 19:25–27*: Crucifixion—The Mother of Jesus

*Acts of the Apostles 1:14*: Mother of the Living, Mary—open, active, contemplative

Paul: *Galatians 4:4*: Means of Jesus' humanity

*Revelation 12:1–6*: Symbol of the Church

## A Dozen Marian Projects

1. Make a mural of the Blessed Mother with torn pieces of paper or used postage stamps to give it a mosaic effect.

2. Collect art reproductions of Mary from used Christmas cards. Make a bulletin board display.

3. Take slide pictures of shrines or statues of Mary from local Churches. (Student and/or teacher project.) Present it to the class.

4. During October or May, create a stained glass window behind the classroom statue of Mary.

5. Collect holy cards of Mary and display them in an arrangement that points out Mary's privileges.

6. Write a brief meditation on each mystery of the rosary based on a quotation from Scripture. Relate it to modern times.

7. Study Mary and report on your findings in:

    a. Literature: *The Mary Book*, compiled by F. J. Sheed; *The Catholic Anthology* by Thomas Walsh; "*The Ballad of the White Horse*" by Chesterton; "*The Mother of God*" by Keats; "*The Coat*" by Dante, "*Rosa Mystica*" by Hopkins; "*The Dry Salvages*" by Eliot; "*A Prayer to the Blessed Virgin*" by Chaucer; and "*Mater Immaculata*" by Wordsworth.

    b. Art: *Mary, God's Masterpiece*. Reproductions of world famous madonnas, published by Perpetual Help Press, N.Y.

    c. Music: Polyphonic music (Palestrina), modern classical music (Gounod's "Ave Maria," Schubert's "Ave Maria"), vernacular hymns to Mary.

8. Compose songs to Mary; use popular tunes.

**13**

9. Arrange a Mary altar at home or school.

10. Write a character sketch of Mary based on a reading of the following Scripture texts: *Luke 1:26–56; 2:1–7, 22–35, 40–52; Matthew 1:18–25; John 2:1–12, 20:25–27; Acts 1:12–14.*

11. The original name of the city of Los Angeles is "Nuestra Senora, La Reina de Los Angeles" (Our Lady, Queen of Angels). List other Marian place names in the United States and in Canada.

12. Write an original poem to Our Lady.

## Statements about Holiness

Discuss each statement until, as a group, you can agree or disagree with it. Give three reasons for your decisions.

1. A holy person cannot be a success in today's world.

2. You have to be a little "different" to be holy.

3. There are no objective standards for holiness.

4. There is a difference between being holy and being good.

5. Everyone, including criminals, has a natural desire for holiness.

## Supplementary Lesson: Christian Prayer Songs

*Approach:*

If you've ever gone camping, or ridden a bus with a group who know one another, you know the importance of song.

What effect does group singing have on its participants? Think of the singing done at sports events.

*Development:*

The psalms are among the oldest and most well-known songs in the world. Originally they were attributed to David, who in his youth soothed the disturbed Saul with his music, and as King, sang and danced before the Ark. Actually the psalms are the liturgical hymns accumulated by the Jewish people over a period of centuries. They expressed the feelings of the Jews toward God and bound them to one another. They also served to boost community morale, especially in moments of pride or despair. Although their melodies have been lost, the lyrics have been preserved in the Book of Psalms in the Old Testament. These poetic prayers express every mood known to human experience, but their predominant spirit is praise. Christ knew and prayed them, invoking one even in his last moments on the cross (*Mark 15:34*).

From the first, Christians met every day at morning and evening to praise God in psalms, adding readings of Scripture, hymns, and other prayers. The morning prayers came to be known as Lauds (praise). The evening prayer was Vespers (evening star). Thus after A.D. 313 when Christians were permitted the open practice of their faith, a prayer liturgy for daytime and nighttime grew up alongside the Eucharistic liturgy. It came to be known as the Divine Office because it was the official praise of God offered by the Church. The Office is a human effort to praise God as continuously as possible in every place on earth. It was solemnly chanted by monks and clerics in monasteries and cathedrals, although parishes celebrated at least Lauds and Vespers together with their pastor.

The Divine Office is a collection of all 150 psalms, hymns, Scriptural and other readings and prayers. It is arranged to be said at different hours during the day. As special ministers of Christ's Body, all in Major Orders, those ordained as deacons, priests or bishops, and certain religious are required to pray this official public prayer of the Church on behalf of all Christians. By reason of their baptismal incorporation into the priesthood of Christ, the laity also truly participate in this official Church prayer when they pray it alone or with others.

During the fifteenth century the psalms were prayed in Latin. Since the lay persons were no longer familiar with the ancient language, the saying of the triple rosary of fifteen decades (150 Hail Marys) substituted for the 150 psalms among the uneducated. Today the Liturgy of the Hours, as it is called, is composed of the Night Office of Readings, Morning Prayer, Daytime Prayer, Evening Prayer, and Night Prayer. Now that the psalms are prayed in the vernacular, and education is universal, more and more lay persons are praying at least some of the Psalter.

The Divine Office is a liturgical prayer because it belongs to the public worship of the Church, whether it is prayed with others or alone. It is considered part of the official prayer of the Church because (a) it contains an arrangement of prayers approved by the Church, (b) it is recited in name of the Church, which means it is offered in the name of Christ, and (c) it is prayed by officially appointed

13

272

persons, those empowered by baptism to praise God in Christ's name. All prayer that fulfills these three functions is the public prayer of the Church: Mass, sacraments, sacramentals, Office, and Benediction. Other prayers are either private when said alone, or communal when recited in a group. The purpose of all prayer is to help us enter more meaningfully into the celebration of the perfect prayer, the Eucharist.

*Activities:*

1. Make a Psalm Source Book.

   a. Write out your favorite psalm or psalms. Label it or them your favorite and tell why you like it or them.

   b. From the psalms gather twenty phrases that mean a great deal to you.

   c. Read through a number of psalms to determine their basic sentiments. Make a psalm directory that tells what psalms to pray for special occasions—for instance, when you are lonely, discouraged, joyful, after receiving a favor, in anger, and so on.

2. Rewrite a psalm in modern-day language, referring to things and places on the contemporary scene. Instead of the Lord destroying the enemies of Moab as the psalm does:

   "I will use Moab as my washbowl and I will throw my sandals on Edom," you might want to have your psalm.

   *say:*

   "I will mop up those who corrupt the young and I will give child abusers a boot."

3. Paraphrase a psalm that appeals to you.

4. Divide the class in two. Let Side I pray the first verse of a psalm you decide on and Side II pray the second. This back-and-forth movement of recitation followed by response is called antiphonal prayer. Discuss the effect this kind of praying has on you. Jewish prayer and poetic forms used a technique known as antithetic

(contrastive) parallelism (similarity). This means that the verses either repeat a thought in different words, or set up a contrast to a parallel thought. Here is an example:

**Psalm 102.1**

| Listen to my prayer, O Lord | statement |
| and hear my cry for help! | repeat |

Analyze any psalm for its use of this technique. Make parallels that are repetitive with a plus sign (+), those that are contrastive with a minus sign (-).

**Psalm 87, 13–14**

| Lord, I call to you for help | statement |
| every morning I pray to you | repeat |
| Why do you reject me, Lord? | contrast |
| Why do you turn away from me? | repeat of contrast |

Select a modern-day, psalm-like hymn to use as a base for a prayer period. A psalm–like hymn is one that has many thoughts or truths in a number of stanzas. Many of Fr. L. Deiss's hymns lend themselves to this purpose.

## Additional Reading

Clark, Elizabeth. *Women in the Early Church.* Message of the Church Fathers 13. Wilmington, DE: Michael Glazier, 1983.

Denny, Frederick, M. *Islam and the Muslim Community.* Religious Traditions of the World. New York: Harper and Row, 1987.

Fishbane, Michael A. *Judaism: Revelations and Traditions.* Religious Traditions of the World. New York: Harper and Row, 1987.

Jeansonne, Sharon Pace. *The Women of Genesis: From Sarah to Potiphar's Wife.* Minneapolis, MN: Augsburg Fortress, 1990.

Tavard, George H. *Women in Christian Tradition.* Notre Dame: University of Notre Dame Press, 1973.

## CHAPTER 14

# Christ Ministering Through His People

(Text pages 382–407)

## FOCUS
**Doctrinal:** All in the Church are called to ministry, each according to his or her own gifts, powers, and ability to be of service.

**Personal:** How do I respond to and envision my own role in a servant Church?

## OBJECTIVES
**Cognitive:** (a) to realize the role and extent of lay ministry in the Church; (b) to understand the Church's hierarchical structure; (c) to be able to explain the Church's gift of infallibility.

**Affective:** (a) to appreciate the variety of roles and ministries found in the Church; (b) to be grateful for Christ's gift of infallibility to his Church.

## Chapter 14  Outline

### SECTION 1
**A Servant Church**

> Total Service
> All Called to Ministry
> The Laity's Essential Mission
> Types of Ministry
> Ministry Within the Church
> *The Church in the Modern World* (text feature)
> Lay Ministries in the World
> *On This Rock* (margin feature)

### SECTION 2
**Christian Leadership: Ordained Ministry**

> Roots of Christian Leadership
> The Bishop
> In Unity with the Bishop
> *Communion of Saints* (margin feature)
> What a Bishop Is and Does
> As Teacher
> As Priest
> *Infallibility—A Gift of the Spirit* (text feature)
> As Shepherd
> The Petrine Ministry

14

275

**SECTION 3**
**A Life of Service**

What a Priest Is and Does
What a Deacon Is and Does
*The Church of the Bishop* (text feature)
*A People at Prayer* (margin feature)
Religious Life and its Role
The Spirit at Work

**14**

# TEACHER'S RESOURCE 14A

## Historical Notes

The Second Vatican Council can be seen as the historical backdrop for much of this chapter. The current teaching of the Church regarding its hierarchical structure and gift of infallibility is contained in the *"Dogmatic Constitution on the Church."* The document clearly defines the role of all Christians in the life of the Church, both local and universal. The Gospel provides fundamental core images that have guided the Church in its self-definition throughout the centuries and will continue to do so into the next century.

## Pedagogical Notes

1. Be sure the doctrine of infallibility is clear, and point out that Vatican II did not intend to proclaim any infallible teaching. Vatican I, in 1870, taught infallibly on "the Holy Father's infallibility."

2. Presenting this chapter requires a balance between introducing many terms and definitions and making those terms meaningful in the lives of your students. Attitudes and motivations can best be formed when proper information is provided that can help students understand these complex processes.

# TEACHER'S RESOURCE 14B

## Theological Notes

One of the most difficult Vatican II teachings for many Catholics to accept is that Christ ministers through his people. Prior to the last council, and even now for many of us, it was assumed that Christ ministers *to* his people through the Church's priests and religious. Catholics thought of themselves as recipients of the sacraments, of grace and of truth mediated by the magisterium.

This understanding, of course, is not entirely incorrect. Insofar as the grace of salvation is a gift, it is quite proper to think of ourselves as receivers or beneficiaries of God's favor. The Church and its ordained ministers are visible signs of God's life, freely given on our behalf. The problem with this approach, however, is two-fold. First, it tends to suggest a rather passive role for the faithful, and it lays a heavy burden on the ordained ministers of the Church.

Priests, according to this view, are considered "all things to all men." If Catholics have a question or problem, they assume that "Father" has the answer or the solution. So, on the one hand, thinking of ourselves solely as recipients can diminish our sense of responsibility for working out our salvation, and on the other it can exaggerate the ability of priests to respond to our needs.

The second problem with this pre-Vatican II understanding is that over the centuries it has lulled Catholics into the mistaken impression that no matter what they do, the Church will always survive. That's simply not true. Whole Churches have vanished from the map. The Church of the Middle East was decimated by the incursion of Islam. The Church of North Africa has also disappeared. Much of Northern Europe was lost to the sixteenth-century reformers, and closer to home, parishes are closing at an alarming rate. It may not be our fault that all these things happen, but these setbacks do indicate that the Church will not magically survive.

In the wake of Vatican II, Catholics have been asked to see themselves not only as recipients of God's gifts, but also as givers of gifts. Theologically, this new emphasis (actually, an ancient biblical emphasis) is grounded in the understanding that the grace of salvation—indeed a gift—also implies a task. From the very beginning of his ministry, Jesus made it clear that all his disciples, not just the twelve apostles, had an obligation to go out "two by two" to preach the Word and overcome the power of evil (*Luke 10:1–20*). The Church of the first century took this responsibility seriously. Those who had been given gifts by the Holy Spirit were expected to exercise them for the good of the community (*1 Corinthians 12 and 14*). To receive a gift and simply to *keep* it was unthinkable.

Now that Jesus is no longer with us physically, he depends on us to be his voice, hands, and feet in the world. We are his Body. (*1 Corinthians 12:27–28*) This means that being a good Catholic involves far more than faithful reception of the Body of Christ in the Holy Eucharist. We must also become Christ's witnesses in our world. This is what ministry is all about. It's taking the responsibility, given to us by Christ and the Holy Spirit, to break and share

**14**

the bread of our lives as a testimony of God's saving presence in history.

When we consider the Vatican II teaching that Christ ministers through his people, one Scripture passage in particular can help us see that Jesus himself intended us to be more than passive recipients of divine life. In the story of the multiplication of loaves and fish, as recorded in Mark 6:34–44, there's a curious exchange between Jesus and the disciples. After noticing how late it was and the number of people who were still listening to Jesus teach, the disciples asked Jesus, "Why do you not dismiss them so that they can go and buy themselves something to eat?" In reply, Jesus said, "You give them something to eat." The disciples were shocked at this response, as we all are when asked to share the bread of our lives in ministry. "Are we to go and spend two hundred days' wages for bread to feed them?"

Jesus didn't even bother to answer their question. He simply showed them that if they gave away what little they had, there would be plenty of food for all—and for leftovers! This is what Jesus challenges us to do in memory of him and this is the challenge of ministry.

14

# The Bishop's Authority

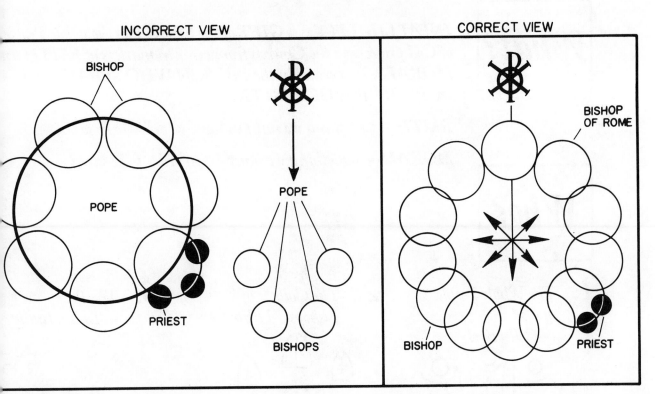

ation: Liz Purcell

Where does the bishop of your diocese get his authority? Above are three different views which attempt to explain this idea.

The first incorrect view shows the pope in the center, around whom all the bishops gather and from whom they get their authority. The second incorrect view shows Jesus giving authority to the pope, who passes on Christ's authority to the bishops. Why are these views incorrect?

The correct view has Christ as the center of the bishops gathered collegially, with the pope present as one among equals.

# Infallibility (transparency)

### What?

**INFALLIBILITY** *is a* **GIFT** *of the* **SPIRIT** *to the whole People of God protecting the Church from error in matters of* **FAITH** *and* **MORALS.** *It operates in the* **PERSON WHO SPEAKS** *and in the* **PEOPLE WHO LISTEN.**

**FAITH**—*something we must* believe *in order to be saved.*

**MORALS**—*something we must* do *in order to be saved.*

### Who?

**1.** *The Whole People of God —Collectively*

*In any truth or moral teaching which the whole Church holds to be true*

*e.g. The Trinity
The Incarnation
The Redemption*

**2.** *The College of Bishops—Unitedly*

*When in union with the Holy Father, they teach the same doctrine*

*e.g. Infallibility of the Holy Father, Vatican I*

**3.** *The Pope —Individually*

*When he proclaims a doctrine of faith or morals, speaking as Chief Shepherd of all the faithful (ex cathedra, from the chair)*

*e.g. Assumption of Mary*

### Why?

*Because Christ promised to be with his Church*
(Matthew 28:20)

*Because of the presence of the Holy Spirit*
(John 16: 7–12)

ame: _____     Score: _____

**udy Sheet**

**10w Your Church Leaders**

*rections:* Indicate the person(s) to whom each statement applies by writing
e classification(s) on the line. Some answers will require multiple
assifications. Since the Holy Father is Bishop of Rome, it is understood that
natever is true of a bishop is true of him. Use the HF classification for
atements that apply **only** to the pope.

⁊ = Holy Father **B** = Bishop **P** = Priest **D** = Deacon **A** = All **N** = None

_1. Exercises the sacred power of Orders within the Christian community.

_2. The chief spiritual leader of each local church or diocese.

_3. Ordained to assist the bishop.

_4. Clarifies issues of faith or morals by writing encyclical letters.

_5. Center of unity in the parish.

_6. Preaches, baptizes, teaches, and presides at marriages.

_7. Has at some period of life been ordained to the diaconate.

_8. His ministry is usually not full time nor top priority in his life.

_9. Must vow poverty, chastity, and obedience.

_10. Forms new parishes, starts religious orders, and sends priests, laity,
and religious to needy areas.

_11. Assembles the bishops in Church Councils to settle questions of
importance.

_12. Is obliged to render service to the Christian community.

_13. Is free from sins and failings.

_14. Holds primacy or authority over the whole Church.

_15. Establishes seminaries and schools.

_16. Has the right and duty to preach the gospel by word and example.

_17. Presides at the Eucharist.

_18. Has the fullness of the sacrament of Orders.

_19. Receives his power from the pope.

_20. Receives his power from the bishop.

_21. Can be married or single.

_22. Successor of the Apostles.

_23. An order which is experiencing rapid growth in the Church.

_24. Must live in community.

_25. Is infallible in faith or morals when speaking in virtue of his office.

_26. Referred to as clergy.

_27. Are called to ministry in the Church.

_28. Has the right to take a stand where the corporate influence of the
Church can make a difference.

_29. The visible source of the unity of the entire Church, both in faith and
communion.

_30. Is responsible that the sacraments are worthily administered and received.

**⑭**

**Study Sheet**

**Know Your Church Leaders**

Answer Key

1. A
2. B
3. P
4. HF
5. P
6. B/P/D
7. A
8. D
9. N
10. B
11. HF
12. A
13. N
14. HF
15. B
16. A
17. B/P
18. B
19. N
20. P/D
21. D
22. B
23. D
24. N
25. HF
26. A
27. A
28. B
29. HF
30. B

**14**

# CHAPTER 14 Test

## Christ Ministering Through His People

I.  **Multiple choice.** Write the letter of the best completion on the blank.

___1.  By his own example, Christ showed us that his Church would be
(a) scholarly, (b) authoritative, (c) servant.

___2.  The call to ministry is directed to (a) priests and religious, (b) all the
baptized, (c) those with special training.

___3.  Lay ministry (a) is experiencing rapid growth, (b) competes with the
ordained ministries, (c) should limit itself to parish involvement.

___4.  Working for peace and justice is (a) the responsibility of elected
leaders,
(b) impossible, (c) an obligation for all Catholics.

___5.  Infallibility means (a) the pope cannot make a mistake in anything,
(b) the pope is free from error when he solemnly proclaims a doctrine
of faith or morals, (c) the Church has never had to change any of its
ordinary teachings.

___6.  The ministry of a bishop involves (a) teaching, (b) building a
community of love, (c) service in relieving human distress, (d) all of
these.

___7.  The Holy Father's chief concern must always be for the good of (a) the
Vatican, (b) his bishops, (c) the whole Church.

___8.  Priests (a) share the Petrine ministry, (b) have full powers of the
priesthood, (c) assist the bishop in carrying out his duties.

___9.  Deacons are ordained (a) for a time, (b) for the service of the diocese,
(c) with the intention that service of the Church will be their top
priority.

___10. Religious life (a) is a special calling to holiness, (b) presupposes active
ministry in the Church, (c) depends entirely on one's personal
decision.

II. **Matching.** On the blank, write the letter of the word defined. There are
extra terms.

14

a. apostolate
b. bishop
c. charism
d. clergy
e. contemplatives

f. counsels
g. deacon
h. infallibility
i. laity

j. *magisterium*
k. ministry
l. Orders
m. priest

___1.  Apostolic service marked by a certain stability

___2.  Vows or promises of chastity, poverty, and obedience made by
religious men and women to God

___3.  The pope and bishops exercising their teaching authority as successors
of the Apostles

___4.  Religious who serve the Church by prayer and penance

Name: _____  Score: _____

___5.  All baptized persons, except clergy and religious men and women

___6.  Ordained bishops, priests, and deacons

___7.  Has the fullness of priesthood and exercises authority in his own right

___8.  A long-term service which carries out the mission of the Church

___9.  The power of priesthood

___10.  A gift to the Church which guarantees immunity from error regarding faith or morals

III. **Essay.** Choose two.

1. To what ministries are the laity of today being called?

2. To what service are those in authority in the Church called?

3. How can you answer the call to ministry in your present lifestyle and vocation?

# CHAPTER 14 Test
## Christ Ministering Through His People

**I.**

1. c
2. b
3. a
4. c
5. b
6. d
7. c
8. c
9. b
10. a

**II.**

1. k
2. f
3. j
4. e
5. i
6. d
7. b
8. a
9. l
10. h

**III.**

Answers will vary.

# CHAPTER 14

## SECTION 1

**Text Questions** (Student text pages 383–389)

**Page 385**

(1) Answers will vary. Tough love is offered and persevering when times are difficult. Love like this may be received from parents, teachers or friends and may be offered to friends or family members.

(2) Answers will vary.

(3) Some roles now being questioned are the roles of women in the workplace and in the Church, of the elderly (over the question of retirement age), and even of young children (to work or care for themselves).

**Page 389**

(4) Answers will vary.

(5) Answers will vary. Families like the Walkers benefit by their meeting many different people. They live their faith and enhance their spirituality by exercising their gifts. The Church benefits by becoming healthier and more alive through the participation of its members.

(6) Answers might include trying to change certain laws, finding cures for disease, legal representation for the poor, and teaching in a parish school.

(7) Keep track of the responses and discuss how the position of each candidate would affect each student's decisions about his or her own voting.

(8) Discuss ways of protesting laws and changing them. When is violence permitted (if at all)? What about the use of non-violent protest or civil disobedience? What forms of protest are not useful?

## SECTION 1 Checkpoint! (page 390)

**Review**

(1) Jesus showed tough love in his ministering to the outcastes of society whom he loved despite everything, and again during his passion and death.

(2) Before Vatican II ministry meant only the work of the clergy. After the Council, all people, lay and religious, should participate in ministry.

(3) A charism could be a gift for politics, science, or business as well as for religious leadership.

(4) An apostolic service is an occasional or spontaneous use of a gift for the Church. An apostolate is the use of a gift or service over a long period of time on a regular basis.

(5) Lay people within the Church can be involved in catechesis, missions, evangelization, or even counseling.

(6) Bringing Christ to the world means that all of one's actions should try to reflect Christ and make Christ present.

**14**

ANSWER
KEY

**(7)** Words to Know: *ministry* (apostolic service marked by a certain stability in time); *tough love* (persevering and courageous caring even when times are difficult); *charism* (gift for the common good); *apostolic service* (short-term use of a gift for the Church); *laity* (all baptized persons except clergy and religious).

## In Your World

**(1)** Whatever cause is chosen, stress the action taken as the goal of this exercise. Discuss the cause as an expression of Christian values and your action as Christian action which reflects Christ in the world. Keep track of class activities and they can be used in future years or as a school display.

**(2)** Encourage both students and the person being interviewed to see the ministry as the use of a gift and how that gift fits into their lives in the Church and in the world.

## Scripture Search

**(1)** In Acts 6 deacons are ministering to widows, distributing food, and waiting on tables. In James, early ministries of prayer are described, as is anointing the sick, and forgiveness of sin. And 1 Corinthians mentions gifts of miracles, prophecy, discernment, tongues, and interpretation of tongues. The ministries were started at the time of Pentecost when the Holy Spirit entered the Apostles and gave each of them special gifts.

**(2)** The store clerk might look at his or her job not only as a way to make money, but also as a way to serve others; the student might see the acquisition of knowledge not only as a way to get a good job or to get into college, but also as a way to learn about righteousness and to search for it; the police officer could see himself or herself as a peacemaker; the landlord would understand the great responsibility of caring for the welfare of others; the mayor could learn the lesson of being meek and working for others; and the journalist might take on the task of seeking out and recognizing the peacemakers, meek, and poor in spirit and act as the conscience of the people.

## SECTION 2
**Text Questions** (Student text pages 391–397)

**Page 393**

**(9)** Answers will vary.

**(10)** Answers will vary.

**Page 396**

**(11)** Answers will vary.

**(12)** Answers might include volunteer work, and adherence to the teachings of the Church and the bishop.

**Page 397**

**(13)** Answers will vary.

## SECTION 2  Checkpoint! (page 398)
### Review

**(1)** Ordained clergy have a special character and unique gift different in degree and essence from the general priesthood of the people. The call of the clergy is in service to the Christian community.

**(2)** As disciple, the bishop leaves all to pattern his life on that of Jesus. As apostle, he is a representative of Christ. As presbyter, he is a leader and is responsible for pastoral care.

**(3)** The main role of a bishop is sacramental ministry—to unify and order the faith community.

**(4)** A bishop has authority in his own right. Priests work in unity with the bishop on the parish level.

**(5)** As teacher the bishop is responsible for all education courses for adults and children. As priest he ordains priests and is responsible for proper administration of the sacraments. As shepherd he provides for the material and spiritual needs of all in his community.

**(6)** The Holy Father is the chief bishop of the Church as the successor of Peter. His is the highest level of authority.

**(7)** Words to Know: *clergy* (ordained ministers); *bishop* (exercises the same office as Christ who is the supreme teacher, priest, and shepherd, exercises authority in his own right); *presbyter* (elder or leader); *pastoral* (refers to shepherding or gentle guidance); *episkopos* (Greek for overseer, bishop); *faculties* (permission granted to a priest to preach or celebrate the sacrament of Penance in that diocese); *pastoral letters* (letters written by bishops to dioceses on issues of importance); *excommunication* (a penalty imposed by the Church which removes a person from Communion with the Church); *Petrine ministry* (ministry of the Bishop of Rome, successor of

**14**

Peter, with primacy over the entire Church); *infallibility* (gift which guarantees immunity from error when believing or teaching a truth of faith or moral).

## In Your World
(1) Include any information available about the background and education of the bishop and his early career in the Church. What does he share in common with the students in terms of background or the conditions of his youth?

(2) Encourage students to be creative and to express themselves in writing, with pictures, or music. Use the images given throughout this section.

## Scripture Search
Matthew refers to Peter as the rock and source of ministry; Luke shows Jesus praying for a disciple; John shows Peter instructed to tend and care for the flock; Acts represents the power of Peter as a representative of Christ and judge; 1 and 2 Peter show Peter giving pastoral instruction, warnings, and offerings of support, and Matthew 16 acknowledges that Peter was the one to recognize Jesus' true identity and he was rewarded in return.

## SECTION 3
### Text Questions (Student text pages 399–404)

**Page 400**

(14) Answers will vary.

**Page 402**

(15) A factory worker might volunteer time to build, repair, or do maintenance work on the church building; a physician could give talks on health care or offer free service for the poor in the church; a bank president could offer to do some of the accounting work for the church; and a salesperson might become involved in some fundraising activities.

## SECTION 3 Checkpoint! (page 405)
### Review
(1) Father Hartman makes friends in the parish and maintains contacts with older priests who offer him support, gets rest, and updates his learning.

(2) Any man who is at least 25 years old if unmarried, or 35 years old if married, may become a deacon.

(3) A deacon is appointed to a particular ministry by the bishop, who allows him to continue his profession and family life.

(4) A deacon may not officiate at the Eucharist, hear confession, or administer the sacrament of the sick.

(5) Religious men and women take vows of chastity, poverty, and obedience.

(6) Taking vows shows that religious men and women offer their lives to God and form a special relationship with God. The vows free the person from some of the obstacles to God's love.

(7) Words to Know: *deacon* (minister ordained to complement the service of priests and bishops in a diocese); *religious* (vowed individuals who act as teachers, nurses, administrators, and in a number of other capacities in the Church).

## In Your World
(1) Find out the special ministry of the deacon and stress the balance made between the religious and other life responsibilities of the deacon.

(2) Remind students of the variety of functions of the office they choose. The symbol should include as many identifying characteristics of the office as possible.

## Scripture Search
Acts shows that the original seven deacons were chosen to distribute the Eucharist in order to leave the disciples free to pray and to be involved in other active ministry.

## CHAPTER 14 Review (pages 406–407)
### Study
(1) All early Christians tried to witness to Jesus' love by spreading the word throughout the world. They all used their gifts.

(2) Saint Paul used the body as an image to illustrate the variety of gifts Christians bring to the Church. We all work together to achieve a common goal just as the various parts of the body work together to make the body function smoothly.

(3) Pius XII said that the role of the laity is in areas where clergy are absent such as politics, the arts, or science.

**14**

(4) Charisms are gifts of the Holy Spirit rooted in one's personality for ministry and service.

(5) Examples of apostolic service are consoling mourners, teaching, or serving the Church with financial or organizational skills.

(6) All baptized persons participate in the priestly, prophetic, and kingly offices of Christ by carrying out the mission of the Christian people in the Church and the world in evangelization, catechesis, and missions.

(7) Baptized persons can be involved in ministries that use their talents and gifts to relate faith to daily life.

(8) People accept their responsibility as Christians by responding to people in need and making a contribution to society through their daily work.

(9) The ordained ministers of the Church are bishops, priests, and deacons.

(10) The offices of the bishop are teacher, priest, and shepherd.

(11) A priest acts as the center of unity in a parish, appointed by the bishop to teach, preach, and minister to the faithful.

(12) The three guiding images of bishops are teacher, priest, and shepherd.

(13) The role of the Holy Father is as chief bishop, successor of Peter, supreme teacher, high priest, and highest authority.

(14) The primary responsibility of priests is celebrating the Eucharist and other sacraments.

(15) A deacon is appointed by the bishop to a particular ministry. Deacons may preach, proclaim the Gospel, baptize, officiate at weddings, and give communion to the sick. Deacons use their work-related skills for the benefit of the Church.

(16) Religious life is a charism which reminds people of Jesus' teachings, and gives service to the Church and community that might not be accomplished otherwise.

## Action

(1) Encourage discussion of both the ups and downs of the life of an ordained minister of the Church. Discuss the growing awareness of a vocation and the path taken to realize it.

(2) Have students who choose this activity prepare the chart so that it can be displayed in the classroom or school. Try to make the chart as complete as possible.

## Prayer

Discuss the need all people have for prayer and the ways prayer can be a way of offering support individually or as a community. This prayer for the pastor should be a way of reminding the class that we all struggle to be what God wants us to be and to live up to our potential.

14

# Christ Ministering Through His People

**OVERVIEW:** This chapter focuses on the roles of ordained and lay ministry in the Church. It aims to clarify the function of each in the life of the Christian community.

**OBJECTIVES: The students will:**

- Offer definitions of the term "minister" and apply them to both lay people and the ordained.
- List the three types of ordained ministers in the Church and discuss the responsibilities of each.
- List and discuss the pros and cons of religious life.

**TIME FRAME: One to one-and-a-half hours.**

**MATERIALS: Paper and pens.**

**PROCEDURE:**

*Into:* Prayer—Begin class with the prayer from "A People at Prayer," page 402.

*Through:*

Activity One:

1. Ask students to define the term "minister" as both a noun and a verb. Put the list on the board.

2. Use question 6 on page 389 to initiate discussion of the types of ministries lay people can have in the life of the Church and in the world.

3. Have each student (or form small groups) list ways they can act as ministers in the Church.

Activity Two:

1. Identify the bishop of your diocese and ask students to describe what he does.

2. Break into three groups and have each group take a piece of paper and write the word teacher, priest, or shepherd on it. Have each group write down a description of the function of that person and apply it to the bishop.

3. As a class discuss the role of the pope. Place him in the hierarchy of the ordained ministry. Use Teacher's Resource 14C.

Activity Three:

1. Break into two groups. Have each discuss the roles of priests and deacons, using the text if necessary.

2. As a class discuss religious life. What vows are taken and why? How does one recognize a calling?

3. List the pros and cons of religious life and its contributions to the life of the Church.

*Beyond:* Suggest that students read "Infallibility—A Gift of the Spirit," on page 395. Also encourage them to complete activity 1 from Section 1, "In Your World," page 390.

*Prayer:* Close class with the prayer in the "Prayer" section, page 407.

289

Name: _____     Score: _____

## CHAPTER 14 QUIZ
# Christ Ministering Through His People

True (+) or false (o).

____**1.** In his own life, Jesus modeled the role of service to which he calls his followers.

____**2.** A variety of lay ministries existed in the early Church.

____**3.** Ministry is how the Church concretely carries out its mission on a day-to-day basis.

____**4.** The laity have always worked closely with the clergy in all forms of ministry.

____**5.** The laity have a share in the priestly, prophetic, and kingly office of Christ.

____**6.** Areas of lay ministry are constantly growing.

____**7.** Ministry extends into the work world and everyday activities.

____**8.** Social justice is best left to the experts.

____**9.** The Church's ordained ministers include bishops, priests, and deacons.

____**10.** Their ministry is service to the Christian community.

____**11.** Bishops are called to be special signs of the Church's unity in Christ.

____**12.** Every bishop receives his power from the pope.

____**13.** Priests preach, teach, and minister to the faithful independently of the bishop.

____**14.** A pastor is meant to call forth and order all the gifts of the members of his parish.

____**15.** The bishops are assistants of the Holy Father.

____**16.** The Holy Father is the visible source of the Church's unity.

____**17.** Bishops are called to be the Church's supreme teachers, high priests, and shepherds.

____**18.** Celebration of the sacraments is the deacon's primary area of ministry.

____**19.** Religious life is a special gift of God to both an individual and the Church.

____**20.** Teen-agers are too young for ministry.

**14**

# CHAPTER 14 QUIZ
Answer Key

1. +
2. +
3. +
4. o
5. +
6. +
7. +
8. o
9. +
10. +
11. +
12. o
13. o
14. +
15. o
16. +
17. +
18. o
19. +
20. o

## A Model for Parish Ministry

The Church of the Savior is a small ecumenical Protestant church which has been in Washington, D.C. for about 30 years. Its eighty members are all fully committed to two goals: the inward spiritual quest to discover their true self and God, and the outward reach to care for human needs either as individuals or in teams.

Although the pastor, Gordon Cosby, uses an evangelical style of preaching, the underlying spirituality is largely drawn from classical Christian tradition. The congregation operates on a "theology of gifts." Since everyone is believed to be gifted, the purpose of the Church is seen as helping its members discover their gifts and using them in service and possibly ministry.

Certain gifted lay people, authorized by pastor Gordon and recognized by the groups, act as group pastor or spiritual director of small groups who meet regularly for spiritual nourishment, sharing, study, and accountability for mission.

Out of this exercise which builds inner spiritual strength flows such ministries as the following:

**FLOC** (For Love of Children) provides actual home and group parents for dependent children in Washington, D.C. It befriends the real parents of the children with the goal of healing and reconciliation. The group homes are supported through prayer and friendship as well as material resources.

**Potters House** is a low-key Christian coffee house, art exhibit, and bookstore located in the heart of the inner city. Over lunch and evening coffee the volunteer staff offer conversation to those who want it and wouldn't come to a "normal" church. Having become aware of a large elderly population in the area, they added free lunches for the elderly poor and have undertaken a housing program for the elderly.

## Helps in Proclaiming the Word of God

1. Become a habitual reader of the Bible to become familiar with its style and themes.

2. In preparing the reading, study not only the assigned passage, but the section into which it fits. Knowing something about the book and author from which you are reading will also help your interpretation.

3. Spend some time meditating on the passage you will read. Practice it aloud several times. Experiment by varying stress, pitch, timing, and phrasing. Don't be afraid to use intelligent pauses.

4. Ask the Holy Spirit to speak through you, but do your part by being well rested, becoming familiar with the podium and the particular book you will read from, and the microphone system. Do not lean into the mike, but stand about six to twelve inches away.

5. Glance up at the congregation, trying to include all areas of the assembly in your glance at one time or another.

6. Identify the passage—for example, "A reading from the first letter of John." You need not give the chapter and verse. Conclude with, "This is the Word of the Lord." You may wish to hold up the book for community veneration as you say these words.

**14**

7. Consult with the liturgists or musicians in advance to find out how the Responsorial Psalm, the Alleluia, and the verse before the Gospel will be handled.

## Student Serves

James Pietrangelo, a student from St. Ignatius High School for boys in Cleveland, Ohio, volunteered as a part-time social worker in an inner city school to tutor kids like Tyrone Blackshear and Thien Tran, who needed help in reading. The almost 300 other high school students also served elderly patients in a nursing home, tutored adults struggling with English as a second language, and worked in hospitals, hunger centers, and social service centers. It is part of a Jesuit program to put their young people in touch with life.

What good do you think the boys do? Why do their teachers consider such service a mandatory part of their religion program?

How do you think their service of others benefits the boys?

## Helping People with Handicaps

Some highlights of a seminar sponsored by the President's Committee on Employment of the Handicapped:

"Handicapped people have to learn to accept themselves fully if they want the rest of the world to accept them" (Harold Russell).

"If you approach handicapped people with respect, if you recognize them as equals—then you will end up considering them truly as persons" (Joan Wadlenger).

"Don't perceive what has to be done for a handicapped person from a negative point of view. Working together on a problem really means working to accommodate to a situation. We accommodate to all kinds of situations all our lives. Let's not perceive them as problems" (Bernadette McCann).

"Handicapped people don't want separate but equal treatment. They want the same opportunities given to others" (Stan Brice).

"It's time we took another look at the word *dis-ability* with those three silly letters at the front end. Let's eliminate those three letters" (Harold Krentz).

"Write [speak] about the handicapped as you would about the nonhandicapped—emphasize similarities rather than differences" (Dr. Harold Yunker).

"Mental illness is an illness, no more. Some people who used to be mentally ill are mentally ill no longer. They're human beings. What they have achieved, they have won the hard way" (Percy Knauth).

"Each of us exists on two levels, a personal level, a public level. Sometimes our private lives are quite far removed from our public lives. When our private and public lives merge, we have it all together. By reducing rejection, we can help the handicapped meld both to bring it all together" (Dr. Herbert Striner).

## Supplementary Projects

1. Highlight the Holy Father

   - Collect articles on the Holy Father, especially on any trip to another country.

   - Summarize each article in a few sentences; include your thoughts and reactions at the end.

   - Write a 250-word composition which surveys the articles on the theme: "Christ Guides His Church Today through Pope John Paul II."

   - Make a map of the pope's travels.

   - Display the articles, map, and your composition on a poster board suitable for viewing.

2. Create a "Model Christian Community (Diocese/Parish)." Specify what you would like it to be in terms of:

   - Geographic area.

   - People.

   - Its bishop or pastor.

   - Liturgy.

   - Education.

   - Lay ministers.

   - Religious.

   - Organizations and activities.

   - Patron saint.

   - Cathedral or church architecture.

14

3. Study your Catholic Diocesan Directory.

   - Give statistics on your diocese: number of Catholics, parishes, priests, deacons, sisters, religious brothers, students going to Catholic Schools.

   - Study the Diocesan office and write a "summary report" that shows the **scope** of activities and interests your Diocese addresses.

   - Find the names of the groups and agencies which help the poor and needy. How many are they? What areas do they cover? Arrange to visit one and report to the class on its history and work.

4. Analyze the churches listed in your telephone book.

   - Look in the yellow pages under "Churches." How many churches are listed? What denominations do they represent?

   - What percentage of the Churches do you find under "Churches—Catholic"?

   - Does the information given lead you to any other conclusions? State your conclusions.

5. Compare parish bulletins.

   - Collect and study the parish bulletins of at least five parishes. Look for the activities sponsored by each parish that really **serve** or **help** the parishioners. List them. Which diocesan activities are mentioned?

   - What kind of parish does each bulletin reflect?

   - Based solely on their bulletin, to which parish would you like to belong? Why?

6. Examine the *Official Catholic Directory* for the current year.

   - How many dioceses are in the United States? How many religious orders of priests, brothers, and sisters in the United States?

   - Refer to the section on diocesan offices. Write down ten offices that truly **serve** the needs of the people.

   - Refer to the information on Chaplains of Public Institutions. How many public institutions are helped by the Catholic Church? List several **kinds** of public institutions.

   - Refer to the directory of Catholic Schools. How many students are being educated in Catholic colleges, high schools, elementary schools?

   - Describe anything else that interests you as you page through.

7. Fold a sheet into three parts horizontally and design a brochure advertising for ministers to carry on Christ's mission in the Church. Make it appealing and contemporary. Name the qualities and persons needed, the tasks to be done, and practical steps needed to apply.

8. Debate: "The pope has very little influence on the life of the average Catholic."

9. Write a job description for the Holy Father.

## Reflection on What it Means to be Pope

1. *Journal of a Soul* by Pope John XXIII

   "Since the Lord chose me for this great service....I see myself only as the humble and unworthy 'servant of the servants of God.' The whole world is my family. This sense of belonging to everyone must give character and vigor to my mind, my heart, and my actions. This vision...will give a new impulse to my constant and continual daily prayer."

2. Selections from a novel about a pope—*Shoes of the Fisherman* by Morris West (New York: William Morrow & Co., 1963)

   The pope speaks: "I see very clearly the shape of a great personal problem for every man who holds this office: how the press of business and the demands of so many people can so impoverish him that he has neither time nor will left to regulate the affairs of his own soul. I long for solitude and the leisure of contemplation."

   A friend speaks to the pope: "I have seen three men sit in this room; you are the last I shall see. Each of them came in his turn to the moment where you stand now—the moment of solitude. I have to tell you that there is no remedy for it, and no escape...Like it or not, you are condemned to a solitary pilgrimage, Your Holiness, and you have just begun the climb. Only God can walk with you all the way, because He took on the flesh to make the same climb Himself...I wish I could tell you differently. I cannot."

   What suffering does the first quotation bring out in the life of a pope?

**14**

The second quotations are taken from a fictional account. Do you think that what is said is true? Explain.

## Requirements for a Permanent Deacon

The permanent deacon is called personally by the Church to serve after the manner of Jesus. First and foremost, he is a Christian man in his usual employment and lifestyle, trained and formed by additional study and prayer for a special ministry to the community as an ordained minister. Candidates in all dioceses pursue an approximately three-year program of theological, pastoral, and spiritual formation before ordination. Specific requirements for acceptance into the permanent diaconate training program may vary from diocese to diocese. In general, requirements would be similar to those for the Diocese of Cleveland, Ohio, which follow.

1. Be at least 32 years old at time of entrance into the program. (Minimum age for ordination is 35.)

2. Be a Roman Catholic of sound moral character, mature faith, and have a sense of vocation to service.

3. Demonstrate prayerfulness and be open to further spiritual formation.

4. Have attained at least a high school diploma (or its equivalency in experience) and have the ability to be trained for quasi-professional service.

5. Be of sound physical and mental health.

6. Be attuned to the needs and the life of the Church today.

7. Have demonstrated active service, apostolic involvement, and leadership among the People of God.

8. Have proven stability in his secular employment and family life.

9. If married, have the enthusiastic support of his wife and family.

10. Demonstrate the basic potential to develop the ministerial skills of relating to people, speaking well, and being a spiritual leader.

11. Have the support of a sponsoring pastor or institution who would welcome his ministry.

12. Be able to represent the Church with intelligence, Christian dignity, and prayerful service.

### Pretest on Religious Life

1. What does the phrase "religious life" mean to you?

2. Name as many religious communities of men and women that you know.

   *Men's Communities:*

   *Women's Communities:*

3. Explain briefly what you think each of the vows mean: chastity, poverty, obedience.

4. Why do people in religious life make these vows?

5. Why are there different communities of religious?

6. How many years, on the average, does the formation program involve?

7. Explain the various stages through which a person passes in becoming a religious.

8. Why do religious pray so much?

9. Why don't religious marry?

10. What would be the signs that a person is called to this vocation?

### Review Exercises
Review I

A. Define the given vertical word.

B. Write the correct answers on the blanks.

1. M _ _ _ _ _ _ _
2. _ A _ _ _ _
3. _ _ _ _ _ G _ _ _ _ _ _
4. _ _ _ _ I _ _ _ _ _
5. _ _ S _ _ _
6. _ _ T _ _ _ _ _
7. _ E _ _ _
8. _ _ _ _  _ R _ _ _ _
9. _ _ _ _ _ I _ _
10. _ _ U _
11. _ _ _ _ _ _ _ M _ _ _ _

1. Service in the Church flowing from Christ's mission.

2. Christian community within a diocese.

3. The union of bishops with one another and the Holy Father.

4. A witness to the Christian life—whether in a foreign land or "at home."

5. The chief spiritual leader of each local church and successor to the Apostles.

6. Another term for universal.

7. Part of the threefold mission of the Church.

8. One of the offices of every bishop.

9. Part of the threefold mission of the Church.

10. Once a doctrine is solemnly defined, it is _____ , that is, it cannot be revoked.

Review II

C. Define the given vertical word.

D. Write the correct answers on the blanks.

1.        _ _ _ _ S _ _
2.        _ _ _ A _ _ _ _ _ _ _ _
3.        _ _ C _ _ _ _ _
4.        _ _ R _ _ _ _
5.        _ _ _ _ A _ _ _ _
6.        _ _ _ _ _ _ M
7.        _ _ E _ _ _ _ _
8.        _ N _
9.        _ _ _ T _ _ _ _ _ _ _ _
10.       _ _ S _ _ _ _ _ _ _

1. Assistants to the bishop, sharing in his ordained ministry.

2. The Spirit's gift of freedom from error in matters of faith and morals.

3. An ordinary teaching of the Church.

4. One of three areas in which the Church is united.

5. The Church's clerical leaders organized into ranks according to ministry.

6. A gift, like infallibility, given to the Church for the welfare of all.

7. One of the three offices of every bishop.

8. A mark of the Church. It is
   _____.

9. A kind of religious order whose main ministry to the Church consists of prayer and penance.

10. People who take private vows and strive to leaven society with Christian values as they work in the world are members of secular
    _____.

Review III

E. Define the given vertical word.

F. Write the correct answers on the blanks.

1.   _ _ U _ _ _ _
2.   _ _ _ _ _ N _ _ _ _
3.   _ I _ _ _ _ _
4.   _ _ V _ _ _
5.   _ _ _ E
6.   _ R _ _ _ _
7.   _ _ _ S _ _ _ _ _
8.   _ _ A _ _ _ _ _
9.   _ _ _ _ _ L _ _ _ _

1. A solemn gathering of bishops with the Holy Father to discuss Church matters.

2. One of the ways in which the Church is one.

3. A local Church.

4. A part of the threefold mission of the Church.

5. The chief bishop of the universal Church; Peter's successor.

6. The sacrament of which the bishop has the fullness.

7. A type of religious life which blends contemplative prayer with active ministry to the Church.

8. One of the ways the Church is one.

9. A letter by the Holy Father to the Universal Church.

## Answers to Review
Review I

A. The Living teaching authority of the Church.

B. 1. ministry, 2. parish, 3. collegiality,
4. missionary 5. bishop, 6. catholic, 7. teach,
8. high priest, 9. sanctity 10. soul, 11. irreformable

Review II

**C.** The Seven liturgical ways of attaining union with Christ.

**D. 1.** priests, **2.** infallibility, **3.** doctrine, **4.** worship **5.** hierarchy, **6.** charism, **7.** shepherd, **8.** one, **9.** contemplative, **10.** institutes

Review III

**E.** Another term for the word "Catholic."

**F. 1.** council, **2.** government, **3.** diocese, **4.** govern, **5.** pope, **6.** orders, **7.** apostolic, **8.** teaching, **9.** encyclical

## A Sinner Called to Heal: Vincent de Paul

From time to time we read of underworld characters who suddenly disappear or get shot. With them, things usually seem to go from bad to worse. But some people's energies work in the reverse direction. They progress from bad to good.

Though ordained early in life, Vincent de Paul was by nature a hard, repulsive, rough, and cross man. His faults were not your everyday defects that we all put up with in one another. They were huge potholes crying out for road repair with every bump.

While working with the most miserably poor of his day, the galley slaves, Vincent encountered Christ who healed him so that he could make the rest of his life a mission of tenderness and healing. God used the boiling energies of this dynamic man to revolutionize health care the world over.

Not until the Christian era were there any social structures for the care of the sick. The Gospels show the afflicted lining the roads of Palestine and even cast out of the towns. Through Vincent de Paul's power of organization and creative thinking the foundation for our present hospital system was laid.

A Frenchman, he was seized and enslaved by Tunisian pirates. His horror at the plight of galley slaves gave him a great desire to help others. After his escape, among the many charities he organized in France, his agencies for the aged, the incurably diseased, and the sick became models for our modern charitable institutions. Until his day, it was unheard of for religious women to leave their cloisters. He fought for and got permission for the Sisters of Charity, an order he founded, to work directly with the poor in the cities. In the secular world, modern nurses and social workers are spin-offs of his efforts and vision.

Today, vowed Vincentian religious, both men and women, bring Christ's healing to people in many lands. Vincent de Paul made it possible for Christ to live in the modern world in new and original ways. With Saint Paul he could say "When I am weak, then I am strong" (2 Corinthians 12:10).

What is the gift (perhaps a fault now) that you can bring to the healing of the world?

While still concerned with charity, the post-Vatican II Church is now focusing on correcting injustice. What is the difference between the two? In their methods?

## Reasons for Church Membership

*Directions: You* have 15 points to divide among the reasons why you think *most people* belong to the Church. You also have 15 points to distribute next to the reasons why you are a member of the Church. You may place all 15 points by one answer or divide possible answers, giving the most points to those you think are most important.

*You/Most People*

___ ___ **1.** I feel that I need God and that the Church is a way to gain God's help.

___ ___ **2.** My parents brought me up in the Church and I don't want to disappoint them.

___ ___ **3.** The Church makes sense to me personally. I will always try to remain an active Church member.

___ ___ **4.** I feel a need to return something to God for all his gifts to me.

___ ___ **5.** I feel a strong attraction to Christ and find his presence in church celebrations and activities.

___ ___ **6.** People might consider me bad or even damned if I didn't belong to the Church.

___ ___ **7.** I believe God wants me to belong to the Church.

___ ___ **8.** The Church gives me a chance to share my faith with others.

___ ___ **9.** In the Church I can do good for others.

___ ___ **10.** I want to be married in a beautiful ceremony and to be buried in the Church and have my children baptized there.

(14)

___ ___ **11.** I would feel guilty if I didn't belong to the Church.

___ ___ **12.** I belong only because I was raised in the Faith and made to go to Church.

___ ___ **13.** Other

## The Church and You

Jesus, during the past days I've been reading and thinking and studying about the Church, the family of those who follow you in love as children of the Father. As I look back over my own experience of "Church" and what it means to me, I remember that as a child and in grade school.... Then during the first two years of high school.... Now, after reading and studying and discussing.... In the future, I would hope.... There are questions and wonderings I have about "Church," such as.... And there are needs that I have that I would hope the experience of Church could meet.... If I were to design or select one symbol to represent "Church" for me, it would be because....

**14**

## HANDBOOK

# Ecumenism—The Call to Unity

(Text pages 408–413)

## FOCUS

**Doctrinal:** Vatican II represented a major adjustment of the Church's view toward the world: we recognize and welcome the workings of the Spirit in other Christian churches.

**Personal:** Am I accepting of members of other churches and open to learning from their holiness?

## OBJECTIVES

**Cognitive:** (a) to know the history, meaning, and aims of ecumenism; (b) to understand the basic Protestant affirmations and the Catholic position on them; (c) to become acquainted with the mainline Protestant churches.

**Affective:** (a) to be aware of mistakes made by the Catholic Church in relation to other churches; (b) to want to share in restoring unity among Christian churches.

## Handbook Outline

Ecumenism — The Call to Unity
The Movement
Comparing Faith Affirmations
Justification
Scripture
Christ's Priesthood
Sacraments
Fellowship of Believers
Christ as Mediator
Mainline Protestant Churches
Lutheran
Presbyterian
Episcopalian (American Anglican)
Methodist

**H**

# TEACHER'S RESOURCE H–A

## Historical Notes

Be mindful that the Protestant churches covered in this short overview do not represent the total of all such churches. There are over 200 different denominations of Protestants in the United States alone. They have all evolved since the time of the Reformation and all share the same fundamental beliefs. They differ in politics, and some changes (such as the ordination of women as ministers) have not been made in all churches.

## Pedagogical Notes

1. Make clear the distinction that ecumenism is a movement aimed at restoring Christian unity, rather than the return of non-Catholics to the Catholic Church.

2. Here is a listing of churches not covered in the Handbook.

**The Baptist Church** was founded in 1570 in Amsterdam by John Smyth. It emphasizes personal salvation through faith, adult Baptism through immersion, and the Bible as the sole authority. There is no binding creed. Its sacraments are Baptism and the Lord's Supper. Membership: 30 million Americans.

**The Disciples of Christ** were formed in America in 1800 by Thomas Campbell against Anglican ritualism. Their creed is Christ, with doctrines from the New Testament. Adult Baptism by immersion and the Lord's Supper are the two sacraments. Membership: 1.2 million Americans.

**Pentecostalism** was started in London in 1832 by John Irving. They believe that true conversion is followed by baptism of the Spirit outwardly manifested by gifts and powers. Membership: 7.2 million Americans among Churches of God, Assemblies of God, and Foursquare Gospel Church.

**The Salvation Army** was founded in London in 1870 by William Booth to care for the poor in the streets. They reject all sacraments, lead strict lives and renounce alcohol. Membership: 400,000 Americans.

**Jehovah's Witnesses** began in 1872 through Charles Russell of Pittsburgh who was said to be the seventh prophet mentioned in Ezekiel. They deny the Trinity and Christ's Divinity. Title comes from a mixing of Hebrew names for God— Jahweh and Elohim. Only 144,000 will be saved. Members give 60–175 hours a month to spreading message, refuse to bear arms or participate in civic events, and forbid blood transfusions. Membership: 600,000 Americans.

**Seventh-Day Adventist** started in the 1840s by William Miller's prediction of the end of the world. Saturday is the Sabbath. Believe that Christ will soon return. They see Christ as divine, and accept Baptism and the Lord's Supper. They abstain from tobacco and stimulants. Membership: 600,000 Americans

**Christian Scientist** was founded in 1879 by Mary Baker Eddy's claim to a cure by prayer. There are no sacraments. They oppose use of medicine. 3000 branches in the United States.

**The Mormon Church (Latter Day Saints)** was founded by Joseph Smith (early 1800s) who received instruction from the angel Moroni to dig up gold plates of Christ's revelation to the ancient people who lived near his Vermont home. These plates, which contain the Old and New Testament as well as legends and other revelations, make up the Mormon Bible. They believe in the pre-existence of the soul, adult baptism by immersion, Lord's Super and, in the early days, polygamy. Membership: 4 million.

**Unitarian Universalists:** Not Protestants, but extremely liberal, with no set doctrine. They are searchers and doubters who gather to pray, think, and discuss religion and philosophical questions. They stress education, fine arts, music, and a questioning attitude about religious matters. Membership: 100,000 in the United States.

Use the *Encyclopedia of Religion* or any other good source to provide additional information about some of these divergent Protestant churches.

# TEACHER'S RESOURCE H–B

## Theological Notes

Some distinctions help to distinguish the Protestant churches. In addition to the mainline churches, there are radical sects (formed by a deeper break with Catholic and Reformed churches) and sects with extremely divergent beliefs. Among the radical sects are Baptists, Disciples of Christ, Pentecostals, the Salvation

Army, Jehovah's Witnesses, and Seventh-Day Adventists. In the group with divergent beliefs are Christian Scientists, Mormons, and Unitarian Universalists.

Within the Protestant churches are found fundamentalists, who literally believe every word of the Bible, evangelists, who emphasize personal religion, and liberals, who remain open to different interpretations of the creed.

Name: _____     Score: _____

## Handbook Test

## Ecumenism: The Call to Unity

### I.   True and false.

If the statement is true, place a plus sign (+) on the line; if it is false, place a zero (o).

____ **1.**  Catholics have always taken the lead in the ecumenical movement.

____ **2.**  Ecumenism applies only to the union of the Christian churches.

____ **3.**  As Catholics, we should not hope for reunion with the separated Churches.

____ **4.**  Christ works through all Churches; each has some of the truth God revealed.

____ **5**  All Protestant churches celebrate baptism and the Lord's Supper, but with different meanings.

____ **6.**  The Catholic Church acknowledges its contribution to disunity.

____ **7.**  Christian unity means that all other religions must become Roman Catholic.

____ **8.**  Catholics still consider all Protestants as heretics.

____ **9.**  Separated Christians have more on which they agree than disagree.

____ **10.**  The wounds of division, which are centuries old, will not be healed by a simple declaration of unity.

### II.  Matching: Write the letter of the correct term on the line. Terms may be used more than once or not at all.

a. Anglicanism
b. baptism by immersion
c. Baptists
d. Calvinism
e. Episcopalians

f. compromise on belief
g. Lutheranism
h. dialog
i. Presbyterians
j. Roman Catholicism

k. Scripture
l. splintering
m. Trent
n. Vatican II

____ **1.**  Another name for Anglicans

____ **2.**  Another name for Calvinists

____ **3.**  Not a mainline Protestant church

____ **4.**  Closest to Roman Catholicism in beliefs and externals

____ **5.**  First of the Protestant groups to break from Rome

____ **6.**  Greatest weakness in Protestantism

____ **7.**  Greatest strength in Protestantism

____ **8.**  Modified the basic belief on which it was founded

____ **9.**  A defensive Catholic response to Protestantism

____ **10.** Protestant, but retains religious orders of men and women

____ **11.** Not one of the means to promote Christian unity

____ **12.** Promoted dialog with all Christians, Jews, non-Christians, and atheists

302

# Handbook Test
## Ecumenism: The Call to Unity
Answer Key

**I.**

1. o
2. +
3. o
4. +
5. +
6. +
7. o
8. o
9. +
10. +

**II.**

1. e
2. i
3. c
4. a
5. g
6. l
7. k
8. d
9. m
10. a
11. f
12. j

# Ecumenism—The Call to Unity

**OVERVIEW:** The goal of this brief handbook is to present the beliefs of some of the mainline Protestant Churches and to compare their beliefs and practices to those of the Catholic Church.

**OBJECTIVES: The students will:**

- Discuss ecumenism and its purpose.
- List as many Protestant churches as they can.
- Present and discuss the beliefs of the mainline Protestant Churches.

**TIME FRAME: One to one-and-a-half hours.**

**MATERIALS: Handbook, song "The Church's One Foundation"**

**PROCEDURE:**

*Into:* Prayer—Lead students in singing "The Church's One Foundation," which was written by Martin Luther.

*Through:*

Activity One:

1. Ask for a definition of ecumenism. Expand the definition and discuss the concept.
2. Ask students how Catholics view (or should view) Protestants and why.
3. Ask what can each individual and the Church as a whole do to encourage unity.

Activity Two:

1. Ask students to name as many types of Protestant churches as they can.
2. Present the basic views of the Protestant churches on Scripture, justification, and sacraments. Be sure this is clear.

Activity Three:

1. Write the words "Lutheran," "Presbyterian," "Episcopalian," and "Methodist" on the board.
2. Present the basic beliefs of each tradition under the appropriate name.
3. Ask students how each church differs and how each are the same. List the similarities. Note that there are definite structural differences among these churches.

*Beyond:* Suggest that students read through the Handbook and compare how each religious tradition is alike and how they differ from each other.

*Prayer:* Close class with the Lord's Prayer which is said by every Christian faith.

## HANDBOOK QUIZ
# Ecumenism: The Call to Unity

Place the letter of the best answer on the line.

___1. The first steps toward ecumenism were taken by (a) Catholics, (b) non-Christians, (c) Anglicans.

___2. Ecumenism is a worldwide movement among Churches to (a) find blame for the separation among them, (b) heal divisions between them, (c) force everyone to join the same Church.

___3. The word *Protestant* mainly means to (a) object, (b) reform, (c) stand up for.

___4. The sacraments that Protestants accept are Baptism and (a) Confirmation, (b) the Lord's Supper, (c) Anointing of the Sick.

___5. Protestants agree on (a) the priesthood of the laity, (b) ordained priesthood, (c) no priesthood.

___6. Protestants (a) accept, (b) reject, (c) disagree on Mary's special power of intercession with God.

___7. The Catholic Church accepts (a) all, (b) most, (c) some blame for the separation of Christian Churches.

___8. Protestants rely for their beliefs almost totally on (a) the Bible, (b) their leaders, (c) personal inspiration.

___9. Devotion to Mary and the saints (a) unites Catholics and Protestants, (b) is distasteful to Protestants, (c) is essential for Catholics.

___10. The pope who rejuvenated Catholic ecumenical activity is (a) John Paul II, (b) John XXIII, (c) Paul VI.

___11. The largest mainline Protestant Church in the United States is the (a) Methodist, (b) Lutheran, (c) Anglican Church.

___12. The founder of the Presbyterian Church was (a) Luther, (b) Calvin, (c) Henry VIII.

___13. The Church that is *not* mainline Protestant is the (a) Lutheran, (b) Anglican, (c) Baptist Church.

___14. Simple trust in Jesus as experienced through the Holy Spirit's action is the emphasis of (a) Methodist, (b) Lutheran (c) Presbyterian spirituality.

___15. That Christ is present *with* and *in* the bread and wine only during Mass is a (a) Catholic, (b) Lutheran, (c) Presbyterian belief.

H

# HANDBOOK QUIZ
Answer Key

**1.** c

**2.** b

**3.** c

**4.** b

**5.** a

**6.** c

**7.** c

**8.** a

**9.** b

**10.** b

**11.** a

**12.** b

**13.** c

**14.** a

**15.** b

## An Ecumenical Litany

"That all may be one, as you, Father, are in me and I in *you*" (*John 17:21*).

For the many times we have looked at the specks in the eyes of our separated brothers and sisters, rather than at their sincere faith, perseverance, and good will, *Lord, forgive us.*

For our sarcasm, narrow-mindedness, and exaggerations in controversy, for our hardness and severe judgments in others' regard, *Lord, forgive us.*

For the bad example that we give in our lives-thereby discouraging, lessening, or even destroying, the effect of your grace in their souls, *Lord forgive us.*

For our forgetfulness to pray for our separated brothers and sisters often, warmly, and with love, *Lord forgive us.*

In spite of differences of language, color, and nationality, *Jesus, make us one.*

In spite of our ignorance of one another, our prejudices, and our dislikes, *Jesus make us one.*

In spite of all spiritual and intellectual barriers, *Jesus make us one.*

O God, for your own greater glory, *bring together separated Christians.*

O God, for the triumph of goodness and truth, *bring together separated Christians.*

O God, that there may be one sheepfold and one Shepherd, *bring together separated Christians.*

O God, that peace may reign in the world, *bring together separated Christians.*

O God, to fill the heart of your Son with joy, *bring together separated Christians.*

—Composed in Antioch of Syria

## Catholic-Protestant Differences
*Spirituality:*

C — Incarnational, the transfiguration of matter by the spirit.

P — Disincarnation, a separation of matter and spirit.

*Focus:*

C — On the altar

P — On the pulpit

*Doctrinal Statements:*

C — Result of consensus, generally approved by the pope

P — Generally the product of a single person's theology

*Salvation:*

C — By faith and good works

P — By faith alone, not good works or sacraments

*Humanity:*

C — Wounded by original sin, hence inclined to evil; creation is good

P — By nature sinful and separated from God

*Scripture:*

C — Normative, but the truth of Scripture lies in the Church, not in private interpretation.

P — Standard or norm of faith, private interpretation

*Priesthood:*

C — The call to universal priesthood exists along with a special ordained priesthood.

P — Every believer is called to priesthood and ministry through baptism; there is no special priesthood.

306

*Sacraments:*

C — Seven sacraments, all encounters with Christ; they cover all the needs of the spiritual life parallel to natural life

P — Limited to Baptism and the Lord's Supper

*Eucharist:*

C — Real Presence

P — A commemoration of the Last Supper

*Papacy:*

C — Pope is accepted as the successor of Peter.

P — Papal authority is rejected.

*Morality:*

C — Based on the gospel law of love, conscience, a sense of community, and the guidance of the Church

P — Based on the gospel law of love and one's individual conscience

*Mary*

C — Honored as the Mother of God and Mother of the Church; prayed to as a mediator

P — Accepted as Mother of Jesus but not given any special honor

## Review of Protestant Denominations

I. What religious founder am I?

1. I am the Father of the Reformation. (**Luther**)

2. I declared myself head of the Catholic Church of England. (**Henry VIII**)

3. I am the founder of Presbyterianism. (**Calvin**)

4. I taught predestination. (**Calvin**)

5. I am the originator of Anglicanism. (**Henry VIII**)

6. I am an Anglican who organized the church that was to become known by reference to my methodical life habits. (**Wesley**)

7. The pope refused to dissolve my marriage. (**Henry VIII**)

II. Which Christian denomination is described?

1. Our creed is the Augsburg Confession. (**Lutherans**)

2. Another of my names is Calvinism. (**Presbyterianism**)

3. Our government is highly organized, with bishops, elders, deacons, and pastors who may be women. (**Methodists**)

4. Our church has all the Catholic sacraments. (**Anglican High Church**)

5. Our organization is similar to that of Catholicism: hierarchical. (**Anglican/Episcopalian**)

6. My three divisions are linked by the Book of Common Prayer, communion with the bishop of Canterbury, and bishops. (**Anglican/Episcopalian**)

7. We insist on adult baptism and only by complete immersion. (**Baptists**)

8. I am the most stable of the Protestant churches. (**Lutheranism**)

9. Ultimate authority rests in a group of laymen. (**Presbyterianism**)

10. A bishop rules elders, and deacons care for temporal needs in our church. (**Presbyterian**)

11. Our church has three types of members: high church, broad church, and low church. (**Anglican**)

12. The Puritans had ties with this Protestant denomination. (**Calvinist/Presbyterian**)

III. What sect did I found?

1. John Smyth (**Baptist**)

2. Charles Russell (**Jehovah's Witnesses**)

3. Mary Baker Eddy (**Christian Science**)

4. William Booth (**Salvation Army**)

5. John Ining (**Pentecostal**)

6. Joseph Smith/Brigham Young (**Mormon**)

7. Thomas Campbell (**Disciples of Christ**)

8. William Miller (**Seventh Day Adventists**)

IV. Which radical sect is described?

1. A "military," missionary society founded to care for the poor in the streets. (**Salvation Army**)

2. A liberal, humanistic group who gather to pray and discuss life's questions. (**Unitarians**)

3. We believe in a return to the utter simplicity of the Gospel. (**Disciples of Christ**)

4. We originated in the United States in 1800 in reaction to ritualism of Anglicanism. (**Disciples of Christ**)

5. We are searchers and doubters of an extremely liberal frame of mind. (**Unitarians**)

Ⓗ

6. We believe that the body is illusion and pain and illness are mental mistakes. (**Christian Scientists**)

7. Our central tenet is the Second Coming and we keep the Sabbath on Saturday. (**Seventh Day Adventists**)

8. Holiness Churches: Churches of God, Assemblies of God, and Foursquare Gospel Churches. (**Pentecostals**)

9. A religion based on revelation received on sacred, golden tablets. (**Mormon**)

10. We deny Christ's divinity. (**Jehovah's Witnesses**)

11. We reject the sacraments but have many rituals. (**Salvation Army**)

12. We believe that only 144,000 will enter heaven. (**Jehovah's Witnesses**)

13. We teach that a true convert will always have externally visible gifts of the Spirit. (**Pentecostals**)

14. We consider secular governments satanic and will never salute the flag. (**Jehovah's Witnesses**)

## Report on a Protestant Church

*Purpose*

1. To become acquainted with and to appreciate the history, worship, and members of another church.

2. To find the similarities and clarify the differences between one Protestant church and yours.

3. To appreciate the devotion Protestants have to Jesus and to the Bible.

4. To understand how Protestants and Catholics are working toward unity (the Ecumenical Movement).

*Procedure*

1. Choose one Protestant church on which to report, preferably one that you can visit.

2. Answer the fifteen questions below, using printed and personal sources. Begin with the article in the *Catholic Encyclopedia*, books and pamphlets dealing with Protestant religions, and materials published by the church itself. Do some reading before you arrange for any personal interviews or visit the church.

3. Attend a church service, preferably a Sunday one and keep a copy of the church program or bulletin. If you cannot attend a service of the church of your report, attend a service in another Protestant church. (Note that this service **does not substitute** for your Sunday mass.) Do not receive communion if it is offered but participate in the prayers and singing.

4. Try to interview one or two members of the church. Ask the minister for materials that will acquaint you with the church's background and with as many activities as possible. Include these materials in your report. After doing the reading, you may wish to call the minister for information you could not locate.

5. At the end of your report, list the sources used. Include the author, title, date, and pages for each book, pamphlet, or magazine article used and identify the people interviewed. Remember to include the church program or bulletin.

*Questions*

1. Briefly explain how this church was founded: person, dates, place, reasons.

2. Which basic Reformation principles does it hold?

3. What is the place of the Bible in the life and worship of its members?

4. What sacraments are received?

5. How often do church members receive the Lord's Supper? What do they believe about it?

6. How are ministers chosen and trained? Are women able to be ministers? bishops?

7. How are children educated in their religion? When and how are they received as full members?

8. What kinds of activities does this church offer: spiritual? charitable? social? youth-centered? ecumenical? other?

9. How widespread is this church in the world? in the United States? Are missionaries sent to other lands? How else are converts made? Is it growing?

10. How does this church show an interest in ecumenical activities?

11. Describe the interior of the church and the order of the ceremony that you attended.

12. What similarities are there between this church and your own?

13. What major differences are there between this church and your own?

14. What impressed you about church members? their service?

15. What did you personally gain from doing this report?

## BIBLIOGRAPHY
### The Nature and Mission of the Church

Aubert, Roger, ed. *History, Self-Understanding of the Church. Concilium.* Vol. 67. New York: Herder and Herder, 1971.

Baum, Gregory and Andrew Greeley, eds. *The Church as Institution. Concilium.* Vol. 10. New York: Herder and Herder, 1974.

Bausch, William J. *The Christian Parish.* Notre Dame, IN: Fides/Claretian, 1980.

*Positioning Belief in the Mid-Seventies.* Notre Dame, IN: Fides Publisher, 1975.

Brown, Raymond, E., S.S. *Priest and Bishop.* New York: Paulist Press, 1970.

*The Community of the Beloved Disciple.* New York: Paulist Press, 1979.

Danfried, Karl P., Reumann, John, eds. *Peter in the New Testament.* New York: Paulist Press, 1973.

Buhlmann, Walbert. *The Coming of the Third Church.* Maryknoll, New York: Orbis Books, 1977.

Champlin, Joseph M. *The Living Parish.* Notre Dame, IN: Ave Maria Press, 1977.

Congar, Yves, O.P. *Power and Poverty in the Church.* Baltimore, MD: Helicon Press, 1965.

*This Church That I Love.* Denville, NJ: Dimension Books, 1969.

deLubac, Henri, S.J. *The Church: Paradox and Mystery.* New York: Alba House, 1969.

Downs, Thomas, *Parish as Learning Community.* West Mystic, CT: Twenty-Third Publications, 1979.

Dulles, Avery, S.J. *A Church to Believe In.* New York: Crossroad Publishing Co., 1982.

*Models of the Church.* Garden City, NY: Image Books, Doubleday & Co., 1978.

*The Resilient Church.* New York: Gill and Macmillan, 1978.

Duquoc, Christian and Casiano Floristan, eds. *Models of Holiness. Concilium.* Vol. 129. New York: Seabury Press, 1979 .

Flannery, Austin, O.P., ed. *Evangelization Today.* Northport, NY: Costello Publishing Co., 1977.

Hale, Russell, J. *Who Are the Unchurched?* Washington, D.C.: Glenmary Research Center, 1977.

Hanson, James E. *I'm a Christian, Why Be a Catholic?* New York: Paulist Press, 1984.

Hater, Robert J. *Religious Education and Catechesis: A Shift in Focus.* A Clarification/Study Paper. Washington, D.C.: National Conference of Diocesan Directors of Religious Education, CCD (NCDD), 1981.

*The Relationship between Evangelization and Catechesis.* A Clarification/Study Paper. Washington, D.C.: National Conference of Diocesan Directors of Religious Education, CCD (NCDD), 1981.

Hebblethwaite, Peter, S.J. *Theology of the Church.* Theology Today Series, No. 8. Hales Corners, WI: Clergy Book Service, 1969.

Herr, Edward C., ed. *Tomorrow's Church: What's Ahead for American Catholics.* Chicago: The Thomas More Press, 1982.

Hurley, Michael, S.J. *Theology of Ecumenism.* Theology Today Series, No. 9. Notre Dame, IN: Fides Publishers, Inc., 1969.

Kahmescher, Matthew F., S.M. *Catholicism Today: A Survey of Catholic Belief and Practice.* New York: Paulist Press, 1980.

Kung, Hans, ed *Apostolic Succession. Concilium.* Vol. 34. New York: Paulist Press, 1968.

Massimini, Anthony T., S.T.D. *The Holiness of the Church.* GlenRock, NJ: Paulist Press, 1965 .

McBrien, Richard P. *Catholicism.* Vols. I, II. Minneapolis: Winston Press, 1980.

Minear, Paul S. *Images of the Church in the New Testament.* Philadelphia: The Westminster Press, 1960.

Pfeifer, Carl J. *Teaching the Church Today.* West Mystic, CT: Twenty-Third Publications, 1978.

Power, David N. *Gifts That Differ: Lay Ministries Established and Unestablished.* New York: Pueblo Publishing Co., 1980.

**H**

Rahner, Karl. *Concern for the Church.* Theological Investigations XX. New York: Crossroad Publishing Co., 1981.

*Foundations of Christian Faith.* New York: The Seabury Press, 1970.

Ranaghan, Kevin and Dorothy. As *the Spirit Leads Us.* New York: Paulist Press, 1971.

*Catholic Pentecostals.* New York: Deus Books, Paulist Press, 1969.

Rauff, Edward A. *Why People Join the Church.* New York: The Pilgrim Press, 1979.

Schelkle, Karl Hermann. *Theology of the New Testament. Vol. IV. The Rule of God: Church—Eschatology.* Collegeville, MN: The Liturgical Press, 1978.

Schillebeeckx, Edward. *Ministry-Leadership in the Community of Jesus Christ.* New York: Crossroad Publishing Co., 1981.

*The Mission of the Church.* New York: The Seabury Press, 1973.

Schmaus, Michael. *Dogma and the Church.* Kansas City, MO: Sheed and Ward, 1972.

Schnackenburg, Rudolf. *The Church in the New Testament.* New York: Herder and Herder, 1965.

Segundo, Juan Luis, S.J. *The Community Called Church.* Maryknoll, New York: Orbis Books, 1973.

Semmelroth, Otto, S.J. *Mary, Archtype of the Church.* New York: Sheed and Ward, 1963.

Stanley, David M. *The Apostolic Church in the New Testament Times.* Westminster, MD: The Newman Press, 1967.

## The Church in History

Aubert, Robert, ed. *Historical Problems of Church Renewal Concilium.* Vol. 7. New York: Paulist Press, 1965.

Bainton, Roland H. *Here I Stand.* New York: Abingdon-Cokesbury Press, 1950.

Bausch, William J. *Pilgrim Church-A Popular History of Catholic Christianity.* West Mystic, CT: Twenty-Third Publications, 1971.

Bokenkotter, Thomas. *A Concise History of the Catholic Church.* Garden City, NY: Doubleday & Co., 1977.

Brown, Raymond E. *The Community of the Beloved Disciple.* New York: Paulist Press, 1979.

Christiani, Leon. *Heresies and Heretics.* Twentieth Century Encyclopedia of Catholicism. Vol. 136. New York: Hawthorn Books, 1959.

Danielou, Jean and Henri Marrou. *The First Six Hundred Years. The Christian Centuries. Vol. 1.* New York: McGraw-Hill Book Co., 1964.

Daniel-Rops, Henri. *Cathedral and Crusade 1050-1350.* London: J.M. Dent and Sons, Ltd., 1957.

*The Church in an Age of Revolution 1789–1870.* New York: E.P. Dutton and Co., 1965.

*The Church in the Dark Ages.* Vol. 1. Garden City, NY: Image Books, 1960.

*The Church in the Eighteenth Century.* New York: E.P. Dutton and Co., 1964.

*The Church of Apostles and Martyrs.* New York: E.P. Dutton and Co., 1960.

*The Protestant Reformation.* Vols. I, 2. New York: Image Books, 1963.

Dawby, Tim *et al.*, eds. *Eerdman's Handbook to the History of Christianity.* Grand Rapids, MI: Wm. B. Eerdman's Publishing Co., 1977.

Dawson, Christopher. *The Dividing of Christendom.* New York: Sheed and Ward, 1965.

Day, Edward. *The Catholic Church Story.* Liguori, MO: Liguori Publications, 1978.

Dulles, Avery, S.J. *Models of the Church.* Garden City, NY: Doubleday & Co., 1974.

Freemantle, Anne, ed. *A Treasury of Early Christianity.* New York: Mentor Books, 1953.

Guitton, Jean. *Great Heresies and Church Councils.* New York: Harper & Row, Publishers, 1965.

Hardon, John, S.J. *Christ to Catholicism.* Unpublished manuscript.

Harney, Martin P., S.J. *The Catholic Church through the Ages.* Boston: Daughters of Saint Paul, 1974.

Hertling, Ludwig, S.J. and Englebert Kirschbaum, S.J. *The Roman Catacombs and Their Martyrs.* Milwaukee: Bruce Publishing Co., 1956.

Homan, Helen Walker. *Letters to the Martyrs.* New York: David McKay Co., 1951.

Hughes, Philip. *A Popular History of the Catholic Church.* New York: Macmillan Co., 1947.

Keller, Werner. *The Bible as History.* New York: William Morrow and Co., 1956.

Lucas, Isidro. *The Browning of America*. Chicago: Fides/Claretian, 1981.

Oleen, John C. *The Catholic Reformation. Savonarola to Ignatius Loyola*. New York: Harper & Row Publishers, 1969.

Plumpe, Joseph C., ed. *Ancient Christian Writers, No. 6. The Works of the Fathers in Translation*. Westminster, MD: The Newman Press, 1948.

Ricciotti, Giuseppe. *The Age of Martyrs*. Milwaukee: Bruce Publishing Co., 1959.

Rice, Edwarn. *The Church: A Pictorial History*. New York: Farrar, Straus and Cudahy, 1954.

Ullmann, Walter. *The Origins of the Great Schism*. Hamden, CT: Shoe String Press, Inc., 1972.

## Documentation

"As One Who Serves." Washington, D.C.: United States Catholic Conference, 1977.

*Behold Your Mother*. Washington, D.C.: National Conference of Catholic Bishops. United States Catholic Conference, 1973.

"Called and Gifted." *Gifts*. Bishops' Committee on the Laity. Washington, D.C.: National Conference of Catholic Bishops, Fall 1980.

*Gifts*. Bishops' Committee on the Laity. Washington D.C.: National Conference of Catholic Bishops Spring 1981, Summer 1981, Winter 1981.

*Modern Ecumenical Documents on the Ministry*. London: S.P.C.K. Publishing Co., 1975.

*The Parish: A People, A Mission, A Structure*. Statement of the Bishop's Committee on the Parish. Washington D.C.: Conference of Catholic Bishops, 1980.

*The Parish: A People, Bishops Reflect on the Challenges and Opportunities of Today's Parishes*. The Parish Project. Washington, D.C.: National Conference of Catholic Bishops, 1980.

*To Build and Be Church*. Lay Ministry Resource Packet. Secretariat for the Laity. Washington, D.C.: United States Catholic Conference, 1980.

## Periodical Literature

"An American Catechism." *Chicago Studies* 12:3 (Fall 1973): 229–366.

Bearsley, Patrick J., S.M. "Mary the Perfect Disciple: A Paradigm for Mariology." *Theological Studies* 41:3 (September 1980): 461–504.

Breig, James. "Let's Listen to the Pope." *U.S. Catholic* 44:11 (November 1979): 12–17.

"Mary, Mary Quite Contemporary." U.S. *Catholic* 42:10 (October 1977): 18–22.

"Our Down-to-Earth Heavenly Queen." U.S. Catholic 45:10 (October 1980): 6–12.

"The Holy Spirit: Let's Get Beyond the Ghost Story." U.S. Catholic 45:5 (May 1980): 6–11 .

Brooker, Betsy. "Lay Ministry: More than a Good Deed Daily." *U.S. Catholic* 44:11 (November 1979): 18–23.

Brown, Raymond E. "Diverse Views of the Spirit in the New Testament." *Worship*. 57:3 (May 1983): 225–336.

*"Episkope– and Episcopos:* The New Testament Evidence." *Theological Studies* 41:2 (June 1980): 322–338.

Chirico, Peter, S.S. "Infallibility between Kung and the Official Church?" *Theological Studies* 42:4 (December 1981): 529–560.

Delaney, John. "Saints: Superstars in the Heavenly Lineup." *U.S. Catholic* 47:11 (November 1982): 12–16.

Dozier, Carroll T. "The Bishop and the Community of the Local Church." *Worship* 57:1 (January 1983): 4–14.

Haughton, Rosemary. "On Discovering Community." *Catholic Mind* 77:1334 (June 1979): 49–57.

Larsen, Kenneth J. "Some Observations About Symbols and Metaphor." *Worship* 54:3 (May 1980): 221–245.

Lyke, James P. "Liturgical Expression in the Black Community." *Worship* 57:1 (January 1983): 14–26.

"The Magisterium, the Theologian and the Educator." *Chicago Studies* 17:2 (Summer 1978).

Mahony, Roger. "The Eucharist and Social Justice." *Worship* 57:1 (January 1983): 52–61.

Marthaler, Berard L., O.F.M. Conv. "Handing on the Symbols of Faith." *Chicago Studies 19:1* (Spring 1980): 21–33.

McBrien, Richard P. "Dogma." *Chicago Studies* 20:2 (Summer 1981): 137–150.

Murphy-O'Connor, Jerome. "Eucharist and Community in First Corinthians." *Worship* 51:1 (January 1977): 56–69.

Power, David N. "Households of Faith in the Coming Church." *Worship* 57:3 (May 1983); 237–255.

Purden, Carolyn. "Six Women: Images of Christ." *U.S. Catholic* 44:4 (April 1979): 24–29.

Ramirez, Ricardo. "Reflections on the Hispanicization of the Liturgy." *Worship* 57:1 (January 1983): 26–34.

Shea, John. "Prayer: Just What Do You Think You're Doing?" *U.S. Catholic* 44:4 (April 1979): 17–23.

Untener, Kenneth. "Local Church and Universal Church," from *America*, 151:10(October 13, 1984): 201–205.

U.S. Catholic Conference Administrative Board. "Statement on Political Responsibility." *Catholic Mind* 78: 1340 (February 1980): 45–56.

Walsh, Sister Mary Ann. "Whatever Happened to Convert-Making?" *U.S. Catholic* 44:10 (October 1979): 26–31.

Whalen, William J. "Do Christians Need a Permit for Intercommunion?" *U.S. Catholic* 45:1 (January 1980): 6–13.

(H)

# Teacher's Notes

# Teacher's Notes

# Teacher's Notes

# Teacher's Notes

# Teacher's Notes

# Teacher's Notes

# Teacher's Notes

# Teacher's Notes